The
INSANITY
DEFENSE

The
INSANITY
DEFENSE

A Critical Assessment
of Law and Policy
in the Post-Hinckley Era

Rita J. Simon
David E. Aaronson

Foreword by Judge Barrington D. Parker

PRAEGER

New York
Westport, Connecticut
London

Copyright Acknowledgments

The author and publisher are grateful to the following for allowing the use of excerpts from:

Norval Morris, *Madness and the Criminal Law* (Chicago: University of Chicago Press, 1982). Reprinted with permission.

John Q. La Fond, "Observations on the Insanity Defense and Involuntary Civil Commitment in Europe," *University of Puget Sound Law Review* (Washington, Spring 1984). Reprinted with permission.

Rita J. Simon, *The Jury and the Defense of Insanity* (Boston: Little, Brown, and Company, 1967). Reprinted with permission.

Library of Congress Cataloging-in-Publication Data

Simon, Rita James.
    The insanity defense: a critical assessment of law and policy in
the post-Hinckley era / Rita J. Simon and David E. Aaronson.

      p.   cm.
    Bibliography: p.
    Includes index.
    ISBN 0-275-92830-6 (alk. paper)
        0-275-92831-4 (pbk.: alk. paper)
    1. Insanity—Jurisprudence—United States.   I. Aaronson, David E.
II. Title.
KF9242.S48   1988
345.73'04—dc19
[347.3054]   87-27890

Library of Congress Catalog Card Number: 87-27890
ISBN: 0-275-92830-6
      0-275-92831-4 (pbk.)

First published in 1988

Praeger Publishers, One Madison Avenue, New York, NY 10010
A division of Greenwood Press, Inc.

Printed in the United States of America

∞

The paper used in this book complies with the
Permanent Paper Standard issued by the National
Information Standards Organization (Z39.48-1984).

10 9 8 7 6 5 4 3 2 1

Contents

Foreword

The American public was stunned when on the fateful afternoon of March 30, 1981, they learned through instant media coverage that John Hinckley Jr. attempted to assassinate President Ronald Reagan. Fifteen months later, when the jurors returned a verdict of "not guilty, by reason of insanity," the American public was stunned even more; the verdict was received with disbelief and bitter criticism. As the presiding judge over Hinckley's trial, within hours of the verdict and for weeks thereafter, I received a flood of mail, expressing outrage and shock that the would-be assassin had been "freed" to an indefinite commitment to a mental hospital.

During the nearly two-month trial, the jurors viewed video accounts of the aborted attempt on the life of the president departing from a speaking engagement at a midtown hotel. They also heard brief testimony from Hinckley's parents describing their son's lifestyle, behavior patterns, and the problems that beset him from early childhood through young adulthood. However, for the greater part of the trial the jurors were exposed to weeks of conflicting and irreconcilable testimony from psychiatrists, psychologists, neuro-psychiatrists and other experts. Even though the experts were cautioned at the outset that the jurors were a group of lay persons, at times, much of their testimony was prolix, toilsome, and far from enlightening.

After several days of careful deliberation, the jurors concluded that they had a reasonable doubt as to Hinckley's mental state at the time of the assassination attempt; therefore, he should not be held criminally responsible for the crimes charged in the indictment. In reaching that verdict, the 12 lay persons respected their sworn obligation as jurors and applied the court's instructions of law to the testimony they had heard during the course of the trial.

In view of the public outrage over the verdict, together with the charged political and social climate of the time, it was not surprising that the insanity plea was the immediate target of relentless attacks from all sources. For many, the defense was a clear manifestation of the failure of our criminal justice system to punish individuals who have clearly violated the law. Others argued stridently that reliance upon the defense was the principal cause for many of our urban crime problems. Condemning a "soft on crime" mentality and crying for "law and order" and a "get tough" policy, the critics mounted a crusade to limit severely the scope of the defense. Expressions of moderation were, for some time, clearly at a minimum.

In the wake of *Hinckley*, the Senate and House Judiciary Committees of the Congress scheduled hearings and considered weeks of diverse testimony from highly qualified experts with varied experiences. Thereafter, Congress enacted the Insanity Defense Reform Act of 1984. That statute represented the first substantive treatment of the insanity defense in the federal criminal code. Following Congress's lead, many state legislatures also introduced important changes in their insanity defense and commitment laws.

Although numerous legal and medical journals have already discussed many of the revisions in our insanity laws, the research presented in *The Insanity Defense* provides a new and invaluable insight to the subject. This interesting book presents a lively account in a thorough fashion of the significant developments since the Hinckley trial. In addition, the authors analyze the provocative proposals that suggest alternatives to the defense or its outright abolition.

The Insanity Defense should prove to be a valuable tool for policymakers, and a practical and useful work for criminal justice practitioners, students, and anyone who seeks to better understand the debate on controversial issues concerning the defense and important changes that have taken place on federal and state levels. What is particularly useful is that the authors provide a readable yet comprehensive overview of central issues and skillfully marshall and analyze relevant data and proposals from the legal, mental health, and social science communities. A variety of perspectives are used to provide a better understanding of the issues, ranging from a historical approach, providing original empirical data from a national survey they conducted of mental health and legal experts, a comparative approach that examines the insanity defense in other countries, and even an inviting discussion as to how the defense has been treated in literature and the theater.

Rita J. Simon and David E. Aaronson are eminently qualified to undertake this study. Each has written and lectured extensively in this area. Rita J. Simon is Dean of the School of Justice at the American University, holding a Ph.D. in sociology. Prior to this present effort, she authored a thoughtful book examining how jurors view the insanity defense, focusing on their understanding of the role of expert testimony and the courts' instructions of law. David Aaronson, a Harvard Law School graduate, is a professor of criminal law at the American University with a joint appointment in the School of Justice. He also holds a Ph.D. in economics. The combination of backgrounds in both social science and law that the authors bring to their research has contributed to the quality and value of their effort.

The *Hinckley* verdict should not cause a rush to judgment and support a reactionary cry for complete abolition of the insanity defense. As the authors demonstrate, the defense is deeply rooted in the cultural and legal tradition of our society. While on the one hand there is a legitimate need to hold and punish criminal defendants who are accountable and responsible for their actions, there is also the long recognized and legitimate view that it is inappropriate to incarcerate persons who are not responsible for their conduct because a mental disability or disease deprives them of the capacity and ability for rational and voluntary choices. The data presented in this work clearly show, as reflected in other sources, that: the insanity defense is infrequently used; acquittals in contested proceedings are rare indeed; a typical defendant who pleads insanity is not a rapist or a murderer; the notion that it is "a rich man's defense" is not supported by credible data. Moreover, commitments following an insanity plea do not necessarily, and as a matter of course, result in early release. Rather, such a defendant may likely be incarcerated for as long a period, if not more, in a mental institution as he would be sentenced in a penal institution, without benefit of an insanity plea.

Whatever opinion or view one may have of the defense, there is a need for a better appreciation, understanding, and knowledge of the issues involved. *The Insanity Defense* should give the reader a deeper understanding and greater appreciation of the issues.

Judge Barrington D. Parker
United States District Court
for the District of Columbia

Preface and Acknowledgments

The attempted assassination of President Reagan by John Hinckley and his subsequent acquittal on grounds of insanity with the resulting changes in federal and state insanity defense laws were the immediate impetus for the study and research that resulted in this book. But both authors have an interest in the moral and legal merits of the insanity defense that extends much farther back in time. Simon's interest was manifest in her doctoral dissertation (University of Chicago, 1957) and in her first book—*The Jury and the Defense of Insanity*—which was published in 1967. Aaronson's involvement stems from his work as an E. Barrett Prettyman Fellow at the Georgetown Graduate Law Center in 1965 and his specialization in criminal law and procedure, including cordirecting the Maryland Criminal Justice Clinic, as a law professor at the Washington College of Law since 1970. His writings on the insanity defense include presentations before the Judicial Conference of the District of Columbia Circuit and at St. Elizabeth's Hospital.

To the extent possible, this book has been a genuine collaboration from designing and pre-testing questionnaires for data collection to the research, writing, and review of individual chapters. As with most joint projects, there was an initial division of labor. Chapters 1, 5, 6, and 9 were joint responsibilities. Rita Simon had primary responsibility for Chapters 4, 7, and 8. David Aaronson had primary responsibility for Chapters 2 and 3.

We note our special appreciation to Eric Yarvin, Nancy Streef, and David Frankel (law students at the Washington College of Law), Paul Schneiderman and Peter Darvas (undergraduate and graduate students at the School of Justice), and Gloria Danziger (freelance writer and Washington attorney) by including their names on the Contents page. But we also owe debts to Julie Henrickson and Kevin Morse, for their help in preparation of the manuscript. The biggest debt of all is owed to Myra (Mike) Schlesinger, who—as she has done with many of Simon's manuscripts—patiently, carefully, and critically typed endless versions and caught mistakes that eluded the rest of us. We take this opportunity to once again express our deep appreciation of her. David Aaronson expresses his appreciation to Dean Fred Anderson of the Washington College of Law for making available summer research grant funds to work on this book.

The
INSANITY
DEFENSE

1

Introduction
and Historical Review

On March 30, 1981, John W. Hinckley, Jr., shot and wounded President Ronald Reagan and three other persons as the president was walking to his limousine after an appearance at a hotel in Washington, D.C. One of the other persons, Press Secretary James Brady, was gravely injured by a head wound. Many eyewitnesses and millions of other persons saw the shooting on television. After a seven-week trial, including three days of jury deliberations, Hinckley was acquitted of 13 crimes. On June 21, 1982, a "not guilty by reason of insanity" verdict was returned against the would-be presidential assassin. Hinckley was then committed to St. Elizabeth's Hospital by presiding Judge Barrington D. Parker, U.S. District Court for the District of Columbia, where Hinckley presently resides.

The acquittal of John Hinckley, Jr., and the jury's verdict of not guilty by reason of insanity set loose a flood of public outcry and a volley of critical statements in the daily press. How could a person be found not guilty and escape punishment for an assassination attempt on the president of the United States seen in plain view by millions of persons on television? For most of the general public, it was puzzling and even baffling to understand a criminal justice system that was unable to immediately and effectively punish a person for a planned assassination attempt resulting in injury to a president and three other persons.

The adverse reaction to the Hinckley acquittal brought forth swift emotional demands for changes in the insanity defense laws. In proposing such changes, Attorney General William French Smith noted that a doctrine that allows a person who has committed a violent crime to then use confusing procedures in order to return to the society he has victimized must be called to an end. Even the secretary of the Treasury took time off from his responsibilities to voice his outrage, and to denounce the verdict, labeling it as "absolutely atrocious."

Immediately following the trial, each house of Congress—through its judiciary committee—scheduled hearings to consider changes in the insanity laws as related to the administration of criminal justice. Within two days of the trial, in a virtually unprecedented action, several members of the jury panel were invited to appear before a subcommittee of the U.S. Senate Judiciary Committee. As a result, Congress enacted the Insanity Defense Reform Act of 1984, and significant changes in the insanity defense laws were also enacted by about half of the states.

How the insanity defense should be formulated and presented has always been a difficult and controversial issue. Perhaps no other area of the criminal law has been subject to more controversy, despite the fact that insanity has been offered as a defense to a charge of crime for centuries. By contrast, when a defendant in a criminal proceeding offers an alibi or an entrapment defense—or indeed any legal defense—and is acquitted, we do not clamor and demand that the alibi or entrapment defense be restricted or abolished.

Difficult issues are involved in the effort to formulate an appropriate insanity defense and to determine the procedures to be used in presentation of this defense. The purpose of this book is to provide a critical assessment and overview of the insanity defense as it exists in the 1980s. One of our goals is to provide the reader with a basis for understanding and evaluating the legislative and judicial responses to the major issues that have stirred such controversy. Some of the questions considered are: What is the purpose and function of the insanity defense in our criminal justice system? What are the differences among the various insanity defense standards, and how important are these differences? What are the variations in the burden of proof, and which side—prosecution or defense—should bear this burden? What should be the role of expert testimony in applying insanity defense standards? Can jurors be relied on to understand and properly apply the judge's instructions and to evaluate conflicting psychological and psychiatric testimony? Is the current public policy wise in its tendency toward significantly narrowing and restricting the insanity defense, or even abolishing it?

In our approach to these and other issues, an effort has been made to draw on a large body of literature and to bring together diverse viewpoints from a variety of disciplines and perspectives. For example, in this introductory chapter, the historical development of the insanity defense is traced, and social science data on the frequency of use of the insanity defense are presented.

Briefly, the remaining chapters focus on the following topics: Chapter 2 reviews the various legal norms that have been adopted by the federal courts since 1954, when the Court of Appeals in the District of Columbia introduced the *Durham* rule, to the passage of the Insanity Defense Act by Congress in 1984. It also reviews the shift in the burdens and standards of proof in federal and state courts. Under the *Durham* rule and the American Law Institute test in the federal courts, the burden was on the government to prove beyond a reasonable doubt that the defendant was *not* insane, once enough evidence was presented to raise the issue. In the Insanity Defense Reform Act of 1984, Congress shifted the burden to the defense to affirmatively prove the existence of the insanity defense by a standard of "clear and convincing" evidence. The reader is referred to the Appendix at the end of the book, where we include a chart that summarizes how the defense of insanity is treated in all 50 states. It contains the most recent legal standards, burdens of proof, and verdict forms.

Chapter 3 analyzes the role that expert witnesses have performed in defense of insanity trials. It reviews the arguments for and against the use and scope of expert testimony and the issues about which expert witnesses should be allowed to testify.

The jury's role in defense of insanity trials is described in Chapter 4. Historical data about how juries have treated defendants who were charged with the assassination or attempted assassination of political leaders and officeholders and who pleaded insanity are reviewed. We offer an assessment (based on experimental juries) of how well juries understand the rules of law and evidence, and of the role of expert witnesses in defense of insanity trials.

Chapter 5 provides the results of a national survey conducted in 1984 by the authors in regard to experts' views on various aspects of the defense of insanity. Respondents included federal and state trial and appellate judges, prosecuting and defense attorneys (private and public defenders), forensic psychologists, psychiatrists, and other mental health officials.

The movements to abolish the defense of insanity and to provide an alternative verdict of "guilty but mentally ill"—which gained considerable support following the verdict in the Hinckley trial—is the focus of chapter 6. It contains the most recent data on those states that have abolished or diminished the defense, the changes in verdict forms from guilty by reason of insanity to guilty but mentally ill, and the reasons for the actions taken. It also assesses the likelihood that the defense of insanity will prevail, at least until the next time it is tested in a major sensational trial.

Chapter 7 provides a rather superficial assessment of how the defense of insanity is used and interpreted in other societies in different parts of the world. We recognize the limitations of the data that are brought to bear in this chapter—in part, because they are derived from formal statutes, with no case analyses or independent assessments of what happens when the defense of insanity is introduced in actual trials or how often it is introduced. Nevertheless, because so little on the subject has been written in a comparative vein, we believe that our bringing together of even the official statutes is a worthwhile and informative endeavor.

Chapter 8 takes a rather unusual twist in that it considers how crime, responsibility, and the insanity defense have been treated in fiction and the theater. Much of the chapter is devoted to two relatively recent U.S. novels; but the authors cast a wide net, and touch briefly on Greek tragedy and on nineteenth-century European fiction.

WHAT IS THE PURPOSE OF THE INSANITY DEFENSE IN THE CRIMINAL PROCESS?

The underlying premise of our criminal law is that a person's conduct must generally be in accordance with the acceptable range of norms of conduct adopted by society. An underlying assumption is that a person in the exercise of free will should be held accountable, because individuals do in fact have at least a minimum capacity for making the voluntary and rational choices required for criminal responsibility. Thus, the ordinary criminal defendant is viewed as "culpable" or "blameworthy" or "responsible," because that person could have chosen to abide by the dictates of the law. However, there are a few individuals who cannot be held accountable. A mental disability or disease deprives them of even the minimal capacity for rational and voluntary choices on which the law's expectation of responsibility is predicated. Because of their incapacity to comply with the law, such persons are not held culpable, nor are criminal sanctions invoked or applied consequent to their conduct.

The insanity defense, therefore, is the exception that "proves" the rule of free will. Supporters of the defense view it as vital to a healthy society, which uses its criminal law to build and buttress self-reliant action on the part of its citizens. Throughout history, it is this vision of law that has rallied supporters to resist efforts to abolish the insanity defense. Eliminating the insanity defense would remove from criminal law and public conscience the vitally important distinction between "illness" and "evil"—or, as one scholar noted, would tuck it away in an administrative process.[1] As evidenced in the discussion of the history of the insanity defense later in this chapter, there is a deeply entrenched human feeling—as old as recorded history—that persons who are grossly disturbed (whether called "madmen," "lunatics," "insane," or "mentally disordered") should not be punished like ordinary criminals.

For these few who cannot be held accountable because of mental disability or disease, social control may be best served by confinement in a secure hospital setting (especially in the case of those who are dangerously insane). Similarly, the general deterrence theory underlying punishment is that a person's awareness and fear of unpleasant consequences will restrain him or her from engaging in criminal behavior. However, this is effective only with persons who can understand the signals directed at them by the criminal code, who can respond to warnings, and who can understand the significance of sanctions imposed on violators. Thus, punishment is not likely to deter seriously disturbed individuals from future antisocial conduct.

Also, the insanity defense is seen by supporters to be quite consistent with the notion of specific deterrence or restraint. If the defense is successfully invoked, the defendant is not merely incarcerated for a fixed period of time, but—instead—can or should be committed until such time as he or she is no longer dangerous.

On the other hand, those who favor abolishing or severely limiting the insanity defense have advanced a number of arguments. These arguments are aired more fully in Chapter 6. We note here that, according to supporters of abolition, the key terms in the various insanity tests are so vague as to invite semantic jousting, speculation, and intuitive moral judgments in the guise of factual determinations. Also, there is little or no basis in psychiatry for allowing expert witnesses to testify—as they often do, in conclusory terms—concerning the differentiation between persons who are personally blameworthy and those who are not. Further, some believe that it is therapeutically more desirable to encourage treatment of persons as responsible for their conduct, rather than as involuntary victims "playing a sick role." In addition, the insanity defense discriminates against persons who commit crimes because of influences on their personalities other than mental disease or defect. Opponents of the defense argue that, if it be therapeutically desirable to provide a medical-custodial disposition, then such a decision should be made directly—immediately following the defendant's conviction—rather than indirectly during the trial. Finally, opponents of the insanity defense claim that, in practice, it is a "rich person's defense" because usually it is only the wealthy who can afford the array of experts needed to mount a convincing defense. These scarce psychiatric resources—they argue—should be spent in treatment of those who have been committed or imprisoned.

Professor Norval Morris, a leading proponent of abolition of the insanity defense, replies to the arguments that it is unjust and unfair to stigmatize the seriously mentally ill as criminals and to punish them for their crimes—and that, if certain mentally ill persons cannot exercise choice, they cannot be deterred and it is therefore a moral outrage to punish them. He argues:

> Choice is neither present nor absent in the typical case where the insanity defense is currently pleaded; what is at issue is the degree of freedom of choice on a continuum from the hypothetically entirely rational to the hypothetically pathologically determined—in states of consciousness neither polar condition exists.
>
> The moral issue sinks into the sands of reality. Certainly it is true that in a situation of total absence of choice it is outrageous to inflict punishment; but the frequency of such situations to the problems of criminal responsibility becomes an issue of fact in which tradition and clinical knowledge and practice are in conflict. The traditions of being possessed of evil spirits, of being bewitched, confront the practices of a mental health system which increasingly fashions therapeutic practices to hold patients responsible for their conduct. . . .
>
> [T]he special defense of insanity may properly be indicted as producing a morally unsatisfactory classification on the continuum between guilt and innocence. It applies in practice to only a few, mentally ill criminals, thus omitting many others with guilt-reducing rela-

tionships between their mental illness and their crime; it exclu[...]
other powerful pressures on human behavior, thus giving excessive
weight to the psychological over the social. It is a false classification in
the sense that if a team of the world's most sensitive and trained psychiatrists and moralists were to select from all those found guilty of felonies and those found not guilty by reason of insanity any given number who should not be stigmatized as criminals, very few of those found
not guilty be reason of insanity would be selected. How to offer proof
of this? The only proof, I regret, is to be found by personal contact
with a flow of felony cases through the courts and into the prisons.
No one of serious perception will fail to recognize both the extent of
mental illness and retardation among the prison population and the
overwhelming weight of adverse social circumstances on criminal behavior. This is, of course, not an argument that social adversities should
lead to acquittals; they should be taken into account in sentencing. And
the same is true of the guilt and sentencing of those pressed by psychological adversities.[2]

Professor Morris believes that mentally disordered offenders who
have the knowledge and intent required by a criminal statute are
morally blameworthy and, thus, should be subject to criminal
sanctions.

HOW FREQUENTLY IS THE
INSANITY DEFENSE USED?

The intense interest and attention that the insanity defense
provokes is somewhat odd when we consider that it is introduced as
a defense in less than 1 percent of all criminal trials. Francis Allen
said of it:

> The issue of criminal responsibility has attracted more attention and
> stimulated more controversy than any other question in the substantive
> criminal law.[3]

Steadman et al. report the results of a mail survey conducted in 1978
of all 50 states and the federal system, in which they found that
there were 1,554 persons committed as not guilty by reason of insanity (NGRI).[4] This figure represents an average of 31 insanity acquittals per state. The number of NGRI admissions per state, however,
varied widely—from 169 in California to 0 in Delaware, Iowa, North

Dakota, South Dakota, West Virginia, and Wyoming. On any given day in 1978, there was an average total of 3,140 persons detained as not guilty by reason of insanity. California had the highest daily census of 569; and, on an average day, seven states had none.

Steadman also compared the number of persons found not guilty by reason of insanity and committed to mental hospitals against the overall number of persons in such institutions. For example, on June 30, 1978, there were 147,283 patients in state and county mental hospitals.[5] The 3,140 NGRIs thus represent only 2 percent of all such residents.

All other data collected in different parts of the country support the conclusion of the American Psychiatric Association in its *Statement on the Insanity Defense* issued in 1982: "[S]uccessful invocation of the defense is rare (probably involving a fraction of one percent of all felony cases). While philosophically important for the criminal law, the insanity defense is empirically unimportant."[6]

For example, an American Bar Association study published in 1970 reported that, during a four-month period in Chicago and San Francisco in 1963, there was one NGRI plea in each city, and each was successful. During a three-month period in New York City, there was one unsuccessful plea; and in a two-month time span in Miami and three months in Detroit, there were none. In Detroit between 1959 and 1963, of the 271 defendants indicted for murder or manslaughter, one was found NGRI. In 1965 in California, 464 defendants introduced a plea of insanity—out of 36,643 felony cases. In two-thirds of those 464 cases, the plea was withdrawn; and in 56, it was dismissed. Of the remaining 195 cases—which comprised 0.53 percent of all felony dispositions—109 resulted in a finding of NGRI, and 86 were convicted.[7]

Steadman reported that, in New York State between April 1965 and June 1978, there were 387 acquittals on grounds of insanity. In a Connecticut study, 25 persons were found NGRI from January 1, 1970, through December 31, 1972. More recent data show a continuation of the trends described above. For example, in 1982 in New Jersey, of the 32,500 cases handled by the offices of the public defender, only 50 entered NGRI pleas. That is less than one-sixth of 1 percent. Of the 50, 15 were found NGRI.[8] Between 1980 and 1983, Maryland averaged 10,000–15,000 felony cases per year. Of those, between 200 and 250 entered pleas of insanity, and between 30 and 40 were found NGRI.[9]

In a letter to Senator Strom Thurmond dated November 4, 1982, the then Assistant Attorney General Robert McConnell wrote that the Justice Department had information on only four federal defendants who were found NGRI in 1981.[10]

Further, in most instances where the insanity defense is successfully invoked, the available evidence of the defendant's abnormal mental state points so overwhelmingly to a conclusion of insanity that the prosecutor agrees not to formally contest the defense. Instead, prosecutors usually enter into a formal or tacit agreement for an acquittal by reason of insanity. Almost always, this decision is based on a report of the federal or state psychiatrists that the defendant meets the criteria for insanity. For example, in Maryland, of the 150–200 cases each year in which the state psychiatrists reject the insanity defense, only two or three defendants are actually found NGRI in a contested trial. On the other hand, about 30–40 defendants are found by state psychiatrists to be insane each year, and most are found NGRI based on findings of fact entered by a judge in a nonjury proceeding.[11] Thus, most successful insanity defense acquittals do not involve controversial trials and the expenditure of substantial psychiatric and judicial resources in court proceedings. The high incidence of uncontested cases undercuts somewhat the argument that the insanity defense is a rich person's defense.

Perhaps the best brief explanation for the intense interest and attention that the defense of insanity attracts is that it touches on ultimate social values. It was founded on the concept of individual responsibility as a prerequisite for criminal punishment. In the words of Alan Stone:

> The defense of insanity purports to draw a line between those who are morally responsible and those who are not, those who are blameworthy and those who are not, those who have free will and those who do not, those who should be punished and those who should not, and those who can be deterred and those who cannot.[12]

Also, historically, the insanity defense has often been used to avoid the harshness of the death penalty. Since the U.S. Supreme Court has apparently given states the green light to proceed with more executions, the insanity defense is likely to take on more practical significance during the 1990s. The mental state of death row prisoners will take on added significance since the U.S. Supreme

Court held in 1986 that the Eighth Amendment prohibits states from inflicting the death penalty on a prisoner who is insane.[13]

THE HISTORICAL DEVELOPMENT OF
THE INSANITY DEFENSE STANDARDS

This section traces the development of the insanity defense. In Chapter 2, the meaning—and limitations—of modern standards for determining criminal responsibility are discussed.

Pre-M'Naghton Insanity Defense Standards

As far back as ancient Rome, legal codes distinguished between those who were mad and therefore not accountable, and those who were sane and responsible. The Justinian code in the sixth century made the distinction in the following manner:

> There are those who are not to be held accountable, such as a madman and a child, who are not capable of wrongful intention. These individuals are able to suffer a wrong but not to produce one. Since a wrong is only able to exist by the intention of those who have committed it, it follows that these persons, whether they have assaulted by blow, or insulted by words, are not considered to have committed a wrong.[14]

In the compendium of Jewish law written in the second century, the Talmud contains the following:

> It is an ill thing to knock against a deaf mute, an imbecile, or a minor. He that wounds them is culpable, but if they wound others they are not culpable . . . for with them only the act is a consequence while the intention is of no consequence.[15]

During the fourteenth century, King Edward III recognized madness as a complete defense to a criminal charge. In Anglo-Saxon law, the earliest record of a jury acquitting a defendant on grounds of insanity occurred in England in 1505. By 1581, the doctrine of the lack of a guilty mind (or felonious intent)—and, hence, lack of criminal responsibility—was well established.

In 1723, a court applied the "wild beast test." An English judge declared in the trial of Edward Arnold: "In order to avail himself of the defense of insanity, a man must be totally deprived of his understanding and memory so as not to know what he is doing, no more than an infant, a brute, or a wild beast."[16] The wild beast test—along with an ability to distinguish good from evil—remained the standards for determining responsibility for three-quarters of a century, until a landmark trial in 1800 set a new standard. These early standards recognized only disorders that totally deprived a person of understanding and memory and that, therefore, precluded the possibility of mens rea (guilty state of mind).

On May 15, 1800, James Hadfield fired a shot at King George III as the king was entering the royal box of the Theatre Royal. Hadfield was tried for high treason. He had been a soldier and had suffered head wounds. Hadfield believed he was the savior of all mankind. He thought that, in order to gain world recognition, it was necessary that he sacrifice himself as had Jesus Christ. In his opening statement, Hadfield's counsel—Thomas Erskine (who later became lord chancellor)—said that Hadfield believed he had been commanded by God to sacrifice himself for the salvation of the world and, rather than commit suicide, had determined to commit a crime that would secure his execution. Hadfield plainly knew what he was doing when he shot at the king—and that it was criminal. Erskine argued that the requirement for a total deprivation of memory and understanding could not be taken literally. The prosecution argued that the defendant's behavior (in the purchase of gun, and powder and slugs for a pistol, and in his concealment of the pistol) showed no indication that Hadfield was either an idiot or a madman "afflicted by the absolute privation of reason."[17]

In fact, Lord Erskine's opening statement anticipated both the *Durham* rule[18] (adopted by the appellate court of the District of Columbia in 1954) and the American Law Institute rule (the rule used by the jury in the *Hinckley* trial) by some 150 years. Erskine argued that a man could know right from wrong; could understand the nature of the act he was about to commit; could manifest a clear design, foresight, and cunning in the planning and executing of it— but that, if his mental condition produced or was the cause of the criminal act, he should not be held legally responsible for it.

Lord Kenyon, the chief justice, recommended to the jury that Hadfield's trial be terminated. The jury accepted the court's suggestion and acquitted the defendant, because "he was under the influence of insanity at the time the act was committed."[19] The Hadfield decision is considered a landmark case because it rejected two well-established concepts. The court rejected the theory that the defendant must be totally deprived of all mental faculty to be acquitted under the insanity defense. Also, it severed the tie between insanity and the ability to distinguish good from evil, or right from wrong.

In the next dozen years, the English courts heard three cases in which the defendants were charged with murder and pleaded insanity. In each case, the English courts returned to the law of criminal responsibility formulated by Mr. Justice Tracy in the *Arnold* case of 1723. All three of the defendants were found guilty and executed. In one of the trials, Lord Chief Justice Mansfield charged the jury as follows:

> [I]t must in fact, be proved beyond all doubt, that at the time he committed the atrocious act with which he stands charged, he did not consider that murder was a crime against the laws of God and nature.[20]

The M'Naghten Insanity Defense Standard

We come, in 1843, to the trial of *The Queen against Daniel M'Naghten*,[21] one of the most thoroughly discussed and controversial cases in English and U.S. law. The case involved a psychotic person—apparently a paranoid schizophrenic—who "intentionally" and with "premeditation" killed an assistant to the prime minister of England because the assailant believed he was being persecuted. Professor Yale Kamisar has observed that this case bears some striking similarities to *United States v. John Hinckley*, especially in terms of the public reaction to the decision and in terms of modifications that resulted in the insanity defense.[22] Daniel M'Naghten—a Scottish woodcutter—assassinated Edward Drummond—secretary to the prime minister, Sir Robert Peel—in the mistaken belief that the secretary was the prime minister. During the trial, nine medical witnesses described M'Naghten as "an extreme paranoiac entangled in an elaborate system of delusions,"[23] who held the prime minister responsible for his continual financial and personal misfortunes. So convincing was the defense's plea that, at the end of the testimony, Lord Chief Justice Tindal—sitting with two other judges—came close to directing the jury's verdict. He told the jury:

> I cannot help remarking in common with my learned brethren that the whole of medical evidence is one side—that it seems almost unnecessary that I should go through the evidence.[24]

He then instructed the jury:

> The point I shall have to submit to you is, whether on the whole of the evidence you have heard, you are satisfied that at the time the act was committed . . . the prisoner had that competent use of his understanding as that he knew what he was doing, by the very act itself, a wicked and a wrong thing? If the prisoner was not sensible at the time he committed the act, that it was a violation of the law of God or of man, undoubtedly he was not responsible for that act or liable to any punishment flowing from that act. . . . If on balancing the evidence in your minds, you think the prisoner capable of distinguishing between right and wrong, then he was a responsible agent and liable to all the penalties the law imposes. If not . . . then you will probably not take upon yourselves to find the prisoner guilty. If this is your opinion, then you will acquit the prisoner.[25]

The jury found the defendant not guilty, on the grounds of insanity. Daniel M'Naghten was committed to Broadmoor Mental Institution, where he remained until his death about 20 years later.

Queen Victoria, the House of Lords, and the newspapers of the day disapproved of the verdict, in angry and bitter tones. M'Naghten's attempted assassination of the prime minister marked the fifth attack on English sovereigns and their ministers since the turn of the century. The government and newspapers interpreted the court's action to be a direct disregard of the dangerous and threatening state of affairs. The press described Broadmoor as a retreat for idlers.

The uproar did not end with official and newspaper disapproval of the verdict. The House of Lords called on the 15 judges of the common law courts to respond to a series of questions on the law applied in the *M'Naghten* case. In effect, the judges had to account for a perceived miscarriage of justice.

The responses of 14 of the judges established a standard for criminal responsibility of the insane. From that time until the present, every case heard in English courts was—and still is—decided along the principles established by the 14 judges' responses to the House of Lords interrogation. Their responses largely crystallized the law as it had been developing for generations, ignoring more recent developments in understanding mental disorders reflected in the *Hadfield* decision and the actual *M'Naghten* trial. Recall that the wild beast test—applied in 1723—provided that, if a person could not distinguish between good and evil and did not know what he or she had done,

there was no "wicked will and intention" (no mens rea). The House
of Lords merely took the next logical step: that persons also lacked
criminal capacity if they did not know what they were doing or were
unable to distinguish between right and wrong, even if their mental
derangement fell a little short of total deprivation of mind and
memory.[26]

Less than a decade later, in 1851, what have become known as
the *M'Naghten* rules were adopted in the federal and most of the
state courts of the United States. Under the prevailing *M'Naghten*
standard—sometimes referred to as the "right–wrong test"—a person
cannot be convicted if, at the time the criminal act was committed,
that person was laboring under such a defect of reason (from a disease
of the mind) as not to know the nature and quality of the act he or
she was doing—or, if that person did know it, as not to know that the
action was wrong. The easy reception of the *M'Naghten* rules into the
law of the United States suggests that there was no well-developed
test of insanity. Before 1800, there were probably not enough reported cases to require—or permit—the law to develop. By 1858, Circuit Justice Clifford was able to observe: "All of the well-considered
cases since 1843, in both countries, are founded upon the doctrine
laid down by the fourteen judges, in the opinion delivered in the
House of Lords at that time."[27]

The word "know" has been the source of much of the controversy and criticism of the *M'Naghten* standard. Critics often assume
that "know" refers only to cognitive or intellectual awareness, and
they argue that there are few—if any—persons who have absolutely
no intellectual awareness of what they are doing. In fact, in most of
the *M'Naghten* jurisdictions, the word "know" is not defined at all,
leaving the jury free to determine the meaning based on the expert
testimony received at trial. Of those jurisdictions that have addressed
the question, the majority have favored a broader construction of the
word. In these states, the word "know" encompasses "affective" or
"emotional" knowledge.[28] As Zilboorg argued in an article written
in 1939, "know" means knowledge "so fused with affect that it becomes a human reality";[29] in the words of Goldstein, "know" refers
to knowledge that "can exist only when the accused is able to evaluate his conduct in terms of its actual impact upon himself and others
and when he is able to appreciate the total setting in which he is
acting."[30] In some of the jurisdictions adopting the restrictive view
of the word "know," the limitation may be of little significance

because of the availability of the "irresistible impulse" control test, in addition to *M'Naghten*.

The irresistible impulse test recognizes insanity as a defense when mental disease prevents the defendant from controlling his or her conduct. The irresistible impulse test predates the *M'Naghten* case. In 1840—just a few years before *M'Naghten*—an English judge instructed the jury in a case where a man named Oxford was charged with treason for firing a pistol at Queen Victoria: "If some controlling disease was, in truth, the acting power within him which he could not resist, then he will not be responsible."[31] The *M'Naghten* rules did not mention this test, probably because the answers to the House of Lords were confined to questions put to the judges in a particular case, which concerned a defendant who had acted because of a delusion. After *M'Naghten*, English trial judges instructed juries only in terms of the right—wrong test, and irresistible impulse was expressly rejected in 1863 as "a most dangerous doctrine."[32]

In the United States, the leading case on the irresistible impulse test came in the 1887 trial of *Parsons v. State*. After instructing the jury on the *M'Naghten* test, the judge stated that, even if this test were not met, the defendant could not be legally responsible: "(1) [i]f by reason of the duress of such mental disease, he had so far lost the power to choose between the right and wrong, and to avoid doing the act in question, as that his free agency was at the time destroyed; (2) and if, at the same time, the alleged crime was so connected with such mental disease, in the relation of cause and effect, as to have been the product of it solely."[33] Jurisdictions using this standard seldom mentioned the phrase "irresistible impulse" in instructions to the jury. The rule is usually stated in terms of a capacity for self-control or free choice. Also, the jury is not ordinarily told that the defendant must have been acting on a sudden impulse or that his or her acts must have been totally irresistible. For this reason, the "irresistible impulse" test is unfortunately named.[34]

In 1946, the U.S. Supreme Court upheld the appellate court's application of the *M'Naghten* standard in *United States v. Fisher*.[35] The Court rejected the doctrine of partial insanity or diminished capacity in the District of Columbia, in the absence of legislation authorizing this doctrine. The question raised was whether it may be possible for a mental disorder to be shown to support a conviction of murder in the second degree, but not of murder in the first degree, on the ground that the defendant's mind at the time was incapable of a deliberate and premeditated design to kill another person.

The *Fisher* case involved the death of the librarian at the Cathedral of St. Peter and St. Paul in Washington, D.C., at the hands of a janitor, Julius Fisher. Psychiatrists testifying for the defense said that Fisher had a mental age of 11 years, a "psychopathic personality of a predominantly aggressive type, and that evidence of a deranged mental condition indicated he was unable to resist the impulse to kill."[36] Counsel for Fisher requested that the jury also be instructed on the question of Fisher's capacity for the premeditation and deliberation necessary to convict for first degree murder, and to take into account the entire personality of the defendant as it was developed by expert evidence in the case. The request was refused.

The jury was charged as follows:

> Insanity, according to the criminal law, is a disease or defect of the mind which renders one incapable to understand the nature and quality of his act, to know that it is wrong, to refrain from doing the wrong act.[37]

Fisher was found guilty of first degree murder, and he was sentenced to die. The U.S. Court of Appeals for the District of Columbia Circuit and the U.S. Supreme Court in a 5–4 vote upheld the verdict.[38]

In a dissenting opinion, Justice Frank Murphy wrote:

> [T]here are persons who, while not totally insane, possess such low mental powers as to be incapable of the deliberation and premeditation requisite to statutory first degree murder. Yet under the rule adopted by the court below, the jury must either condemn such persons to death on the false premise that they possess the mental requirements for a first degree murderer or free them completely from criminal responsibility and turn them loose among society. The jury is forbidden to find them guilty of a lesser degree of murder by reason of their generally weakened or disordered intellect. Common sense and logic recoil at such a rule.[39]

Other state courts have reached the opposite conclusion and recognized the possibility of such unsoundness of mind as to constitute partial diminished capacity, without establishing a total lack of criminal responsibility. It is argued that, just as intoxication—while not an excuse for crime—may disprove the presence of some particular state of mind, a mental disorder could be of such a nature as to produce the same result. If the state of mind required for the guilt of the particular grade or degree of the offense charged be missing—whether because of mental disease or defect or for any other reason—that crime has not been committed.

THE DURHAM RULE AND OTHER RECENT DEVELOPMENTS

The next chapter provides a detailed analysis of the development of insanity defense standards in the federal courts, from the *Durham* rule to the adoption of the American Law Institute's rule in 1962, and—most recently—the enactment of the Insanity Defense Reform Act of 1984. This section merely highlights the major changes between 1954 and 1984.

In the years following *M'Naghten*, only one state—New Hampshire—adopted a rule that was not in line with this standard. The New Hampshire rule was later adopted and modified as the *Durham* rule. In 1868, a New Hampshire jury was trying to decide whether a defendant who had killed his victim with an ax in the course of a robbery was insane. Chief Justice Perley instructed the jury along the following lines:

> If [the jury] found that the defendant killed Brown in a manner that would be criminal and unlawful if the defendant were sane, the verdict should be "not guilty by reason of insanity" if the killing was the offspring or product of mental disease in the defendant; that neither delusion, nor knowledge of right and wrong, nor design, nor cunning in planning and executing the killing, and escaping or avoiding detection, nor ability to recognize acquaintances, or to labor or transact business or manage affairs, is, *as a matter of law*, a test of mental disease; but that *all* symptoms and *all* tests of mental disease are *purely matters of fact* to be determined by the jury.[40]

Under such instructions, the issue of the accused's mental condition—whether he had the capacity for criminal intent—became a question of fact and, therefore, a matter for the jury to determine, not for the court to define.

A few years later, the New Hampshire court made this point even more explicit, when it used the following analogy in its instructions to the jury:

Whether the defendant had a mental disease seems as much a question of fact as whether he had a bodily disease; and whether the killing of his wife was the product of that disease was also as clearly a matter of fact as whether thirst and a quickened pulse are the product of a fever.[41]

The decisions in *State v. Pike* (1870)[42] and *State v. Jones* (1871)[43] are today the law in New Hampshire. But the New Hampshire rule has had little impact outside the borders of that state, and failed to gain adoption in any other jurisdiction for almost a century. Other jurisdictions continued to adhere to the *M'Naghten* "right from wrong" formula.

In 1954, the U.S. Court of Appeals for the District of Columbia handed down its decision discarding the *M'Naghten* rule and introducing a different legal basis for determining criminal responsibility, in *Durham v. United States.*[44]

Unlike many trials involving a defense of insanity, Monte Durham's crime was housebreaking, rather than murder. The defendant, a 26-year-old resident of the District of Columbia, had a long history of mental disorder and petty thievery. He had been committed on several occasions to mental hospitals and had served time in prison for passing bad checks. He received a medical discharge from the navy. On at least two occasions, he had attempted suicide. The judge in the district court instructed the jury along the lines of the *M'Naghten* rule, and the defendant was found guilty.

On appeal, after deciding to grant the defendant a new trial on other grounds, the court went on to announce its new rule for insanity. Speaking for the court, Judge David L. Bazelon stated the new formula:

> The rule we now hold must be applied on the retrial of this case and in future cases is not unlike that followed by the New Hampshire court since 1870. It is simply that an accused is not criminally responsible if his unlawful act was *the product of mental disease or mental defect*. We use "disease" in the sense of a condition which is considered capable of either improving or deteriorating. We use "defect" in the sense of a condition which is not considered capable of either improving or deteriorating and which may be either congenital, or the result of injury, or the residual effect of a physical or mental disease.
>
> Thus your task would not be completed upon finding, if you did find, that the accused suffered from a mental disease or defect. He would still be responsible for his unlawful act if there was not a causal connection between such mental abnormality and the act. These questions must be

determined by you from the facts which you find to be fairly deducible from the testimony and the evidence in this case.[45]

The adoption of the *Durham* rule in the District of Columbia was widely hailed in most psychiatric and some legal circles as the beginning of a new era. As Seymour Halleck stated in 1960: "It is doubtful whether any single case in the criminal law has stirred more comment than *Durham*."[46] The *Durham* decision was regarded as a sign that the law would recognize the growing prestige and knowledge of psychiatry, and would work with it in the disposition of criminal cases, especially those in which the issue of insanity was introduced.

The *Durham* rule, however, did not gain wide acceptance. In the decade following its adoption in the District of Columbia, 30 state and 5 federal courts reviewed and rejected the rule. Two states—Vermont and Maine—adopted it for civil actions, but retained *M'Naghten* for criminal cases.

Twenty-eight years later in the district court in Washington, D.C., a jury found John Hinckley not guilty by reason of insanity, under still another set of legal rules. The *Hinckley* jury was instructed along these lines:

> A person is not responsible for criminal conduct if at the time of such conduct, as a result of mental disease or defect, he lacks substantial capacity either to appreciate the criminality (wrongfulness) of his conduct or to conform his conduct to the requirement of law.[47]

With slight alterations, this formulation—which was written by the American Law Institute in 1962—became the law in a majority of the states and, until October 1984, in the federal circuits. In the words of Judge Irving Kaufman of the appellate bench:

> This test focuses not only on the defendant's understanding of his conduct, which remains a key element in any inquiry into mental capacity, but also on the defendant's ability to control his actions. It would absolve from criminal punishment an individual who knows what he is doing yet is driven to crime by delusions, fears or compulsions. This result conforms to the modern view of the mind as a unified entity whose functioning may be impaired in numerous ways.[48]

Following the controversy over the *Hinckley* verdict, various professional associations convened special committees to study and recommend adoption of a policy vis-à-vis the retention or abolition of the defense of insanity. The National Mental Health Association, the American Psychiatric Association, and the American Bar Association all came out in favor of retaining the defense. The National Mental Health Association noted:

> The Commission strongly believes that this virtual elimination of the insanity defense is unnecessary for the protection of the public, unwise as a matter of public policy and a radical departure from one of the basic precepts of our jurisprudence . . . . [T]he insanity defense, in some form, has been a part of our Anglo-American justice system for centuries.
>
> Certainly proposals which seek to abolish this defense should bear a significant burden of proof in order to demonstrate the urgent need to simply eliminate this concept from our jurisprudence. The Commission does not believe that the proponents of abolition have demonstrated in any fashion that they have met that burden.[49]

The American Psychiatric Association statement contained the following:

> The insanity defense rests upon one of the fundamental premises of the criminal law, that punishment for wrongful deeds should be predicated upon moral culpability. However, within the framework of English and American law, defendants who lack the ability (the capacity) to rationally control their behavior do not possess free will. They cannot be said to have "chosen to do wrong." Therefore, they should not be punished or handled similarly to all other criminal defendants. Retention of the insanity defense is essential to the moral integrity of the criminal law.[50]

The American Bar Association supported retention, and approved the following new test for insanity:

> RESOLVED, that the American Bar Association approves, in principle, a defense of nonresponsibility for a crime which focuses solely on whether the defendant, as a result of mental disease or defect, was unable to appreciate the wrongfulness of his or her conduct at the time of the offense charged.[51]

After reviewing the American Bar Association policy positions and the position statement of the American Psychiatric Association, the Committee on Legal Issues of the American Psychological Association endorsed in principle the position of the American Bar Association that the insanity defense be retained. Swimming against the tide of this professional opinion, the American Medical Association adopted a policy favoring abolition of the insanity defense. The report on which the AMA's policy was based concluded:

> [The insanity defense] has outlived its principal utility, it invites continuing expansion and corresponding abuse, it requires juries to decide cases on the basis of criteria that defy intelligent resolution in the adversary forum of the courtroom, and it impedes efforts to provide needed treatment to mentally ill offenders. As a result, it inspires public cynicism and contributes to erosion of confidence in the law's rationality, fairness, and efficiency.[52]

Within the Reagan administration, there were strong sentiments in favor of abolishing the defense of insanity. Precedent for this position dates back to the Nixon administration. In congressional deliberations over revising the federal criminal code, the Nixon administration included a provision in a proposed comprehensive criminal code reform bill that would have abolished the insanity defense, as follows:

> Section 501. Insanity.
> It is a defense to a prosecution under any federal statute that the defendant, as a result of mental disease or defect, lacked the state of mind required as an element of the offense charged. Mental disease or defect does not otherwise constitute a defense.[53]

Professor Alan Dershowitz has argued that, under the above proposal, a defendant accused—for example—of first degree murder could be convicted even if he were grossly psychotic, so long as he killed "intentionally" and with "premeditation." In his view, the *M'Naghten* case itself illustrates this point. Under the Nixon proposal, M'Naghten would probably have been convicted—even though he was apparently psychotic at the time he pulled the trigger—because the killing was committed intentionally and with premeditation.[54] It follows that, in the *Hinckley* case, evidence of Hinckley's mental condition would have been admissible only if it could show that Hinckley did not intend to kill the president. If such evidence were admitted even by the trial judge, and the jury found that Hinckley intended to kill

the president, it would not have mattered whether Hinckley appreciated the significance of his acts or whether he may not have been
able to control his impulse to commit them. Under this proposal,
insanity is not recognized as a separate defense.

During the debate over the Crime Control Act of 1984, there
existed some congressional sentiment to abolish the insanity defense.
The U.S. Department of Justice formally proposed retaining the
insanity defense but returning to a restrictive standard patterned on
the *M'Naghten* rule. The Insanity Defense Reform Act was passed by
Congress on October 12, 1984, as one part of the Comprehensive
Crime Control Act of 1984.[55]

The Insanity Defense Reform Act of 1984 represents the first
federal codification of the insanity defense. The new standard provides for the affirmative defense that "the defendant, as a result of a
severe mental disease or defect, was unable to appreciate the nature
and quality or the wrongfulness of his acts." This formulation does
not allow an insanity defense based on a defendant's inability to conform his conduct to the requirements of the law, as provided by the
American Law Institute standard.

The act also shifts the burden of proof from the prosecution to
the defendant, who must prove insanity by a standard of clear and
convincing evidence. It changes the verdict form to not guilty *only* by
reason of insanity, and establishes a federal procedure for commitment of persons who have been found not guilty only by reason of
insanity.

The act also limits the role of experts, such that:

> No expert witness testifying with respect to the mental state or condi-
> tion of a defendant in a criminal case may state an opinion or inference
> as to whether the defendant did or did not have the mental state or
> condition constituting an element of the crime charged or of a defense
> thereto. Such ultimate issues are matters for the trier of fact alone.

During the three-year period after the *Hinckley* acquittal, approximately half of the states enacted some limitations on the insanity
defense. Congress restricted the insanity standard on the federal level;
nine states also narrowed the substantive test of insanity. Seven states
shifted the burden of proof to the defendant. Prior to *Hinckley*, a
bare majority of the states had placed the burden of proof on the
prosecution to disprove a defendant's insanity claim beyond a reason-

able doubt, after sufficient evidence of mental disorder had been produced to raise the defense. Presently, two-thirds of the states require that the defendant bear the ultimate burden of persuasion that he or she was insane. Most states require that the defendant prove insanity "by a preponderance of the evidence"—a lower standard than the federal standard of "clear and convincing evidence." Further, 8 states have supplemented the insanity verdict with a separate verdict of guilty but mentally ill, bringing to 12 the number of states using this approach.[56] The guilty but mentally ill statutes are discussed in Chapter 6 of this book. Finally, one state—Utah—abolished the insanity defense altogether, joining two other states—Montana and Idaho—which had abolished the defense earlier. These states do admit evidence of mental disorder for the narrow purpose of proving that the defendant did not have the special knowledge or intent required for conviction of the offense charged—similar to the Nixon administration proposal discussed above.

NOTES

1. Abraham S. Goldstein, *The Insanity Defense* (New Haven: Yale University Press, 1967), p. 223.

2. Norval Morris, *Madness and the Criminal Law* (Chicago: University of Chicago Press, 1982), pp. 61–64.

3. Francis Allen, *The Borderline of Criminal Justice* (Chicago: University of Chicago Press, 1964), p. 105.

4. Henry J. Steadman, "Empirical Research on the Insanity Defense," *Annals of American Academy of Political and Social Sciences* 2 (January 1985).

5. Ibid., p. 3.

6. Board of Trustees of the American Psychiatric Association (APA), *American Psychiatric Association Statement on the Insanity Defense* 5 (December 1982).

7. Richard A. Pasewark, "Insanity Plea: A Review of the Research Literature," *Law and Psychiatry* 362–63 (1982).

8. Henry J. Steadman, "Insanity Acquittals in New York State," *American Journal of Psychiatry* 324 (March 1980).

9. David E. Aaronson, "Maryland Responds to the *Hinckley* Case: Changes in the Insanity Defense," 85 *Maryland Bar Journal* 33, 35 (1985).

10. David E. Aaronson, "The Insanity Defense: Law and Policy," 111 *Federal Rules Decisions* 223 (1986) (panelist presenter, Judicial Conference, District of Columbia Circuit).

11. Governor's Task Force to Review the Defense of Insanity, Executive Department, State of Maryland, *Report to the Governor* (1984), p. 20.

12. Alan Stone, *Mental Health and Law: A System in Transition*, DHEW pub. no. (ADM) 75-176 (Rockville, Md.: NIMH 1975), p. 218.

13. *Ford v. Wainwright*, U.S., 106 S. Ct. 2595 (1986).

14. David W. Carrither, "The Defense of Insanity and Presidential Peril," *Society* 23-27.6 (July/August 1985).

15. Barbara A. Weiner, "Not Guilty by Reason of Insanity: A Sane Approach," *Chicago-Kent Law Review* 1057-85 (1980).

16. Rita J. Simon, *The Jury and the Defense of Insanity* (Boston: Little, Brown, 1967), p. 17.

17. *Rex v. Hadfield* (K.B. 1800), 27 St. Tr. 1281, 1312-15 (1820).

18. *Durham v. United States*, 94 U.S. App. D.C. 228, 214 F.2d 862 (D.C. Cir. 1954).

19. 27 *Hadfield* St. Tr. 1281 (1800), as quoted in Pasewark, "Insanity Plea."

20. Simon, *Jury and Insanity*, p. 19.

21. *Regina v. M'Naghten*, 10 Cl. and F. 200, 8 Eng. Rep. 718 (1843).

22. Yale Kamisar, "The Assassination Attempt," University of Michigan Law School *Law Quadrangle Notes* 1 (Fall 1982).

23. Simon, *Jury and Insanity*, p. 20.

24. Ibid.

25. Ibid., p. 21.

26. Rollin M. Perkins and Ronald N. Boyce, *Criminal Law* (3d ed., Mineola, N.Y.: Foundation Press, 1982), p. 960. At a meeting of the Association of Medical Officers of Hospitals and Asylums for the Insane on July 14, 1864, Dr. Harrington Tuke moved and the assembly adopted a resolution:

> That so much of the legal test of the mental condition of an alleged criminal lunatic as renders him a responsible agent, because he knows the difference between right and wrong, is inconsistent with the fact well known to every member of this meeting, that the power of distinguishing between right and wrong exists very frequently among those who are undoubtedly insane, and is often associated with dangerous and uncontrollable delusions.

27. *United States v. Holmes*, 26 F. Cas. 349, 358 (No. 15,382) (Cir. Ct. D. Me.).

28. Wayne R. LaFave and Austin W. Scott, Jr., *Handbook on Criminal Law* (St. Paul, Mn.: West Publishing Co., 1972), pp. 276-77.

29. Gregory Zilboorg, M.D., "Misconceptions of Legal Insanity," 9 *Am. J. Orthopsychiatry* 540, 552-53 (1939).

30. Goldstein, *Insanity Defense*, p. 49.

31. *Regina v. Oxford*, 175 Eng. Rep. 941, 950 (1840).

32. *Regina v. Burton*, 176 Eng. Rep. 354, 357 (1863).

33. *Parsons v. State*, 81 Ala. 577, 2 So. 854 (1887).

34. LaFave and Scott, *Criminal Law*, p. 284.

35. *United States v. Fisher*, 328 U.S. 463, 66 S. Ct. 1318 (1946).

36. John Biggs, *The Guilty Mind* (New York: Harcourt, Brace, 1955), pp. 138–39.

37. Ibid., pp. 142–43.

38. Ibid., p. 143.

39. Ibid., pp. 143–44.

40. Simon, *Jury and Insanity*, p. 25.

41. Ibid., p. 31. Emphasis in original.

42. *State v. Pike*, 49 N.H. 399 (1870).

43. *State v. Jones*, 50 N.H. 369 (1871).

44. *Durham v. United States*, 94 U.S. App. D.C. 228, 214 F.2d 862 (1954). Emphasis in original.

45. Simon, *Jury and Insanity*, p. 32.

46. Seymour Halleck, "Insanity Defense in the District of Columbia—A Legal Lorelie," 49 *Geo. L. J.* 294 (1950).

47. American Law Institute, *Model Penal Code*, sec. 4.01 (Philadelphia: ALI, 1962).

48. Irving Kaufman, "The Insanity Plea on Trial," *New York Times Magazine*, August 8, 1982, p. 18.

49. Ingo Kelitz and Junius P. Fulton, *The Insanity Defense and Its Alternatives: A Guide for Policy Makers* (Williamsburg, Va.: Institute on Mental Disability and the Law, National Center for State Courts, 1984).

50. APA, *Statement on the Insanity Defense.*

51. American Bar Association, *American Bar Association Policy on the Insanity Defense* (approved by the ABA House of Delegates on February 9, 1983).

52. Committee on Medicolegal Problems, American Medical Association, "Insanity Defense in Criminal Trials and Limitations of Psychiatric Testimony: Report of Board of Trustees," 251 *J.A.M.A.* 2967 (1984).

53. Criminal Code Reform Act of 1973, S. 1400, 93d Cong., 1st sess. (March 17, 1973). See also Heathcote W. Wales, "An Analysis of the Proposal to 'Abolish' the Insanity Defense in S.1: Squeezing a Lemon," 124 *U. Pa. L. Rev.* 687 (1976).

54. Alan Dershowitz, "Abolishing the Insanity Defense: The Most Significant Feature of the Administration's Proposed Criminal Code—An Essay," 9 *Crim. L. Bull.* 434 (1973).

55. The Comprehensive Crime Control Act of 1984 is title II of Public Law 98–473, 98 Stat. 1837, 1976, enacted October 12, 1984. The act comprises 23 chapters. Chapter IV of the Crime Control Act deals with offenders with mental disease or defect. The revised insanity defense standard appears in 18 U.S.C., sec. 20 (1984).

56. Peter W. Low, John Calvin Jeffries, Jr., and Richard J. Bonnie, *The Trial of John W. Hinckley, Jr.: A Case Study in the Insanity Defense* (Mineola, N.Y.: Foundation Press, 1986), pp. 126–27, 130, 132.

2

Rules of Law and Burdens of Proof: From *Durham* to the Insanity Defense Reform Act of 1984 *(with the assistance of Eric Yarvin)*

This chapter provides a detailed analysis of post–World War II developments in the insanity defense. The focus is on the more recent evolution of insanity defense standards and on burdens of proof. In content and style, this is the most traditionally "legal" chapter in the book. The case law discussed has provided the basis of the judge's instructions to the jury on the law of insanity.

The first part of the chapter continues our discussion of the evolution of insanity defense standards. Because the *Durham* rule was a federal case and because significant refinements to the American Law Institute (ALI) test occurred in the federal courts, the discussion here is based on federal case law. The first section concludes with an analysis of the revised standard in the Insanity Defense Reform Act of 1984. As mentioned earlier, several states have adopted so-called guilty but mentally ill statutes in response to the *Hinckley* verdict. These statutes are discussed in Chapter 6.

The second part of the chapter examines the burdens of proof in the presentation of the insanity defense, both on the federal and state level. While the controversy now appears to be settled on the federal level, constitutional issues are analyzed.

In connection with this chapter, the Appendix at the end of the book is a chart that summarizes how the defense of insanity is treated in all 50 states. It includes the most recent legal standards, burdens of proof, and verdict forms.

FROM DURHAM TO THE INSANITY DEFENSE
REFORM ACT OF 1984

The Durham Rule

In the period preceding adoption of the *Durham* test for criminal responsibility, the District of Columbia Circuit Court had used the predominant standard of the times: the *M'Naghten* rule supplemented by the irresistible impulse test.[1] In 1954, however, the District of Columbia Circuit embarked on a new course for determining the appropriate standard of insanity—in response to increasing criticism directed toward the *M'Naghten* rule—when it overruled *M'Naghten* in *Durham v. United States.*[2] While the *Durham* rule is no longer law,[3] it enjoyed a turbulent 18-year existence, which produced a wealth of insanity defense jurisprudence unrivalled elsewhere.[4] Moreover, some of the solutions to issues developed during this period have been adopted in other insanity defense formulations.

The *Durham* rule differed from previous tests of insanity in at least one significant respect. While most other tests of criminal responsibility emphasized an incapacitating or debilitating condition—cognitive (intellectual)/volitional (control) impairment—resulting from mental illness, *Durham* was unconcerned with any incapacitating condition other than the mental illness itself. Thus, the test was quite broad, if applied according to its literal meaning. Many observers criticized this aspect of the rule because, if literally applied, it could have effectively operated to exculpate large numbers of defendants previously held culpable for their criminal acts. For this reason, many members of the legal and psychiatric professions reacted to the *Durham* standard with skepticism and hostility. Attempts to limit and redefine its potentially broad application commenced immediately after announcement of the new test. Before we address these issues, we examine the *Durham* decision itself.

A U.S. district judge sitting without a jury convicted Monte Durham of housebreaking. At the time that *Durham* was decided, the federal courts in the District of Columbia had jurisdiction over federal offenses as well as felonies committed in violation of local law. The only defense asserted at trial was that the defendant was of "unsound mind" at the time of the offense. As noted in Chapter 1, Durham had a long history of imprisonment and psychiatric hospitalization. On numerous occasions preceding the charge of housebreaking, psychiatrists had diagnosed Durham as suffering from a

"personality disorder" or "psychosis with psychopathic personality."
On several occasions, he was committed to mental institutions after
being adjudged "incompetent to stand trial."[5] Against this background, the trial began.

The trial court rejected the defendant's defense of insanity and
convicted him of the offense charged. The trial judge made the following observation:

> I don't think it has been established that the defendant was of unsound
> mind as of July 13, 1951, in the sense that he didn't know the differ-
> ence between right and wrong or that even if he did, he was subject to
> an irresistible impulse by reason of the derangement of mind.
>
> While, of course, the burden of proof on the issue of mental capacity
> to commit a crime is upon the Government, just as it is on every other
> issue, nevertheless, the Court finds that there is not sufficient evidence
> to contradict the usual presumption of the usual inference of sanity.
>
> *There is no testimony concerning the mental state of the defendant
> of July 13, 1951, and therefore the usual presumption of sanity governs.*
>
> *While if there was some testimony as to his mental state as of that
> date to the effect that he was incompetent on that date, the burden of
> proof would be on the Government to overcome it. There has been no
> such testimony, and the usual presumption of sanity prevails.*[6]

Based on this statement, a court of appeals then reversed Durham's conviction, because the trial judge had improperly decided that
the burden of proof did not shift to the government. Under the prevailing view—the court observed—"as soon as some evidence of mental disorder is introduced" by the defendant, "sanity, like any other
fact must be proved as part of the prosecutor's case beyond a reasonable doubt."[7] For this and other reasons, the appellate court reversed
the conviction, and remanded for a new trial. The court then went on
to consider whether a new test for criminal responsibility should replace the *M'Naghten* rule.

After reviewing the history of the insanity defense in the United
States and addressing the criticisms of the *M'Naghten* and irresistible
impulse tests, the court found that "as an exclusive criterion the
right–wrong test is inadequate in that (a) it does not take sufficient
account of psychic realities and scientific knowledge, and (b) it is
based upon one symptom and so cannot validly be applied in all circumstances."[8] The court also found the irresistible impulse test
invalid partly because it "gives no recognition to mental illness

characterized by brooding and reflection and so relegates acts caused by such illness to the application of the inadequate right–wrong test."[9] As a result, the court concluded that "a broader test should be adopted."[10]

The court stated a new test: "[A]n accused is not criminally responsible if his unlawful act was the product of mental disease or mental defect."[11] As noted in Chapter 1, the court then explained its definition of mental disease or defect as follows:

> We use "disease" in the sense of a condition which is considered capable of either improving or deteriorating. We use "defect" in the sense of a condition which is not considered capable of either improving or deteriorating and which may be either congenital, or the result of injury, or the residual effect of a physical or mental disease.[12]

The court formulated the following general instructions for the jury to follow:

> If you the jury believe beyond a reasonable doubt that the accused was not suffering from a diseased or defective mental condition at the time he committed the criminal act charged, you may find him guilty. If you believe he was suffering from a disease or defective mental condition when he committed the act, but believe beyond a reasonable doubt that the act was not the product of such mental abnormality, you may find him guilty. Unless you believe beyond a reasonable doubt either that he was not suffering from a diseased or defective mental condition, or that the act was not the product of such abnormality, you must find the accused not guilty by reason of insanity. Thus your task would not be completed upon finding, if you did find, that the accused suffered from a mental disease or defect. He would still be responsible for his unlawful act if there was no causal connection between such mental abnormality and the act.[13]

The jury—the court declared—is not required to depend on "selected symptoms, phases or manifestations."[14] The inquiry permits the jury to consider "whether an accused, who suffered from a mental disease or defect, did not know the difference between right and wrong, acted under the compulsion of an irresistible impulse or had been deprived of or lost the power of his will."[15] In this manner—the court concluded—the jury will be most able to perform its function in making its judgment and "will be guided by wider horizons of knowledge concerning mental life. The question will be simply whether the accused acted because of a mental disorder, and not whether the accused displayed particular symptoms which medical science has long recognized do not necessarily, or even typically, accompany even the most serious mental disorder."[16]

In the aftermath of the announcement of the *Durham* decision, many members of the legal community sought to narrow the *Durham* rule, in fear of its broad application. These steps focused on two key issues: (1) how to determine what acts were "products" of mental disease, defect, or disorder; and (2) how to define "mental disease" and "mental defect." Before the court had the opportunity to consider these issues, the question of *Durham's* relation to other insanity defense standards was addressed.

In *Douglas v. United States*,[17] the defendant was convicted of two robberies in separate trials. During the appeals trial, the defendant offered testimony of his insanity, through psychiatrists who had examined him prior to trial. The appellate court reversed the conviction and held that the *Durham* rule was not intended to bar all reference to either the *M'Naghten* or irresistible impulse tests. Rather, testimony couched in terms of the defendant's ability to distinguish between right and wrong and the ability to refrain from doing the unlawful act may still be used by the trial court, despite the fact that *Durham* rejected such testimony as the *sole* criteria for determining criminal responsibility. *Durham*—the court noted—"gives greater latitude" to the jury. Therefore, although no longer used as the exclusive test for criminal responsibility, such evidence may be considered by the trier of fact, to determine whether the accused acted because of mental disease or defect.

The flood of critical commentary on the *Durham* rule increased in 1957 when the same court enunciated a broad test of causation, in defining the phrase "product of" in *Carter v. United States*: "The simple fact that a person has a mental disease or defect is not enough to relieve him of responsibility for a crime." Rather, "[t]here must be a relationship between the disease and the criminal act; and the relationship must be such as to justify a reasonable inference that the act would not have been committed if the person had not been suffering from the disease."[18] The court then explained what it meant by "product of":

When we say the defense of insanity requires that the act be a "product of" a disease, we do not mean that it must be a direct emission, or a proximate creation, or an immediate issue of the disease. . . . We do not mean to restrict this defense to such cases; many mental diseases so affect areas of the mind that some or all of the mental elements requisite to criminal liability under the law are lacking. We mean to include such cases.

When we say the defense of insanity requires that the act be a "product of" a disease, we mean that the facts on the record are such that the trier of the facts is enabled to draw a reasonable inference that the accused would not have committed the act he did commit if he had not been diseased as he was. *There must be a relationship between the disease and the act, and that relationship, whatever it may be in degree, must be, as we have already said, critical in its effect in respect to the act. By "critical" we mean decisive, determinative, causal; we mean to convey the idea inherent in the phrases "because of," "except for," "without which," "but for," "effect of," "result of," "causative factor"; the disease made the effective or decisive difference between doing and not doing the act.* The short phrases "product of" and "causal connection" are not intended to be precise, as though they were chemical formulae. They mean that the facts concerning the disease and the facts concerning the act are such as to justify reasonably the conclusion that "but for this disease the act would not have been committed."[19]

In stating the causal relation required under *Durham*, the court observed that this inference necessarily involved the "trait assumption" that, if the disease had not existed, the person would have been a law-abiding citizen. The court, however, did note that such an assumption is not necessarily true, and can rarely—if ever—be proved.[20]

The court's broad definition of the phrase "product of" as a but-for test of causation generated significant criticism, both from without and within the court. In a concurring opinion in 1961 in *Blocker v. United States*, Judge Burger (later to become chief justice of the U.S. Supreme Court) voiced his criticism:

Apart from all other objections, the product aspect of *Durham* is a fallacy in this: assuming arguendo that a criminal act can be the "product" of a "mental disease" that fact should not per se excuse the defendant; it should exculpate only if the condition described as a "mental disease" affected him so substantially that he could not appreciate the nature of the illegal act or could not control his conduct.[21]

Another criticism of the broad definition of the term "product"—as noted in *Frigillana v. United States* in 1962[22]—was that it placed an almost impossible burden on the prosecution to prove beyond a reasonable doubt that the unlawful act and the mental disease were *not* causally related. The then U.S. attorney for the District of Columbia noted that, if a psychiatrist can come to a firm opinion on the product issue, it is almost invariably in the defendant's favor: "While occasionally one can say that an act *was* a product of mental disease, one can rarely if ever say that an act was *not* a product. To analogize, one can sometimes find a needle in the haystack, but one cannot find that there is *not* a needle in the haystack."[23] A case decided under the *Durham* rule illustrates that this criticism has some merit. In 1957, the court in *Wright v. United States* held that the government had not sustained its burden of proof. Of 11 testifying psychiatrists, no opinion on the product issue was elicited from 5; 2 said they had insufficient data to support a conclusion; 1 said it was "likely" that there was a causal connection; another said there "could very well be" a causal connection; still another, that it was "surely possible"; and the last answered "yes" to a hypothetical question on the matter.[24] It has been argued that this case was not unusual in the degree of its ambiguity on the product issue.[25]

The term "product" was also criticized as having no clinical significance for psychiatrists and psychologists. Once an opinion had been given by a psychiatrist, its broad definition made it even more difficult for jurors to make an independent assessment of the weight to attach to the expert's opinion. In 1967, the District of Columbia Circuit Court of Appeals responded to these criticisms in the landmark case of *Washington v. United States.*[26] The court held that psychiatrists may no longer give a conclusion to the jury as to whether the alleged offense was the product of a mental illness:

> The term "product" has no clinical significance for psychiatrists. Thus, there is no justification for permitting psychiatrists to testify on the ultimate issue. Psychiatrists should explain how defendant's disease or defect relates to his alleged offense, that is, how the development, adaptation and functioning of defendant's behavioral processes may have influenced his conduct. But psychiatrists should not speak directly in terms of "product," or even "result" or "cause."[27]

Part of the underpinning of the *Durham* rule was that the *M'Nagh-ten* and irresistible impulse tests—as applied by many trial judges—placed undue restrictions on expert testimony. The *Washington* opinion recognized that *Durham* had given expert witnesses too much authority; and, as a result, it placed clear limits on the role of the expert while testifying. As the court noted in *Washington*, its opinion was designed to eliminate a fundamental cause of unsatisfactory expert testimony—namely, the tendency of the expert to use "concepts [which] can become slogans, hiding facts and representing nothing more than the witness's own conclusion about the defendant's criminal responsibility." It recognized that—while psychiatrists and psychologists are called to testify about the medical component of the responsibility issue—by testifying in terms of a nonmedical construct ("product"), they express conclusions that—in essence—embody ethical and legal conclusions.

While criticism of the product test of causation was mounting, critics of the *Durham* rule also sought to limit or modify the broad and general definitions of "disease" and "defect." Critics asserted that the *Durham* definition simply differentiated between "disease" and "defect," and failed to define the terms in any useful way—especially in light of the sweeping broadness of the concept of mental illness as used by the majority of the psychiatric profession who were called on to assist the jury in its ultimate determination. In the minds of some observers, the phrase "mental disease or defect" could include not only psychotic manifestations—which other tests were specifically limited to—but also various forms of neurosis, personality defects, and other relatively minor disorders. In 1957, the court suggested that, indeed, the term "mental disease" had no clear boundaries. In *Briscoe v. United States*, the court stated that "[t]he assumption that psychosis is a legally sufficient mental disease and that other illnesses are not is clearly erroneous."[28]

In the absence of definition for "mental disease or defect," medical experts attached to it meanings that would naturally occur to them—medical meanings. In test cases under *Durham*, disputes about nomenclature arose: such as whether "psychopath," "sociopath," or other types of "neuroses" were mental diseases. This problem was dramatically highlighted by the weekend flip-flop case, *In re Rosenfield*.[29] The petitioner was described as a "sociopath." A St. Elizabeth's Hospital psychiatrist testified that a person with a sociopathic personality was not suffering from a mental disease. That was on a

Friday afternoon. On the following Monday morning—through a policy change at St. Elizabeth's Hospital—it was determined as an administrative matter that the state of a psychopathic or sociopathic personality did constitute a mental disease.[30] Cases such as *In re Rosenfield* intensified the criticism that the undefined phrase "mental disease or defect" left the jury without standards to guide it and made it unduly dependent on the experts' classifications of mental abnormalities.

The concern that medical terminology not control legal outcomes resulted in a major modification of the *Durham* test in 1962. In *McDonald v. United States*,[31] the court recognized that the phrase "mental disease or defect" has various meanings—depending on how and why it is used, and by whom. "Mental disease" means one thing in the situation of a physician—where medical terms are developed to facilitate treatment—but something different—even if somewhat overlapping—to a court of law seeking to define a standard of criminal responsibility. *McDonald* set out to give the phrase a legal definition. "Our purpose"—the court stated—"is to make it very clear that neither the court nor the jury is bound by *ad hoc* definitions or conclusions as to what experts say is a disease or defect. What psychiatrists may consider a 'mental disease or defect' for clinical purposes . . . may or may not be the same as mental disease or defect for the jury's purpose."[32]

In defining mental illness under *Durham* for purposes of the jury's determination of the criminal responsibility of the accused, the jury should be instructed that:

> A mental disease or defect includes any abnormal condition of the mind which substantially affects mental or emotional processes and substantially impairs behavior controls. Thus the jury would consider testimony concerning the development, adaptation and functioning of these processes and controls.[33]

The court emphasized that psychiatric opinion or definitions should not control the jury in its determination. In the court's view, since the jury ultimately decides the question of whether the defendant has a mental disease or defect, the jury itself must determine from all the expert and lay testimony "whether the nature and degree of the disability are sufficient to establish a mental disease or defect," as defined by the court.[34]

Two observations may be noted about the legal definition of "mental disease or defect" enunciated in *McDonald*. First, while the court did not directly abandon the but-for definition of "product," this definition of "mental disease or defect" indirectly responded to the criticism discussed earlier—such as Judge Burger's comments in the *Blocker* case—by requiring a substantial relationship between the mental disease and the unlawful act. Second, because a mental condition must have behavioral consequences to qualify as a mental disease or defect, *Durham* was limited in such a way that it closely resembled the American Law Institute "substantial capacity test" discussed below.

In *Washington v. United States*—which prohibited expert witnesses from testifying directly in terms of product—the court also criticized the practice of experts couching their testimony in terms of medical labels. The court admonished psychiatrists and psychologists to limit the use of medical labels "such as schizophrenia or neurosis" as much as is practical.[35] As discussed in the next chapter on expert witnesses, the court appended to its decision an instruction for the benefit of jurors about the role of expert witnesses who testify in insanity defense trials, which has now become a standard jury instruction in the District of Columbia. The court stated that the expert could still testify as to whether the defendant was suffering from a "mental disease or defect," since the term used may have some "clinical significance"—unlike the term "product," which has only legal significance.

As demonstrated by the above discussion, *McDonald* in 1962 and *Washington* in 1967 together significantly modified the test for criminal responsibility announced in 1954 in *Durham*. By the end of the 1960s, it was abundantly clear that *Durham*—even as modified—was creating more problems than solutions. In 1972, the court in *United States v. Brawner*[36] finally rejected *Durham* as a workable standard for determining criminal responsibility, and adopted the ALI test.

While *Brawner* is mostly concerned with laying the groundwork for adoption of the ALI standard, the court did indicate why it decided to abandon *Durham*. The principal reason given was the "undesirable characteristic" or "undue dominance by the experts giving testimony."[37] Although the court had tried to alleviate this problem in *McDonald* and *Washington*, the difficulty in separating the roles of expert witness and jury remained unresolvable. "The more we have pondered the problem," the court noted, "the more convinced we have become that the sound solution lies not in further shaping of the *Durham* 'product' approach in more refined molds, but in adopting the ALI's formulation as the linchpin of our jurisprudence."[38]

The court accepted the objective of *Durham* as still sound—in that it permitted the jury to consider all the relevant information within the expert's professional judgment—but concluded that the ALI formulation permitted a reasonable accommodation between the experts, the jury, and the judges and lawyers, while retaining the beneficial relationship between the mental illness and the criminal act.

In sum, while *Durham* may be considered a failure in the sense that the same court that made the decision ultimately rejected it and that no other federal court ever accepted the decision, the *Durham* years produced a wealth of insanity defense jurisprudence unrivalled elsewhere. Its solutions to some of the issues are reflected in other insanity defense formulations. Thus, *Durham* can be viewed as having made a major contribution to the development of the law relating to the insanity defense.

The American Law Institute (ALI) Test

In 1953—one year prior to the District of Columbia Circuit's holding in *Durham*—a group of distinguished members of the legal and medical professions began an intensive study on the problem of criminal responsibility, under the auspices of the American Law Institute (ALI). After considerable debate and the submission of a number of proposed drafts, the ALI drafted the Model Penal Code test for criminal responsibility in 1962. Section 4.01 of the Model Penal Code sets forth the applicable standard of insanity:

> Section 4.01 (1) A person is not responsible for criminal conduct if at the time of such conduct as a result of mental disease or defect he lacks substantial capacity either to appreciate the criminality (wrongfulness) of his conduct or to conform his conduct to the requirements of law. (2) As used in this Article, the terms "mental disease or defect" do not include an abnormality manifested only by repeated criminal or otherwise anti-social conduct.[39]

The ALI test can best be understood by examining its five operative concepts. These concepts together represent a critical difference from previous efforts at defining legal insanity: (1) mental disease or defect; (2) lack of substantial capacity; (3) appreciation; (4) criminality/wrongfulness; and (5) conformity of conduct to the requirements of the law. The changes that these concepts brought to the *M'Naghten* rule, the *Durham* rule, and the irresistible impulse test are discussed below.

The ALI test incorporates basic underlying theories concerning cognitive (intellectual) and volitional (ability to choose or control) aspects of the human personality—theories that *M'Naghten* and the irresistible impulse test had recognized earlier. Therefore, Subsection 1 above excuses a defendant from criminal responsibility when he or she "lacks substantial capacity to appreciate the criminality (wrongfulness) of his [or her] conduct." This is an expression of the test's recognition of a defendant's cognitive incapacity. Likewise, the ALI test recognizes a defendant's volitional incapacity, by the phrase "lacks substantial capacity . . . to conform his [or her] conduct to the requirements of law." Again, while it may appear that the Model Penal Code's recognition of the cognitive and volitional elements closely resembles the *M'Naghten* rule supplemented by the irresistible impulse test, the authors' carefully chosen language differentiates the Model Penal Code from previous tests of insanity.

By the early 1970s, every federal circuit with the exception of the First Circuit and the District of Columbia had abandoned the *M'Naghten* rule—whether standing alone or supplemented by the irresistible impulse test—and had adopted the ALI test.[40] As noted above, the District of Columbia Circuit rejected the *Durham* rule in favor of the ALI test in 1972.[41] Although a majority of the federal circuits eventually adopted the ALI test without modification, some circuits modified the test, either by expressly omitting some portion or by substituting its own definitions in place of the Model Penal Code definitions. The following discussion addresses the relevant case law of various federal courts, regarding the ALI test. We first examine the reasons justifying the switch from the earlier tests of insanity to the Model Penal Code formulation, with emphasis on those federal circuits that adopted the test without modification. Then, we shift focus to explain why some circuits felt compelled to modify the ALI standard.

Generally speaking, the ALI test—like *Durham*—sought to implement some of the scientific advancements that the psychiatric profession had made during the first half of the twentieth century. At the same time, the test was designed to avoid the causation problem inherent in the "product" approach of the *Durham* rule, and the single-minded emphasis on the concept of right and wrong commonly associated with the *M'Naghten* rule. Thus, the federal circuits believed that the ALI test—although not a perfect solution—substantially improved the legal standard of insanity, and they quickly accepted it as a viable alternative to the earlier standards of legal insanity.

In *United States v. Freeman*,[42] the Second Circuit rejected the *M'Naghten* test and instead opted for the ALI standard as "the soundest yet formulated." The court explained that the *M'Naghten* rule was incompatible with modern psychiatric theory because it focused solely on the cognitive or intellectual component of the mind—the ability to distinguish between right and wrong. In contrast, the ALI formulation "views the mind as a unified entity and recognizes that mental disease or defect may impair its functioning in numerous ways."[43]

Another reason why the court adopted the ALI test is its explicit recognition of degrees of incapacity. The *M'Naghten* rule required a complete and total lack of capacity to distinguish between right and wrong. A primary virtue of the ALI test was its use of the adjective "substantial" to describe incapacity.[44] In the court's view, this modifying adjective broadened *M'Naghten* and, thus, while "'any' incapacity is not sufficient to justify avoidance of criminal responsibility . . . 'total' incapacity is also unnecessary."[45]

The court also noted that use of the term "appreciate" in the Model Penal Code test rather than "know" was a significant change from the *M'Naghten* rule.[46] "[M]ere intellectual awareness that conduct is wrongful, when divorced from appreciation or understanding of the moral or legal import of behavior, can have little significance," the court explained.[47] Thus, the ALI test further expanded the *M'Naghten* rule by requiring a failure to apprehend the significance of one's actions in some deeper sense involving "affect" or "emotional appreciation," rather than some surface understanding or verbalization of knowledge.[48]

Apart from the beneficial aspects that the ALI standard had in comparison to the *M'Naghten* rule, the *Freeman* court also expressed its preference for the new formulation because it was "free of many of the defects which accompanied *Durham*"—primarily the problem of expert testimony.[49] While the court viewed expert testimony as indispensable to the determination of criminal responsibility, it found that the ALI formulation provided the jury with a workable standard—

in more understandable terms—without relying on conclusions based on causal relationships made by the expert. As the court concluded: "Relieved of their burden of divining precise causal relationships, the judge or jury can concentrate upon the ultimate decisions which are properly theirs, fully informed as to the facts."[50]

Other federal circuits that considered adopting the ALI test generally accepted the Second Circuit's views. For instance, the Fourth Circuit adopted the ALI formulation without modification, in *United States v. Chandler*.[51] There, the court declared that the ALI test—although not perfect—substantially rectified the dangers and problems of the earlier tests of insanity. Recognizing both the cognitive and volitional elements, the court observed that the test requires an unrestricted inquiry into the entire personality of the defendant. The ALI test allows considerable expert testimony, while avoiding a diagnostic approach; and it leaves the jury free to make its findings in terms of a standard that jurors can more easily comprehend and apply.[52]

Like the *Freeman* court, other federal circuits adopting the ALI test without modification placed strong emphasis on the phrase "lacks substantial capacity" as the primary factor mandating departure from the earlier tests of insanity. In *United States v. Shapiro*[53]— for example—the court found the ALI test preferable to the *M'Naghten* rule, since it "does not require the total incapacity [of the defendant] in the cognitive area."[54]

Discussing the volitional component of the ALI test, the court stated that the most notable and critical difference between the two tests is that *M'Naghten* supplemented by the irresistible impulse test "requires complete destruction of the power of self-control, where ALI requires only that the defendant have less than 'substantial capacity' to conform his conduct."[55] Contrary to the government's contention that use of the term "substantial" in the ALI test makes it too "liberal" because "it creates the real danger that a jury might acquit those, who while morally responsible for their conduct are nonetheless in need of psychiatric treatment,"[56] the court concluded "that in this difficult field absolutes are not realistic . . . and the ALI approach is preferable."[57]

In *Blake v. United States*,[58] the Fifth Circuit adopted the ALI formulation without modification, for precisely the same reasons cited in other circuits. Noting that one of the primary questions in the administration of the defense of insanity was whether legal insanity should be defined in terms of substantial or total lack of mental capacity, the court held that "a substantiality type standard is called for in light of current knowledge regarding mental illness."[59] The court reasoned that the term "substantial" permits the jury to determine whether the alleged mental defect was related to the conduct in question under all the evidence—expert and lay. The court concluded that the Model Code's definition of insanity enables "the court and jury to give effect to the defense of insanity in terms of what is now known about diseases of the mind."[60]

Lastly, the Eighth Circuit in *United States v. Frazier*[61] rejected the *M'Naghten* rule as modified by the irresistible impulse test, and accepted the ALI test. In *Frazier*, the court examined both prongs of the ALI test in relation to the *M'Naghten*/irresistible impulse approach. The court found the *M'Naghten* cognitive test "inappropriate," since "all psychiatric evidence under the traditional M'Naghten test tends to be narrow—relating only to the defendant's intellectual reasoning."[62] This approach was inconsistent with the court's previous observation that all evidence relevant to the defendant's mental capacity should be considered by the jury. Along with other circuits reviewing the irresistible impulse test, the court found that it is defined in absolute terms and is equated with the complete destruction of the governing power of the mind. The ALI test recognizes that a defendant need not have total incapacity to be found criminally irresponsible.[63]

Therefore, the court concluded that the ALI test presented a better solution, since it addressed the problems raised by the earlier standards of insanity:

> [W]e simply find that the substance of the ALI rule invites a broader medical-legal investigation, provides improved means for communication by medical specialists, offers a better basis for understanding of complex issues by triers of fact and overall serves the desired end in the administration of our criminal laws.[64]

All the federal circuits adopted the ALI test for many of the reasons mentioned above. Some circuits, however, adopted the test in a slightly modified version, by either omitting certain provisions of the test or by supplementing it with their own definitions of terms. In *United States v. Currens*,[65] the Third Circuit adopted a modified version that expressly removed from the standard of insanity any reference to the defendant's cognitive capacity—that is, the defendant's ability to appreciate the criminality/wrongfulness of his or her conduct—and defined insanity in terms of the defendant's capacity to conform his or her conduct to the requirements of the law. Thus, the court adopted the following formula as the test for criminal responsibility:

> The jury must be satisfied that at the time of committing the prohibited act the defendant, as a result of mental disease or defect, lacked substantial capacity to conform his conduct to the requirements of the law which he is alleged to have violated.[66]

In formulating this modified test of insanity, the court explained that its primary reason for excluding the cognitive prong from the ALI test was that it tended to overemphasize the defendant's ability to distinguish between right and wrong.[67] It distracted the jury from the critical issues (that is, the total personality of the defendant). Thus, in the court's opinion, the cognitive element "would rarely be significant."[68]

While *Currens* appears to be the only federal case to specifically reject the cognitive element of the ALI formulation, a number of circuits adopted the first subsection of the test—including both the cognitive and volitional prongs—but rejected the so-called caveat paragraph of the test, which excludes from the definition of "mental disease or defect" abnormalities manifested by repeated criminal (recidivistic) or otherwise antisocial (psychopathic/sociopathic) conduct.

For example, in *United States v Smith*,[69] the court rejected the *M'Naghten* rule supplemented by the irresistible impulse test and adopted the ALI formulation because the latter can be readily understood by lay jurors, comports with and makes available modern scientific knowledge, and serves to aid the continuing development of the federal law. However, the Sixth Circuit refused to endorse the Model Penal Code's supplemental definition of "mental disease or defect" as set forth in subsection 2 of the test, observing that there is "great dispute over the psychiatric soundness" of this portion of the test.[70]

The sentiment expressed by the Sixth Circuit in *Smith* was embraced by the Ninth Circuit in *Wade v. United States*,[71] where the court adopted the ALI test except for the second subsection—which excludes certain psychopathic personalities from the definition of "mental disease or defect." First, the court believed that the definition supplied by the authors of the ALI test was not meaningful and that many noted medical authorities had questioned the validity of the definition.[72] Second, the court pointed out that the exclusion of persons who are diagnosed as psychopathic but are nonetheless "seriously ill and . . . incapable of persistent, ordered living of any kind" leaves society unprotected from potential recidivists, since—if sent to prison—they normally would be released after serving some fixed period of time.[73] Moreover, the court noted that inclusion of the ALI's definition of mental disease or defect in a jury instruction on the issue of insanity would have "little or no impact on the determination of the criminal responsibility of any mentally deranged defendant, whether psychopathic or not, since it is practically inconceivable that mental disease or defect would, in the terms of paragraph (2), be 'manifested *only* by repeated criminal or otherwise antisocial conduct.'"[74] Finally, the court was concerned that the definition was ambiguous and would only tend to confuse the jury. Thus, on balance, the Ninth Circuit—while adopting the first paragraph of the Model Penal Code test for criminal responsibility—decided to reject the second paragraph.

A second class of cases that departed from the standard Model Penal Code language are those that substituted the definition of certain phrases or terms as used in the ALI test. As discussed in the previous section on the *Durham* rule, the District of Columbia in 1972 adopted the ALI test in place of the *Durham* test in *United States v. Brawner*.[75] However, the court modified the ALI definition of "mental disease or defect" by substituting the definition initially formulated in *McDonald v. United States*.[76] In retaining the *McDonald* definition of "mental disease or defect," the court stated that the ALI definition of this phrase "contains an inherent ambiguity."[77] In the court's view, any alleged disadvantage found in incorporating the *McDonald* definition into the ALI test was overridden by its advantages:

> The *McDonald* rule has helped accomplish the objective of securing expert testimony needed on the subject of mental illness, while guarding against the undue dominance of expert testimony or specialized labels. It has thus permitted the kind of communication without encroachment, as between experts and juries, that has prompted us to adopt the ALI rule, and hence will help us realize our objective.[78]

In addition to changing the definition of "mental disease or defect," the District of Columbia Circuit—like many other federal circuits[79]—also substituted the term "wrongfulness" as an alternative to the suggested word "criminality" in the first subsection of the ALI test. Noting that the authors of the ALI test provided a choice of terminology in defining the cognitive prong,[80] the court opted for the term "wrongfulness" on "pragmatic grounds . . . since the resulting jury instruction is more like that conventionally given and applied by the jury."[81] While such an instruction admittedly "lacks complete precision," it serves the objective of calling on the jury to provide a community judgment on a combination of factors."[82]

Finally, the Ninth Circuit—in adopting the ALI test—also used the term "wrongfulness" rather than "criminality," and further modified the test by providing a supplemental definition of "wrongfulness," in *Wade v. United States.*[83] The court concluded that the alternate word—"wrongfulness"—was more appropriate, since the term "criminality" necessarily excluded from the category of the criminally irresponsible those defendants "who, knowing an act to be criminal, committed it because of a delusion that the act was morally justified."[84] For example, if A kills B—knowing that he is killing B, and knowing that it is illegal to kill B—and if A acts under an insane delusion that the salvation of the human race will be obtained by his execution for the murder of B and that God has commanded him to kill B, then A's act is a crime if the test of whether A appreciated the criminality of his acts or if the word "wrong" is narrowly interpreted to mean illegal. It is not a crime if the word "wrong" means morally wrong. Under the *M'Naghten* test, in England, the word "wrong" is narrowly interpreted to mean legally wrong.[85] In the United States, the question of *M'Naghten*'s jurisdiction has been resolved variously among the few courts that have addressed this issue. The Ninth Circuit adopted a broad definition of the term "wrongfulness"—permitting a jury to apply community moral standards in looking beyond whether the defendant realized, understood, or appreciated that the offense was legally wrong (illegal) and to find the defendant not responsible if he or she lacks substantial capacity to appreciate the moral wrongfulness of the conduct in question.

In summary, by the early 1970s, all federal circuits (except possibly the First Circuit)[86] had adopted the ALI test in one form or another, as the sole test for criminal responsibility. Also, by 1980, the ALI test had been adopted—by legislation or by judicial ruling—

in more than half of the states. The ALI has been characterized as a modernized amalgam of the *M'Naghten* and irresistible impulse tests. It uses the term "appreciate" rather than "know" in the *M'Naghten* prong of the test. The ALI test recognizes that there is no bright line between the sane and the insane and that a standard for criminal responsibility need not be expressed solely in terms of absolute or total incapacity. In asking whether the defendant lacked "substantial capacity" to appreciate wrongfulness or to exercise control, the authors intended to limit the insanity defense to persons whose mental disorders were characteristic of the most severe afflictions of the mind. Proponents of the ALI test hailed it as fostering a new era in the history of the insanity defense; they argued that its language is more easily understood and applied by the average lay juror, while permitting a thorough broad examination into the defendant's psychiatric profile without undue dominance by the psychiatric expert.

In the main, the test drew praise from the commentators, but it was not without its critics. Weihofen argued that the ALI test is only a "refurbishing" of the two traditional tests and that it fails to "bridge the gap that now exists between legal and psychiatric thinking."[87] Others have argued the ALI standard is ambiguous. It has been argued that use of the word "result" introduces the most objectionable aspects of the *Durham* product test. The words "substantial capacity" and "appreciate" do not have common, absolute meanings; they are bound to encourage differences among expert witnesses and also among jurors, over whether a defendant's degree of impairment or depth of awareness was sufficient to apply.[88]

The attempted assassination of President Ronald Reagan and related wounding of three other persons on March 30, 1981, created an uproar not merely concerning the ALI standard, but the entire concept of the defense of insanity. As a consequence, in October 1984, Congress passed the Insanity Defense Reform Act, abolishing the ALI test as the standard used in the federal courts on the question of criminal responsibility. This was the first time that Congress had ever addressed the content of the insanity defense.

The Insanity Defense Reform Act of 1984

In 1984, the U.S. Congress passed the Insanity Defense Reform Act of 1984[89]—the first federal codification of the insanity defense. Applicable solely to defendants in federal court, the new law legislatively alters the definition of insanity that had gradually developed through the process of judicial decision making. It represents the fifth major attempt—following *M'Naghten*, irresistible impulse, *Durham*, and the American Law Institute standards—in the United States at determining the nature of criminal responsibility and the kinds of conduct deserving of the defense of insanity.

A number of events occurring during the preceding decade or so predisposed Congress to act where it had never acted before. Commencing with the administration of President Richard Nixon, renewed efforts were underway to reform the federal criminal code. President Nixon called for abolition of the insanity defense as one of the central features of his administration's effort to reform the federal criminal law and to get tough on crime in the streets. At the same time, a national movement toward deinstitutionalization of "status offenders" and "civil committees" led to the release of thousands of mentally handicapped individuals on the streets. A large number of outdated mental institutions were being replaced by smaller, community-based mental facilities. This led to increasing public concern about the premature release of dangerous persons, including defendants who had been acquitted by reason of insanity. These events coincided with the growing national conservative consensus, which advocated strict criminal laws and penalties.

Against this background, the unexpected verdict of not guilty by reason of insanity in the trial of John W. Hinckley, Jr., sparked a new and intensive debate concerning the insanity defense. Following the jury's verdict, 26 bills to modify the insanity defense were introduced in the U.S. House of Representatives. In his opening remarks on this issue to the House Judiciary Subcommittee on Criminal Justice, its chairman—John Conyers (D. Mich.)—suggested that the number of introduced bills was a symptom of members' concern. He noted that the verdict in the *Hinckley* case had fostered public disrespect for the criminal justice system.[90] In the U.S. Senate, Arlen Spector (R. Pa.) suggested that "we proceed most expeditiously to hearings in order to show the public that the law and law-makers are not helpless to correct inequities in our criminal justice system." Congressman John Myers (R. Ind.) argued before the House Judiciary Subcommittee on Criminal Justice that legislation was necessary "to dispel the view of the public that the laws we pass here and elsewhere are only for the poor to obey."[91]

Hearings were held in both houses of Congress during the summer of 1982. Action was not completed as the Ninety-seventh Congress adjourned. During the Ninety-eighth Congress, insanity defense legislation was actively considered in both houses. Positions varied: from abolition of the insanity defense, to an additional verdict of "guilty but mentally ill," to procedural changes such as shifting the burden of proof from the prosecution to the defense. Testimony was offered by such organizations as the U.S. Department of Justice, the Federal Judicial Conference, the National Association of Attorneys General, the American Bar Association, the American Psychiatric Association, the National Legal Aid and Public Defender Association, the American Civil Liberties Union, a number of academics, and members of Congress.[92]

The *Hinckley* verdict was unquestionably the decisive influence on congressional modifications to the insanity defense. The atmosphere surrounding the congressional hearings and debates has been characterized as one of consensus, rather than brokerage politics. The impetus to pass a crime package just before a national election suggests that a majority of members felt a need to reassure the public. Neither Democrats nor Republicans wanted to appear to be "soft on crime." A widely shared perception was that an insanity defense law provided a confusing message—at best—to the general public, as to which persons should be held blameworthy. At worst, it communicated the message that there was a great loophole in existing law, allowing some persons who should be held blameworthy to escape criminal punishment. Thus, the primary modifications of the insanity defense focused on changing those factors that Congressional members felt contributed to Hinckley's "getting off": (1) the volitional test; (2) the placing of the burden of proof on the prosecution; and (3) confusion created by contradictory "conclusory" testimony by psychiatrists.[93]

The legislative history of the Insanity Defense Reform Act of 1984 shows that the final language for its historic changes in the insanity defense was developed by a conference committee of the appropriations—not judiciary—committee. The timing for the changes came at the close of a legislative session—shortly before elections—as one part of a major revision of the federal criminal code, in a process that provided little opportunity for members of Congress to consider its final provisions. Specific insanity defense concerns were lost in the debate over the crime package. A brief review of this legislative history follows.

The insanity defense provisions were one part of a comprehensive

bill involving 23 chapters. The Senate changes were incorporated in
S. 1762, the Comprehensive Crime Control Act of 1984. It passed
the full Senate on February 2, 1984. On May 1, 1984, the House Subcommittee on Criminal Justice favorably reported a bill—H.R. 3336—
to modify the insanity defense. On June 26, 1984, the House Rules
Committee considered the bill, but—because of a procedural problem
and concerns unrelated to the content of the bill—it was not given a
rule. On September 18, 1984—with the legislative session drawing to
a close—the Democratic House leadership brought the bill up on a
suspension of the rules. Under this procedure, the debate was limited,
amendments were prohibited, and a two-thirds majority was required
for passage. The bill failed to achieve the required super majority,
with a vote of 225-171. Because of the rush to adjourn so that members could return to their districts to campaign and because of the
need to concentrate on budgetary matters in the remaining days of
the session, the legislation appeared dead.[94]

The crime issue resurfaced during the congressional debate on the
continuing budget resolution. On September 25, 1984, House Republicans—by a procedural motion—attached the crime bill to the continuing budget resolution.[95] Representative Daniel Lungren (R. Ca.)
led the effort, presenting the vote as the final opportunity for House
members to send a message on crime to the public before the election. He argued:

> If we have an opportunity, as we did today, to attach the foreign aid
> bill and the public works bill, we should do no less than attach this bill
> since the American people have shown in the latest poll this is the
> number 1 issue facing them.
>   You cannot dodge it; this is your chance to do it. I would hope that
> we would have an overwhelming yes vote on behalf of the American
> people in favor of the comprehensive Crime Control Act of 1984.[96]

On October 2, 1984, the House Anti-Crime Act of 1984—H.R. 5690—
passed by a vote of 406-16.[97] The Senate ultimately attached an
amended S. 1762—their crime package—to their spending bill, on
October 4, 1984.[98]

Because the anticrime provisions were attached to the House and
Senate spending bills, the bills were sent to a conference committee
consisting of members of the appropriations committees, not the

judiciary committees. In particular, there were no House conferees knowledgeable on the insanity defense. The conference report included the slightly more conservative Senate version of the insanity defense. Both houses approved this report on October 11, 1984. The legislation was signed into law by the president on the following day.[99] As noted below, the content of at least one provision of the Insanity Defense Reform Act—relating to the burden of proof—may have been affected by the fact that the bill was not considered by conferees from the judiciary committees.

Subsection (a) of the Insanity Defense Reform Act of 1984 sets forth the new federal insanity defense standard:

> (a) Affirmative defense. It is an affirmative defense to a prosecution under any Federal statute that, at the time of the commission of the acts constituting the offense, the defendant, as a result of a severe mental disease or defect, was unable to appreciate the nature and quality or the wrongfulness of his acts. Mental disease or defect does not otherwise constitute a defense.[100]

The new standard changes the law previously adhered to in all federal circuits (except the Fifth Circuit[101]), from a standard based on the ALI model to one patterned along the lines of the *M'Naghten* rule. The new standard changes the ALI test in three principal ways.

First, the act eliminates the "volitional" prong of the ALI test. The volitional prong—which grew out of the irresistible impulse test—permitted the defendant to be found not guilty by reason of insanity when the defendant could not "conform his conduct to the requirements of the law" as a result of a mental disease or defect. In the view of the Senate Judiciary Committee—whose bill was reported in Congress—the volitional component of the insanity defense standard has received "particularly strong criticism" since "*all* criminal conduct is evidence of lack of power to conform behavior to the requirements of the law."[102] Perhaps the most influential of the academic witnesses to testify before Congress—Professor Richard J. Bonnie—explained the problem as follows:

> Unfortunately, however, there is no scientific basis for measuring a person's capacity for self-control or for calibrating the impairment of such capacity. There is, in short, no objective basis for distinguishing

between offenders who were undeterrable and those who were merely undeterred, between the impulse that was irresistible and the impulse not resisted, or between substantial impairment of capacity and some lesser impairment. Whatever the precise terms of the volition test, the question is unanswerable—or can be answered only by "moral guesses." To ask it at all, in my opinion, invites fabricated claims, undermines equal administration of the penal law, and compromises its deterrent effect.[103]

The American Psychiatric Association also noted that many psychiatrists believe that psychiatric information relevant to whether a defendant understood the nature of his act and whether he appreciated its wrongfulness has a stronger basis and is more reliable than information relevant to whether a defendant was able to control his behavior. They also noted that, in practice, there is considerable overlap between a psychotic person's defective understanding or appreciation and his ability to control his behavior, so that dropping the volitional prong should not have a substantial impact on insanity defense outcomes.[104]

Richard J. Wilson, on behalf of the National Legal Aid and Defender Association, replied to Professor Bonnie's arguments in testimony before a subcommittee of the Senate Judiciary Committee:

Furthermore, this proposal suffers from an internal contradiction, for it seems to suggest that a more "accurate scientific basis" exists for measuring one's capacity for "appreciation of the wrongfulness of one's conduct" as distinguished from one's "capacity for self-control." I question whether there is any more scientific support for "measuring" such "cognitive" disease. If not, what's to prevent the argument from being turned around to support total elimination of the insanity defense?[105]

Also, it has been suggested that there are clinically compelling cases of volitional impairment involving so-called impulse disorders—pyromania, kleptomania, and the like—that may not qualify under the cognitive prong. These disorders involve severely abnormal compulsions. Where such disorders can be shown—and their relationship to criminal conduct, established—is it just that criminal law should invoke society's moral condemnation of such persons and merely consider this evidence of compulsion only at the time of sentencing?[106]

Moreover, Congress abolished the volitional prong without the benefit of any studies of the potential impact of such a change on the outcome of forensic psychiatric evaluations and opinions. Such a study was recently undertaken, and its results question the wisdom of dropping the volitional prong. Recently, Maryland established a Governor's Task Force to Review the Defense of Insanity. At the request of the task force, the professional staff of the Clifton T. Perkins Hospital Center—Maryland's evaluation center for serious offenders—carried out a retrospective reassessment of those cases reported "not responsible" between July 1, 1981, and June 30, 1982. The object was to discover whether the proposed elimination of the volitional prong would yield the results anticipated by its proponents: screening less seriously ill offenders, promoting more consistent psychiatric opinion, and diminishing the frequency of courtroom "battles of the experts." A pool of nine experienced forensic psychiatrists participated in the assessment of the charts of 42 cases reported as not responsible. In each case, the chart was assessed by three reviewing psychiatrists, one of whom was present at the original forensic staffing. The ALI standard was divided into its cognitive and volitional prongs.

The study found that, indeed, there are individuals whose severe mental illness is primarily reflected in their inability to control their behavior. The task force report stated:

> Manic patients often may be severely impaired in their capacity to control behavior, while their cognitive disruption may be less striking. To advocate removing the volitional prong ignores understandings of the mind as a unified entity which may be impaired in many ways.
>
> The Perkins study found that elimination of the volitional prong of the test of criminal responsibility could systematically exclude from a vindicated plea of not criminally responsible a "class of psychotic patients whose illness is clearest in symptomatology, most likely biologic in origin, most eminently treatable and potentially most disruptive in penal detention."
>
> The Perkins study also indicates that deleting the volitional prong would result in less uniformity of the State's evaluation which would, in turn, encourage the defense to more frequently contest the report and result in more trials with conflicting psychiatric testimony.[107]

Based in part on the results of this study, the Maryland Governor's Task Force to Review the Defense of Insanity recommended retaining the volitional prong of its version of the ALI standard.[108] The Perkins study suggests that eliminating the volitional prong of the

ALI test may not achieve the results intended by Congress. Had Congress had the benefit of the results of the Perkins study, would that have affected the decision to drop the volitional prong of the ALI test? Probably not. In correspondence with one of the reform act's authors, Elyce H. Zenoff—Professor of Law at George Washington University—commented:

> The Perkins material was fascinating. However, I'm not sure that the proponents of eliminating the volitional test would feel they had erred. I think many of them simply want to reduce the case of the insanity defense, no matter how sick the offender is. Today, I think most people no longer think Hinckley was a malingerer and would accept the fact that he was and is severely mentally ill. Yet most of them probably still think he should have been found guilty.[109]

Professor Zenoff has a very interesting insight. Arguably, the message behind the public reaction to the *Hinckley* verdict is that— while John W. Hinckley, Jr., may have been very sick and in need of psychiatric treatment—nevertheless, he should be held morally responsible for his unlawful acts. It is apparently safe to exempt from punishment those who do not know what they are doing, for such persons are quite clearly not deterrable and may be exculpated without diminishing the pressure on ordinary persons to conform to the law. This is not true—so the argument goes—if the exculpation is predicated on lack of self-control. Further, how is moral responsibility to be determined? One commentator answers in a manner that may be relevant to assessing the public reaction to the *Hinckley* case:

> Not by asking whether it was reasonable, on the facts of the individual case, to expect compliance with the law, for the criminal law frequently imposes condemnation in the absence of such an expectation [citing in a footnote the cases of conviction for taking the life of another to save one's own life in a nondefensive situation and conviction under a penal statute of which the defendant was reasonably ignorant]. Instead, moral blameworthiness "is less a quality of the offender, resting on his actual ability or inability to conform, than of the normative judgment of others that he ought to have been able to conform."[110]

Thus, a person may be deemed to be sick—in the sense that medical treatment and care is needed—but also be deemed to be morally responsible, for purposes of the minimum standards of the criminal law. An argument in support of the standard of the Insanity Defense Reform Act is that—like the *M'Naghten* rule—it may be an appropriate device for identifying those without moral blame, because it isolates "that group that is popularly viewed as insane" and whose "acquittal will not offend the community sense of justice."[111]

The degree of impact of the new standard will partly depend on how expansively the appellate courts interpret the word "appreciate," and on the extent to which trial judges will permit psychiatrists and psychologists to present their theories of the defendant's mental condition under the variation of the so-called cognitive prong, as adopted by Congress.

Second, the Insanity Defense Reform Act of 1984 also modifies the "cognitive" prong of the ALI test by substituting the phrase "unable to appreciate" for "lacks substantial capacity . . . to appreciate." Presumably, Congress intended that the change tighten the requirement to a total lack of ability to appreciate the nature and quality or the wrongfulness of the criminal act. Also, in the view of the U.S. Department of Justice, the term "appreciate" should be subject to a very narrow interpretation consistent with the overall intent of the legislation:

> Although a defendant can be acquitted on grounds of insanity if he cannot appreciate either the nature and quality of his acts or their wrongfulness, the term "appreciate" should be construed as meaning only cognitive appreciation. Attorneys for the Government should argue that "emotional" or "subjective" appreciation is not covered by the new standard, and that the only purpose of the new test is to determine whether the defendant had the cognition or reasoning ability to understand his acts. The "appreciation prong" of the ALI test was similarly limited, as was the rule established in *M'Naghten's* Case, 8 Eng. Rep. 716 (H.L. 1843), upon which this prong of the ALI test was based. Accordingly, attempts to introduce evidence of "emotional" or "subjective" appreciation should be resisted on the grounds that such evidence would resurrect a test based on volition, which Congress has now rejected.[112]

Recall, however, that the ALI test was found more appealing than restrictive interpretations of the word "know" in *M'Naghten*, partly because—as Judge Kaufman noted—the ALI test broadened the term "know" to "appreciate" so as to make clear that it includes emotional or affective understanding.[113]

Until the new law is subject to the interpretation of the federal courts, it will remain unclear whether the restrictive interpretation of the word "appreciate" favored by the U.S. Department of Justice or the broader interpretation under the ALI standard will prevail. The American Bar Association—in a policy statement approved by its house of delegates in 1983—urged a broader definition, in order to facilitate a full clinical description of the defendant's perceptions and understanding at the time of the offense. The ABA observed that such a broader interpretation is needed to allow flexibility, since the term "unable to appreciate" replaces the ALI test of lacking "substantial capacity . . . to appreciate."[114]

Third, the new act requires that the mental disease or defect be "severe," thus changing the broad definition established in *McDonald v. United States.*[115] The committee noted that the word "severe" was added to the text of the new standard to "emphasize" that certain behavioral disorders should not constitute the defense. The committee was particularly concerned with such "non-psychotic" behavioral disorders as "inadequate personality," "immature personality," "neurosis," and a "pattern of antisocial tendencies."[116] The Senate Judiciary Committee felt that these "illnesses" were subject to abuse under the old standard and were undeserving of the insanity defense. The use of a word such as "severe" invites appellate litigation concerning the scope of the new standard.

The Insanity Defense Reform Act also abolishes the concept of "diminished capacity." Both the ALI test and many of the circuit courts—such as the District of Columbia in *United States v. Brawner*[117]—had recognized, as an adjunct to the insanity defense, that a defendant could claim diminished capacity (also called "diminished responsibility"). This is a partial insanity defense, which allowed a defendant to show that, as a result of a mental disease or defect, the defendant lacked the capacity to have the required mental state (or mens rea) of a specific intent crime—such as the capacity to premeditate and deliberate required for first degree murder. In this example, the result of a successful diminished capacity defense would mean that the defendant would be convicted of second degree murder, instead of first degree.[118] The legislative history of the reform act states that this provision is intended to assure "that the insanity defense is not improperly resurrected in the guise of showing some other affirmative defense, such as that the defendant had a 'diminished responsibility.'"[119]

Moreover, the Insanity Defense Reform Act makes substantial changes in the presentation of the insanity defense. As discussed in the next section of this chapter, Congress shifted the burden of proof from the prosecution to the defendant. The standard of proof that must be borne by the defendant is to prove the insanity defense by "clear and convincing evidence." Also, as discussed in Chapter 3 on expert witnesses, Congress amended Rule 704 of the Federal Rules of Evidence to prevent expert witnesses in insanity defense trials from testifying to conclusions on the ultimate issues.

Further, the form of verdict has been changed to a special verdict. Before enactment of the Insanity Defense Reform Act, all federal cases except those prosecuted in the District of Columbia had only the two verdict options traditionally available in criminal cases: guilty or not guilty. The new act adds a special verdict of "not guilty only by reason of insanity" to federal law. Thus, a defendant who raises the issue of insanity in federal courts will now present the jury with three verdict options.

Finally, the Insanity Defense Reform Act establishes for the first time a federal procedure for commitment of persons who have been found guilty only by reason of insanity. The commitment provisions respond to what many observers feel was the most serious dissatisfaction with the insanity defense: the potential for premature release of dangerous persons acquitted by reason of insanity. After a hearing, a defendant who needs care or treatment may be committed by the trial judge to the custody of the attorney general for treatment at a "suitable facility." The defendant is given a provisional sentence for the maximum term authorized for the offense. If the defendant recovers before the expiration of the term, the court proceeds to final sentence, and may modify the provisional sentence.

In summary, the Insanity Defense Reform Act of 1984 reflects the view that—while our social, moral, and legal traditions require that crimes resulting from mental disease or defect be not deserving of moral blame and, hence, no criminal responsibility should attach—this concept is an ever expanding and contracting notion dependent on the social and political climate in which we live. The new standard reflects Congress's present determination that the defense of insanity—while remaining a viable concept in the nation's criminal law—

should be applied in only those extreme circumstances that clearly merit its application. Until the new law is subjected to interpretation by the federal courts, it will remain unclear as to whether its effect on the defense of insanity will be substantial.

BURDENS OF PROOF

The remainder of this chapter examines the burdens of proof in the presentation of the insanity defense, both on the federal and state levels. The first section distinguishes between the burden of going forward with the evidence and the burden of persuasion. The second section reviews the federal and state laws on burdens of proof, and discusses the policy issues that arise in allocating the burden of persuasion to prove the insanity defense. The final section analyzes the controversy concerning the constitutionality of placing the burden of persuasion on the defendant. While it appears that the present U.S. Supreme Court would uphold placing the burden of persuasion on the defendant, state courts—interpreting corresponding provisions in their state constitutions—can provide a more expansive interpretation of relevant constitutional provisions.

Understanding Burdens of Proof

When discussing the phrase "burdens of proof," it is important to distinguish between: (1) the burden of going forward with the evidence (sometimes referred to as the "burden of production"), and (2) the burden of persuasion.[120] In all U.S. jurisdictions, a criminal defendant who raises the defense of legal insanity has the initial burden of going forward with the evidence. This proposition is most often stated in terms of the presumption of sanity: That is, in all criminal prosecutions, the defendant is presumed to be sane at the outset of the litigation. Thus, where a defendant wishes to show that— due to a defective mental state—he or she is not criminally responsible for an offense, that defendant must satisfy the burden of going forward. This means that some evidence must be produced at trial, to show that the defendant was insane at the time of the commission of the criminal act. When the burden of going forward with the evidence is satisfied, the presumption of sanity is said to "burst"—which means the presumption has been rebutted. If, however, the defendant fails to produce a sufficient amount of evidence to meet this burden, the sanity of the defendant is presumed for all legal purposes. In other words, where the defendant fails to satisfy the burden of going forward, the question of the defendant's insanity is adversely foreclosed to him or her during the trial, and the jury is instructed to presume the defendant's sanity when it deliberates on the verdict.

There are two practical reasons for placing the burden of going forward on the defendant. The first reason is that, if the prosecution were required to prove the sanity of each defendant in all criminal cases without any evidence to indicate the defendant may have been insane, it would place an intolerable burden on the prosecution. This point is reinforced by the fact that only a substantial minority of defendants claim insanity as a defense to a criminal charge. The second reason often given to justify placing the burden of going forward on the defendant is that many jurisdictions consider the defense of insanity to be an affirmative defense, so that—at the very least—the defendant should bear the burden of producing some evidence tending to show that he or she was insane when the offense occurred.

The ways in which a criminal defendant can satisfy the burden of going forward are theoretically infinite. The most common way is through testimony elicited by expert or lay witnesses for the defense. This procedure is normally sufficient to meet the burden of going forward. However, this is by no means the only way to put the defendant's mental condition in issue at trial. Many times, questions as to the defendant's criminal culpability will be raised through the testimony of the prosecution's witnesses, either on direct or cross examination.[121]

As to the question of how much evidence is needed to satisfy the burden of going forward, there is considerable disagreement. Some jurisdictions require the defendant to produce "some" evidence of legal insanity, while others express this burden in terms of a "scintilla" of evidence. The remaining jurisdictions provide that the defendant must present a sufficient amount or quantum of evidence to raise a reasonable doubt as to his or her mental responsibility for the criminal act.[122]

Once the defendant produces a sufficient amount of evidence to satisfy the burden of going forward with the evidence, the presumption of sanity is considered rebutted. When this occurs, two additional evidentiary issues are raised in relation to the insanity defense: (1) Which party—prosecution or defense—should carry the burden of persuasion on the ultimate issue of the sanity or insanity of the defendant; and (2) what quantum of evidence is needed to satisfy this burden?

In the United States, two views have developed concerning the question of which party to a criminal trial bears the burden of persuasion on the issue of legal insanity. Generally speaking, one view takes the position that the burden of persuasion should rest on the prosecution. When the defendant introduces sufficient evidence to satisfy the burden of going forward with the evidence, the burden shifts to the prosecution to prove that the defendant was legally sane at the time of the offense. In order to satisfy the burden of persuasion, the prosecution must prove the defendant's sanity beyond a reasonable doubt.[123] This approach is based on the notion that criminal intent—or mens rea—is an essential element of all criminal offenses. Since the prosecution is constitutionally required to bear the burden of proving all the elements of an offense beyond a reasonable doubt[124] and since—arguably—there can be no mens rea without sanity, a reasonable doubt concerning the sanity of the accused is equivalent to a reasonable doubt respecting guilt. Thus, an acquittal is mandated where there exists in the collective mind of the triers of fact a reasonable doubt as to the defendant's insanity.

In contrast, the second view holds that, where insanity is raised as a defense to a criminal charge, the defendant must establish his or her insanity under various standards of proof, depending on the jurisdiction.[125] This position proceeds on the theory that the sanity of the criminal defendant is not an element of criminality. Rather, legal insanity is viewed as an affirmative defense to a specific charge, which—like many other such defenses—must be established by the defendant. Which of the two views should prevail may depend—at least in part—on the content and scope of the insanity defense standard that a jurisdiction adopts.

Present Status of Burdens of Proof and the Insanity Defense

Burden of Persuasion in the Federal Courts

As in the state courts, the defendant has always carried the burden of going forward with evidence to rebut the presumption of sanity. In 1895, the U.S. Supreme Court held in *Davis v. United States*[126] that—once the defendant has met his or her burden of going forward to raise the insanity defense issue—the burden of persuasion in the federal courts is on the prosecution to prove the defendant's sanity beyond a reaonable doubt. As made clear by subsequent decisions, this conclusion was not constitutionally based, but rested on the Court's inherent supervisory powers over the federal court system.

One of the major changes in federal insanity defense law in the Insanity Defense Reform Act of 1984 was the shifting of the burden of proof from the prosecution to the defense—thus, in effect, abolishing the *Davis* rule. Subsection (b) of the act states: "The defendant has the burden of proving the defense of insanity by clear and convincing evidence."[127]

An examination of the legislative history of the act explains how this provision became the new federal standard of proof and reveals the policy issues involved in the decision. The insanity defense law under which Mr. Hinckley was convicted had followed the *Davis* rule in placing the burden of persuasion on the prosecution. After Hinckley's trial, there was bitter reaction concerning the fact that the prosecution had the responsibility to prove beyond a reasonable doubt that Hinckley was sane. Within days of the verdict, several members of the jury panel were invited to testify before a subcommittee of the Senate Judiciary Committee. Some of the jurors testified that the judge's instruction on the burden of proof played a role in their verdict.

The House and Senate judiciary committees were presented with a variety of arguments and positions in regard to allocating the burden of proof. The American Bar Association argued that allocation of the burden of proof—and establishment of the standard of proof— was essentially a public policy issue. The *Davis* doctrine reflects a policy that the "risk of error" remain with the prosecution. The ABA recommended that the burden of proof depend on whether a jurisdiction adopted the ALI test or a version of the *M'Naghten* rule. Recommendation Two of the ABA stated:

> That in Jurisdictions utilizing any test for insanity which focuses solely on whether the defendant, as a result of mental disease or defect, was unable to know, understand or appreciate the wrongfulness of his or her conduct at the time of the offense charged, the prosecution should have the burden of disproving the defendant's claim of insanity beyond a reasonable doubt; and second, that in jurisdictions utilizing the ALI-Model Penal Code test for insanity the defendant should have the burden of proving by a preponderance of the evidence his or her claim of insanity.[128]

The ABA argued that mistakes in the administration of the insanity defense occur primarily when the volitional prong is used; and, in such cases, the ABA would have the burden of persuasion shift to the defendant by a preponderance of the evidence.

The use of a "volitional test"—especially when coupled with placing the burden of persuasion on the prosecution—can "lend itself to fabrication and produce jury confusion."[129] A narrowing of the insanity test—the ABA argued—requires that the "risk of error" remain with the prosecution. Further, if exculpation is morally required when certain facts exist, then—as a general rule—the prosecution should be required to negate the existence of these facts beyond a reasonable doubt.[130]

The American Psychiatric Association stated that it was "exceedingly reluctant to take a position about assigning the burden of proof in insanity cases." The APA stated:

> For public policy, the issue is, in part, whether the rights of the individual or the rights of the state are to be given more or less weight in criminal insanity trials, or as is sometimes stated, which type of errors do we deem more or less tolerable in insanity trials. Given the inherent uncertainties involved in psychiatric testimony regarding the defense and the ever-present problems relating abstract legal principles to controversies of such emotion, who bears the burden of proof in insanity trials may be quite important. This is particularly so when what must be proved must also be proved "beyond a reasonable doubt." As suggested by the U.S. Supreme Court in the *Addington* case, usually psychiatric evidence is not sufficiently clear-cut to prove or disprove many legal facts "beyond a reasonable doubt."
>
> It is commonly believed that the likely effect of assigning the burden of proof (burden of persuasion) to defendants rather than to the state in insanity trials will be to decrease the number of such successful defense. This matter clearly requires further empirical study.[131]

The American Psychiatric Association statement highlights a key question in assigning the burden of persuasion: whether the desired policy outcome is to increase, keep constant, or reduce the number of insanity acquittals in contested cases.

Another important policy issue involved in allocating the burden of persuasion is which party has control of the relevant facts. Other things being equal, it is argued that the burden of proof should be placed on the party who is in the better position to produce the facts.

This is the major reason that underlies placing the burden of going forward with the evidence on the defendant in an insanity defense, as discussed above. The testimony of a representative of the National District Attorneys Association before the Senate Judiciary Committee was based, in part, on this policy argument:

> A most vital feature of this Act is the allocation of the burden of proof of insanity to the defendant. The most widely criticized aspect of the insanity law in some jurisdictions is the impossible burden sometimes placed on the Government of proving someone's sanity beyond a reasonable doubt. . . . A defendant is required to present the evidence in all other affirmative defenses and this is particularly fitting in the case of insanity. Such evidence is peculiarly available, if at all, to the defendant. On the other hand, evidence to establish sanity—beyond any reasonable doubt—is frequently unavailable to the prosecution.
>
> I have heard judges, prosecutors and defense counsel roundly denounce the Herculean task of requiring the Government to prove anyone is not insane beyond a reasonable doubt. The single most attractive provision of this Act is to fairly require the accused to prove his insanity by the lesser standard of clear and convincing evidence.[132]

In response to the above argument, a representative of the National Legal Aid and Defender Association testified before the Senate Judiciary Committee as follows:

> It is, I believe, wrong to think that the defense inherently enjoys such an advantage when insanity is raised that the ordinary rule, placing the burden of proof on the prosecution, should be reversed. On the contrary, the prosecution already holds advantages when it tries to rebut a claim of insanity that it has in no other kind of case.
>
> Whether or not a statute or rule specifically authorizes the practice, prosecutors have traditionally been able to secure court orders requiring defendants who raise insanity to speak at length with the government's own psychiatrists and psychologists. And the courts have consistently sustained this practice against self-incrimination. I am aware of no comparable power the prosecution has to compel the defendants to cooperate in such a way with the government's efforts to secure his conviction. This practice is unheard of when, for example, the defense is alibi or self-defense.
>
> Further, the prosecution frequently reaps the fruits of a court-ordered hospitalization and study of the defendant at a government-run facility. It is often able to call on the testimony of government employees who

have observed, spoken with, and evaluated a defendant 24 hours a day at a hospital where the defendant has been placed, whether to evaluate his competency to stand trial or his responsibility for his acts. But the government's advantage is the greatest in those cases ... where the defendant is too poor to afford to pay for his own defense. Even with court-authorized expert services under the Criminal Justice Act, it is very doubtful that he can summon comparable resources to those available to the government. This defendant is unlikely to match the government in either the choice of experts available to him or in their number.[133]

It is noteworthy that both the bills that emerged from the House and Senate judiciary committees shifted the burden of persuasion to the defendant, but the bills differed on the standard of proof. The House bill required the defendant to prove the existence of the defense "by a preponderance of the evidence." The Senate bill demanded proof by "clear and convincing evidence." At the time of the *Hinckley* case, no state placing the burden of persuasion on the defendant used a higher standard than preponderance of the evidence. (As the Appendix shows, Arizona adopted this standard of proof in 1983.) Yet, the Senate Judiciary Committee concluded "that a more rigorous requirement ... is necessary to assure that only those defendants who plainly satisfy the requirements of the defense are exonerated from what is otherwise culpable criminal behavior."[134]

As noted earlier, the final bill was sent to a conference committee composed of conferees from the House and Senate appropriations committees—not the judiciary committees—because the crime bill was attached to a continuing budget resolution. Not one House conferee knowledgeable on the insanity defense was present. The conference report included the Senate version of the insanity defense, with the standard of clear and convincing evidence. Based on interviews with key staff members, one researcher has speculated that, had the conferees consisted of judiciary committee members, the House's standard of preponderance of the evidence would have been included in the final bill.[135]

Burden of Persuasion in the States

As discussed below in the final section of this chapter, a state probably may constitutionally impose the burden of persuasion on the defendant to prove his or her insanity, so long as the prosecution is required to prove every element of the crime—as defined by state law—beyond a reasonable doubt. Further, this burden can apparently be satisfied by a standard of proof ranging from a preponderance of the evidence to proof beyond a reasonable doubt. Thus, while a state may place this burden on the prosecution, the U.S. Constitution does not require it to do so.

Wide variations exist among the states as to whether the prosecution or the defense must bear the ultimate burden of persuasion in the insanity defense. Prior to the *Hinckley* case, a bare majority of the states placed the burden of persuasion on the prosecution. After the defendant had produced sufficient evidence of a mental disorder to raise the insanity defense, the prosecution had to prove the defendant's sanity beyond a reasonable doubt.

The Appendix at the end of this book is a chart that shows the present status of burden of proof, on a state-by-state basis. In the aftermath of the *Hinckley* case, at least seven states have shifted the burden of persuasion to the defendant. Presently, about two-thirds of the states require that the defendant bear the ultimate burden of persuading the jury that he or she was insane. Almost all of these states require that the defendant prove insanity by a preponderance of the evidence. One state—Arizona—requires that the defendant prove his or her insanity by clear and convincing evidence.

THE CONSTITUTIONAL CONTROVERSY IN ALLOCATING THE BURDEN OF PERSUASION

While the constitutionality of placing the burden of going forward on the criminal defendant to rebut the presumption of sanity has rarely been seriously questioned,[136] the constitutionality of requiring the defendant to carry the burden of persuasion has been subject to much debate and controversy. In 1983, the U.S. Supreme Court in *Jones v. United States*[137] observed *in dictum* that the burden of persuasion could be placed on the defendant and that the defendant could be required to prove his or her insanity by a higher standard than preponderance of the evidence. Probably, most observers would conclude that the present U.S. Supreme Court would uphold the constitutionality of the burden of persuasion provisions of the Insanity Defense Reform Act of 1984. However, the Court's decisional law interpreting the due process clause has hardly been clear-cut. Also, state courts are free to provide more expansive interpretations of similar provisions in their own state constitutions.

Davis v. United States[138] presented the first opportunity for the Supreme Court to consider the constitutionality of placing the burden of persuasion on the defendant, in an issue of legal insanity. In *Davis*, the defendant was indicted in federal court for murder, which the law defined as the felonious and willful killing of another with malice aforethought. At trial, the defendant introduced evidence tending to show that, at the time of the offense, he was not criminally responsible "by reason of unsoundness or weakness of mind."[139] At the same time, however, the government proved that the defendant did commit the act, but was unable to prove that the defendant possessed the required criminal intent beyond a reasonable doubt.

In its instructions to the jury on the applicable law, the trial court declared in part:

> [T]he law presumes every man is sane, and the burden of showing it is not true is upon the party who asserts it. The responsibility of overturning that presumption . . . is with the party who sets it up as a defense. The government is not required to show it. . . .
>
> So that when, as in this case, insanity is interposed as a defense, the fact of the existence of such insanity at the time of the commission of the offense charged, must be established by the evidence to the reasonable satisfaction of a jury, and the burden of proof of the insanity rests with the defendant.[140]

Based on this statement of the law, the jury returned a verdict of guilty, and the defendant subsequently received a sentence of death.

The defendant appealed his conviction to the U.S. Supreme Court, which inquired whether a jury can find a defendant guilty of the specific crime charged—under circumstances that prove a case of murder—but "upon the whole evidence . . . they have a reasonable doubt whether at the time of killing the accused was mentally competent to distinguish between right and wrong or to understand the nature of the act he was committing."[141]

Reversing the conviction, the Court laid out the rule that a criminal defendant who satisfies his or her burden of going forward on the issue of insanity is entitled to a judgment of acquittal "[i]f the whole evidence, including that supplied by the presumption of sanity does not exclude beyond a reasonable doubt the hypothesis of insanity, of which some proof is adduced. . . . His guilt cannot be said to have been proved beyond a reasonable doubt—his will and his acts cannot be held to have joined in perpetrating the [crime] charged—if the jury, upon all the evidence, have a reasonable doubt whether he was legally capable of committing crime."[142]

In short, *Davis* held that, in the federal courts, sanity is an element of the crime of murder. Like any other element of the crime, the prosecution has to prove it, beyond a reasonable doubt. In federal prosecutions, after the defendant has satisfied the burden of going forward, the prosecution bears the burden of persuasion to prove the defendant's sanity beyond a reasonable doubt, when sanity is an essential element of the offense. At the conclusion of the trial, the jury must find that the defendant was mentally incompetent to legally commit the crime, if a reasonable doubt exists as to the defendant's sanity.

After the Court's opinion in *Davis*, there continued to be some question as to whether the states had to follow the principle announced in *Davis*, or whether the holding was limited to federal prosecutions. During this period, a number of states enacted statutes that placed the burden of persuasion on the defendant to prove insanity. Most often, these statutes required the defendant to prove his or her insanity by a preponderance of the evidence. Oregon—however—went one step further, and provided that the defendant establish his or her legal insanity beyond a reasonable doubt. The constitutionality of this statutory scheme was challenged in the Supreme Court in the landmark case of *Leland v. Oregon.*[143]

In *Leland*, a state court tried the defendant for the crime of first degree murder. The operative statute provided:

When the commission of the act charged as a crime is proven, and the defense sought to be established is the insanity of the defendant, the same must be proven beyond a reasonable doubt.[144]

At the conclusion of the trial, the court instructed the jury that the prosecution had to prove all the elements necessary to establish guilt, including "premeditation, deliberation, malice and intent."[145] On the issue of the defendant's insanity, the court instructed the jury that—if the prosecution had proved beyond a reasonable doubt all the essential elements of the crime of murder—for the defendant to prevail, he had the burden of proving insanity beyond a reasonable doubt. In other words, these issues had to be separately considered. The defendant was subsequently convicted.

On appeal, the defendant contended that the Oregon statutory scheme violated his Fourteenth Amendment right to due process of law, in requiring him to establish his innocence by disproving beyond a reasonable doubt an element of the crime necessary for a verdict of guilty.[146] Rejecting this argument, the Supreme Court observed that *Davis* "establishes no constitutional doctrine, but only the rule to be followed in federal courts" based on the Court's supervisory powers. As such, "the rule is not in question here."[147] Accordingly, the Court held that, so long as the prosecution is required to prove beyond a reasonable doubt every element of the offense charged, the state can constitutionally place the burden of persuasion on the defendant to prove his or her insanity beyond a reasonable doubt. In the Court's view, such a policy did not violate "generally accepted concepts of basic standards of justice."[148]

Davis and *Leland* arguably represent two alternative—but constitutionally consistent—approaches to the insanity defense. In *Davis*, the government had an affirmative duty to prove sanity beyond a reasonable doubt, because sanity was considered an element of the crime. In *Leland*, however, the burden of persuasion on insanity could be constitutionally placed on the accused, since Oregon did not define sanity to be an element of the crime. In light of this distinction, *Leland* apparently authorized each state to define the elements of each crime and thereby determine which party carries the burden of persuasion on insanity. From a constitutional perspective, the only restraints on this power are the fundamental notions of justice embodied in the Fourteenth Amendment's due process clause.[149] Hence, the definition of "guilt" remains a matter of state law.

After the Court's holding in *Leland*, the controversy concerning the burden of persuasion in relation to the insanity defense was indirectly revived in *In re Winship* (1970)[150] and *Mullaney v. Wilbur*,[151] although—factually—these cases did not involve the defense of insanity.

In *Winship*, the state charged a juvenile with delinquency such that, had an adult committed the act, it would have constituted the crime of larceny. At the delinquency hearing, the judge rejected the juvenile's contention that his guilt must be established beyond a reasonable doubt, as required by the due process clause of the Fourteenth Amendment. Instead, the judge applied a statutory standard stipulating that "any determination at the conclusion of [an adjudicatory hearing] that a [juvenile] did an act or acts must be based on a preponderance of the evidence."[152]

The Supreme Court reversed the state court's determination of delinquency, and held that—in all cases involving criminality—proof beyond a reasonable doubt is constitutionally required as a matter of due process of law.[153] "[I]t is critical," the Court noted, "that the moral force of the criminal law not be diluted by a standard of proof that leaves people in doubt whether innocent men are being condemned."[154] Proof of guilt beyond a reasonable doubt safeguards the crucial interests of liberty, reputation, and the moral force of the law without displacing any of the substantive benefits of state law. As the Court concluded, this standard "lies at the foundation of the administration of the criminal law," and implements and provides concrete substance for the presumption of innocence.[155]

By holding that due process required proof beyond a reasonable doubt of every fact necessary to constitute the crime charged, many thought that *Winship* implicitly conflicted with *Leland*. However, *Winship* did not affect the rule announced in *Leland* or the states' power to impose the burden of persuasion on a defendant in regard to issues that were not elements of a crime as defined by state law. Rather, the import of *Winship* with regard to the insanity defense was to uphold *Leland*, because a state could still define a crime to include the element of sanity, in which case the burden of persuasion remained with the prosecution to prove sanity beyond a reasonable doubt. If, however, the state excluded sanity from its definition of the crime—but considered insanity as a factor for avoiding punishment—then the burden of persuasion could constitutionally be placed on the defendant. As one court observed in holding that *Winship* did not overrule *Leland*:

> *Winship* . . . did not undertake to demand that the states require any particular facts as elements of the crime. . . . It is one thing to say that proof of every element of the crime beyond a reasonable doubt is constitutionally mandated; it is quite a different thing to say the Constitution requires that a state define the elements of its own internal crimes in a particular way. From *Leland* it seems clear that there is no constitutional interdiction that would prevent a state from fashioning its own rule whereby sanity is not an ingredient of the crime, but is instead an affirmative defense designed to avoid punishment.[156]

Thus, after *Winship*, it was evident that the due process clause protects the accused against conviction except upon proof beyond a reasonable doubt of every element necessary to constitute the crime with which he or she has been charged. Where a state considered insanity as a factor independent of the elements of the crime, the burden of persuasion could then constitutionally be placed on the defendant asserting the defense.

Five years after *Winship*, the Supreme Court in *Mullaney* extended the rationale of *Winship* to invalidate Maine's statutory scheme for felonious homicide, which required the defendant to prove by a pre-ponderance of the evidence the mitigating defense of heat of passion on sudden provocation. Under this statute, the state defined the crime of murder as the killing of a human being "with malice afore-thought, either express or implied." Under Maine case law, malice aforethought—as an element of the crime—required the state to prove beyond a reasonable doubt that the defendant had killed another human being without *mitigation*, justification, or excuse. Yet, Maine's statutory scheme cast the burden of persuasion on the de-fendant to prove a mitigating defense—that the killing was committed in a heat of passion on sudden provocation—to reduce the degree of criminal culpability or blameworthiness to the lesser crime of man-slaughter.[157]

In *Mullaney v. Wilbur*, the Supreme Court held that Wilbur's due process rights had been violated by placing on the defendant the burden of proving by a preponderance of the evidence that the action had been committed in a heat of passion on sudden provocation. Under the state law definition of "malice aforethought," the absence of heat of passion is an element "critical to criminal culpability"—an element that directly affects the severity of the punishment im-posed.[158] The due process clause requires the prosecution to prove beyond a reasonable doubt the absence of heat of passion on sudden provocation as a fact necessary to constitute the crime of murder.[159]

Although *Mullaney* did not involve the insanity defense per se, in its aftermath some commentators argued that the Court's analysis raised "substantial doubt as to the continued viability of *Leland*."[160] The basis of this theory rested on three concepts: First, *Winship* undoubtedly required the state to prove every fact necessary to con-stitute the crime, beyond a reasonable doubt. Second, *Winship* clearly did not overrule *Leland*, in that a state need not disprove an affirmative defense—such as insanity—that was unrelated to guilt or innocence as defined by state law. Third, *Mullaney* extended *Winship* whenever the state makes a distinction—defined in terms of culpability, guilt, or blameworthiness—that necessarily affects the punishment of the defendant, even when that fact (for example, insanity) is not formally defined by the state as an element of the crime.[161]

Accordingly, some commentators argued that—whenever a state defines a crime not to include the defendant's sanity, and places the burden of persuasion on the defendant to prove insanity (like the statute considered in *Leland*)—under *Mullaney* that statute is unconstitutional, since insanity by its very nature is a fact "critical to criminal culpability" and necessarily affects the punishment of the defendant. Thus, any statute that places the burden of persuasion on the defendant to prove his or her insanity—regardless of whether sanity is defined by the state as an essential element of a crime—should be held to be unconstitutional under the due process clause of the Fourteenth Amendment.

One year after *Mullaney*, the Supreme Court had the opportunity to test the applicability of this argument to the insanity defense, in *Rivera v. Delaware*.[162] There, the state had indicted the defendant for first degree murder. However, the defendant was convicted of murder in the second degree. During her trial, the defendant raised insanity as a defense to the crime. The applicable Delaware statute classified the insanity defense as an affirmative defense, which the defendant had to prove by a preponderance of the evidence. Relying on *Leland*, the Delaware Supreme Court had upheld the constitutionality of the Delaware law, explicitly rejecting the contention that *Mullaney* overruled *Leland*.[163]

The U.S. Supreme Court dismissed the appeal "for want of a substantial federal question,"[164] thus implying that *Winship* and *Mullaney* had not overruled *Leland*. Justices Brennan and Marshall dissented, contending that—in light of the *Winship* and *Mullaney* decisions—the Court should decide the question of whether *Leland* had continuing validity.[165]

The next opportunity for the Court to question the validity of *Leland* occurred in *Patterson v. New York*.[166] In *Patterson*, the state had charged the defendant with second degree murder. The statutory scheme for murder in New York differed from the Maine statute considered by the Supreme Court in *Mullaney v. Wilbur*. Murder was defined by the New York legislature as consisting of two elements: (1) intent to cause the death of another person, and (2) causing the death of such person or of a third person. Unlike the Maine statute, "malice aforethought" (which, in Maine, required the state to prove an intentional killing as well as the absence of any factors of mitigation, excuse, or justification—once the defendant had satisfied the burden of going forward with some evidence of such factors) was not an element of the crime of murder in New York.[167] New York law permitted a person accused of murder to raise an affirmative defense that he or she had "acted under the influence of extreme emotional disturbance for which there was a reasonable explanation or excuse." Under New York law, killing under such circumstances constituted the lesser crime of manslaughter.

Before trial, the defendant confessed to the killing. At trial, the defendant raised the affirmative defense of extreme emotional disturbance, which permitted "the defendant to show that his actions were caused by a mental infirmity not arising to the level of insanity, and that he is less culpable for having committed them."[168] The trial judge instructed the jury that the prosecution had to establish all of the elements of the crime beyond a reasonable doubt, but that "the defendant had the burden of proving his affirmative defense by a preponderance of the evidence."[169] The jury found the defendant guilty of murder.

On appeal, the defendant argued that the New York statutory scheme violated the due process clause of the Fourteenth Amendment. The Supreme Court affirmed the conviction. Noting that the affirmative defense of extreme emotional disturbance "constitutes a separate issue" and "does not serve to negate any facts of the crime which the State is to prove in order to convict for murder,"[170] the Court distinguished *Patterson* from *Mullaney*. The Court recognized that, in *Mullaney*, murder as defined by the state included "malice"— expressed or implied—and that the defense of heat of passion on sudden provocation was necessarily inconsistent with malice. Thus, requiring the defendant to prove the latter would necessarily negate the former, which the prosecution was required to prove.[171] This procedure—the Court affirmed— was "impermissible."[172] Under the New York scheme, however, this problem was not presented, because "nothing was presumed or implied against Patterson."[173]

Moreover—contrary to the defendant's contention that "*Mullaney's* holding . . . is that the State may not permit the blameworthiness of an act or the severity of punishment . . . to depend on the presence or absence of an identified fact without assuming the burden of proving the presence or absence of that fact . . . beyond a reasonable doubt"—in the Court's view, such an interpretation of *Mullaney* was too broad and far-reaching, which the Court had not intended.[174]

Thus, in determining that the New York statutory scheme did not violate the defendant's right to due process, the Court dispelled the theory that *Mullaney* implicitly—if not explicitly—overruled *Leland*. In effect, the Court reaffirmed the principles that had been announced in *Leland* and implicitly endorsed in *Rivera*, and seemed to settle the issue of the constitutionality of requiring the defendant to bear the burden of persuasion on the sanity issue.

Any doubt that may have remained after *Patterson* in regard to the constitutionality of placing the burden of persuasion on a defendant to prove insanity was put to rest in *Jones v. United States*.[175] In *Jones*, the state had charged the defendant with attempted petit larceny, a misdemeanor punishable by a maximum prison sentence of one year. At trial, the defendant had successfully proved his insanity by a preponderance of the evidence, and was found not guilty by reason of insanity. The defendant was subsequently committed to a public mental institution. Under the District of Columbia code in these circumstances, a defendant is automatically committed to a mental hospital, but is entitled to a judicial hearing within 50 days to determine his eligibility for release. At this hearing, the defendant has the burden of proving by a preponderance of the evidence that he is no longer mentally ill. The code also provides that the defendant is entitled to a judicial hearing every six months, at which he may establish by a preponderance of the evidence that he is entitled to be released.

At Jones's 50-day hearing, the court found that he remained mentally ill and constituted a danger to himself and others. A second release hearing was held after he had been hospitalized for more than one year—the maximum period he could have spent in prison if he had been convicted. On that basis, the defendant demanded to be either released unconditionally or recommitted under civil commitment procedures, which would include a jury trial and would require that the government prove his mental illness and dangerousness by clear and convincing evidence. The trial court denied his request, reaffirmed its finding made at the 50-day hearing, and ordered that his hospital confinement be continued.[176]

The Supreme Court affirmed. It approved automatic commitment under the due process clause, because the inference is permissible that the individual was continuing to suffer from the mental disorder that the defense had affirmatively established at trial by a preponderance of the evidence.[177] Also, since the state had established at trial that the defendant committed the criminal act charged, the inference is permissible that the individual was continuing to be dangerous. In reaching its decision, the Court noted that "[a] defendant could be required to prove his insanity by a higher standard than a preponderance of evidence."[178]

Thus, while the issue involved in *Jones* did not deal with the question of whether the burden of persuasion could constitutionally be imposed on a defendant to prove his or her insanity, the Court implicitly reaffirmed the continued viability of *Leland*. Also, *Jones* provided a practical incentive for states to shift the burden of persuasion on the issue of insanity to the defendant. Where the defendant must prove his own insanity by at least a preponderance of the evidence (as contrasted with merely raising a reasonable doubt, where the state bears the burden of persuasion), this amounts to an affirmative finding on the record of the defendant's insanity—which justifies automatic commitment, because the inference is permissible that the defendant continues to be insane.[179]

In conclusion, the battle in the federal courts over the constitutionality of placing the burden of persuasion on the defendant to prove the existence of insanity appears to be over. The Supreme Court's broad language in *In re Winship* and *Mullaney v. Wilbur* suggested that the 1952 decision in *Leland v. Oregon* might be reconsidered. In more recent decisions, the failure to consider the appeal in *Rivera v. Delaware* ("for want of a substantial federal question") and the language in the *Patterson* and *Jones* decisions indicates that the U.S. Supreme Court would probably reject a challenge to the burden of persuasion provision in the Insanity Defense Reform Act of 1984. As in other areas of criminal law and procedure, given identical provisions of state constitutions, those state supreme courts with more moderate–liberal judges are more likely than their conservative brethren to be receptive to arguments that state statutes allocating the burden of persuasion to the defendant in insanity defense cases violate due process of law.

NOTES

1. *Smith v. United States*, 36 F.2d 548, 59 U.S. App. D.C. 144, 70 A.L.R. 654 (1929); *Hollaway v. United States*, 148 F.2d 665, 80 U.S. App. D.C. 3 (1945), cert. den., 334 U.S. 852 (1948).

2. *Durham v. United States*, 94 U.S. App. D.C. 228, 214 F.2d 862 (D.C. Cir. 1954).

3. *Durham* was finally rejected by a unanimous court as unworkable, in *United States v. Brawner*, 471 F.2d 969 (*en banc*, D.C. Cir. 1972)–wherein the D.C. Circuit adopted the ALI standard.

4. During its existence, only the D.C. Circuit adopted the *Durham* test for criminal responsibility. Some federal circuit courts explicitly rejected it. See, for example, *United States v. Freeman*, 357 F.2d 606 (2d Cir. 1966); *Howard v. United States*, 232 F.2d 274 (5th Cir. 1956); *Anderson v. United States*, 237 F.2d 118 (9th Cir. 1957); *Wion v. United States*, 325 F.2d 420, cert. den., 377 U.S. 946 (10th Cir. 1963). Other jurisdictions implicitly rejected it, by adopting the subsequent ALI standard. See, for example, *United States v. Freeman*, supra; *United States v. Currens*, 290 F.2d 751 (3d Cir. 1961); *United States v. Chandler*, 393 F.2d 920 (4th Cir. 1968); *Blake v. United States*, 407 F.2d 908 (5th Cir. 1969); *United States v. Smith*, 404 F.2d 720 (6th Cir. 1968); *United States v. Shapiro*, 383 F.2d 680 (7th Cir. 1967); *Pope v. United States*, 372 F.2d 710 (8th Cir. 1967); *Wade v. United States*, 426 F.2d 64 (9th Cir. 1970); *Wion v. United States*, supra.

5. *Durham v. United States*, 94 U.S. App. D.C. 228, 214 F.2d 862, 964 (D.C. Cir. 1954).

6. Ibid., pp. 865–66. Emphasis in the original.

7. Ibid., p. 866 (citations omitted). See the following section on burdens of proof.

8. Ibid., p. 874.

9. Ibid.

10. Ibid.

11. Ibid., pp. 874–75.

12. Ibid., p. 875.

13. Ibid.

14. Ibid.

15. Ibid., p. 876.

16. Ibid.

17. *Douglas v. United States*, 239 F.2d 52, 57–59 (1956).

18. *Carter v. United States*, 252 F.2d 608, 615 (1957).

19. Ibid., pp. 616–17. Emphasis added.

20. Ibid., p. 617.

21. *Blocker v. United States*, 110 U.S. App. D.C. 41, 288 F.2d 853, 862 (1961) (Justice Burger concurring). It is interesting to note that Judge Burger's

opinion foreshadowed the later development of the insanity law in the District of Columbia and elsewhere.

22. *Frigillana v. United States*, 307 F.2d 665 (D.C. Cir. 1962).

23. David C. Acheson, *"McDonald v. United States*: The *Durham* Rule Redefined," 51 *Geo. L. J.* 580, 583 (1963). Emphasis in original.

24. *Wright v. United States*, 102 U.S. App. D.C. 36, 250 F.2d 4 (1957).

25. Acheson, *"Durham* Redefined," p. 584.

26. *Washington v. United States*, 129 U.S. App. D.C. 29, 390 F.2d 444 (D.C. Cir. 1967).

27. Ibid.

28. *Briscoe v. United States*, 248 F.2d 640, 641 (D.C. Cir. 1957).

29. *In re Rosenfield*, 157 F. Supp. 18 (D.D.C. 1957).

30. It should be noted that disputes about nomenclature also were common in insanity defense trials under the *M'Naghten* standard. Prosecution psychiatrists would classify the defendant's behavior as not psychotic. On the other hand, defense psychiatrists would claim that the defendant's behavior was psychotic, or the result of another mental disorder claimed to qualify. Abraham S. Goldstein, *The Insanity Defense* (New Haven: Yale University Press, 1967), p. 85.

31. *McDonald v. United States*, 312 F.2d 847, 851 (*en banc*, 61 D.C. Cir. 1962).

32. Ibid. Emphasis in original.

33. Ibid.

34. Ibid.

35. *Washington v. United States*, 129 U.S. App. D.C. 29, 390 F.2d 444, 454 (D.C. Cir. 1967).

36. *United States v. Brawner*, 471 F.2d 969 (*en banc*, D.C. Cir. 1972).

37. Ibid., p. 981.

38. Ibid., p. 986.

39. American Law Institute, *Model Penal Code*, sec. 4.01 (Philadelphia: A.L.I., 1962).

40. See Annot., 56 A.L.R. Fed. 326 (1982), for citations to specific circuits.

41. See *United States v. Brawner*, 471 F.2d 969 (*en banc*, D.C. Cir. 1972).

42. *United States v. Freeman*, 357 F.2d 622 (2d Cir. 1966).

43. Ibid., pp. 622-23.

44. Ibid. In this respect, it is interesting to note that the court's interpretation is on target with the intention of the drafters of the Model Penal Code. See American Law Institute, "Model Penal Code," sec. 4.01(1), tent. draft no. 4, comment at pp. 157-59 (1955). In *United States v. Freeman*, supra, the court said:

Nothing makes the inquiry into responsibility more unreal for the psychiatrist than limitation of the issue to some ultimate extreme of total incapacity, when clinical experience reveals only a graded scale with marks along the way. . . . The law must recognize that when there is no black and white it must content itself with different shades of gray. The draft, accordingly, does not demand *complete* impairment of capacity. It asks instead for *substantial* impairment. [emphasis in the original]

45. *United States v. Freeman*, 357 F.2d 622–23 (2d Cir. 1966).
46. See American Law Institute, "Model Penal Code," sec. 4.01(1), proposed official draft, expl. n. at p. 62 (1962).
47. *United States v. Freeman*, 357 F.2d 623 (2d Cir. 1966).
48. Ibid.
49. Ibid.
50. Ibid.
51. *United States v. Chandler*, 393 F.2d 920 (4th Cir. 1968).
52. This last point was the primary focus of the Tenth Circuit in *Wion v. United States*, 325 F.2d 420, cert. den., 377 U.S. 946 (10th Cir. 1963). In *Wion*, the court—in adopting the ALI test—noted that it was similar to the *M'Naghten* and irresistible impulse tests previously used by the Tenth Circuit. The primary advantage that the court found in the ALI test was its simple and comprehensible language for the lay juror. This factor—the court concluded—permits the jury to apply the test to the expert testimony more intelligently, while allowing psychiatrists enough leeway in testifying about their findings and conclusions.
53. *United States v. Shapiro*, 383 F.2d 680 (7th Cir. 1967).
54. Ibid., p. 685.
55. Ibid.
56. Ibid., p. 686.
57. Ibid., pp. 685–86.
58. *Blake v. United States*, 407 F.2d 908 (5th Cir. 1969).
59. Ibid., p. 914.
60. Ibid., p. 915.
61. *United States v. Frazier*, 458 F.2d 911 (8th Cir. 1972).
62. Ibid., p. 915.
63. Ibid., p. 917.
64. Ibid.
65. *United States v. Currens*, 290 F.2d 751 (3d Cir. 1961).
66. Ibid., p. 774. See also *United States v. Brawner*, 471 F.2d 969 (*en banc*, D.C. Cir. 1972), where—although the court adopted both prongs of the ALI test—it suggested that, in a particular case, the accused may specifically request omission of the cognitive prong in the instruction to the jury, if it is wholly unrelated to the facts of the case and if the accused fears that a jury might be unable to understand the details of the instruction on insanity, and might thus infer that the defense has lost on the issue if the defendant "appreciates" the wrongfulness of his conduct.
67. *United States v. Currens*, 290 F.2d 774 (3d Cir. 1961), n. 32.
68. Ibid.
69. *United States v. Smith*, 404 F.2d 720, 727 (6th Cir. 1968).

70. Ibid, p. 727, n. 8. In *United States v. Gray*, 522 F.2d 429 (6th Cir. 1975), the court refined the meaning of its holding in *Smith* (see note 69 above) by noting that every defendant diagnosed as having a psychopathic or antisocial personality is not—as a matter of law—suffering from a "mental disease or defect," as that phrase is defined by the ALI test. Rather, it is ultimately left to the jury to decide whether the defendant was suffering from a mental illness at the time of the criminal act, and—if so—whether such mental illness so affected the defendant's conduct as to excuse him or her from criminal responsibility, by reason of insanity.

71. *Wade v. United States*, 426 F.2d 64 (9th Cir. 1970).

72. Ibid., p. 72.

73. Ibid.

74. Ibid, pp. 72-73. Emphasis in original. Since a psychiatrist is unlikely to base his diagnosis of the criminal psychopath or sociopath solely on the patient's criminal or antisocial conduct, it is argued that the actual impact of paragraph (2) may be to exclude only those psychopaths who receive a routine examination, but not those affluent and fortunate enough to receive a more careful diagnosis. Bernard Diamond, "From *M'Naghten* to *Currens*, and Beyond," 50 *Calif. L. Rev.* 189, 194 (1962).

75. *United States v. Brawner*, 471 F.2d 969 (*en banc*, D.C. Cir. 1972).

76. *McDonald v. United States*, 312 F.2d 847 (*en banc*, 61 D.C. Cir. 1962). As noted earlier, in *McDonald*, the District of Columbia Circuit defined "mental disease or defect" as used in the *Durham* rule as "*any* abnormal condition of the mind which substantially affects mental or emotional processes and substantially impairs behavioral controls" (p. 851, emphasis added).

77. *United States v. Brawner*, 471 F.2d 969, 983 (*en banc*, D.C. Cir. 1972).

78. Ibid., p. 984.

79. See, for example, *United States v. Freeman*, 357 F.2d 606 (2d Cir. 1966); *Blake v. United States*, 407 F.2d 908 (5th Cir. 1969); *United States v. Shapiro*, 383 F.2d 680 (7th Cir. 1967); *United States v. Frazier*, 458 F.2d 911 (8th Cir. 1972); *Wion v. United States*, 325 F.2d 420, cert. den. 377 U.S. 946 (10th Cir. 1963). The Fourth Circuit adopted the suggested term "criminality." See *United States v. Chandler*, 393 F.2d 920 (4th Cir. 1968).

80. See ALI, *Code*, sec. 4.01(1): "he lacks substantial capacity to appreciate the criminality (wrongfulness) of his conduct."

81. *United States v. Brawner*, 471 F.2d 992 (*en banc*, D.C. Cir. 1972).

82. Ibid.

83. *Wade v. United States*, 426 F.2d 64 (9th Cir. 1970).

84. Ibid., p. 71.

85. *Regina v. Windle*, 2 Q.B. 826, 2 All Eng. Rep. 1 (1952).

86. At that time, the standard used by the First Circuit was unclear. See *Beltron v. United States*, 802 F.2d 48 (1st Cir. 1962).

87. Henry Weihofen, *The Urge to Punish* (New York: Farrar, Straus, and Cudahy, 1956), pp. 99-100.

88. Wayne R. LaFave and Austin W. Scott, Jr., *Handbook on Criminal Law* (1972), p. 294.

89. The Comprehensive Crime Control Act of 1984 is title II of Public Law 98–473, 98 Stat. 1837, 1976, enacted October 12, 1984. The act comprises 23 chapters, some of which have their own titles. Chapter IV is entitled "Insanity Defense Reform Act of 1984," appearing in 18 U.S.C., sec. 20 (1984).

90. U.S. Congress, House of Representatives, Subcommittee on Criminal Justice, *Hearings on H.R. 67883* (1982), p. 1. The authors express their appreciation to Dr. Barbara Ann Stolz, a staff member of the U.S. House of Representatives Select Committee on Narcotics Abuse and Control, for providing us with a draft of her article on the legislative history of the Insanity Defense Reform Act of 1984: Barbara Ann Stolz, "Congress and Criminal Justice Policy-Making: The Federal Insanity Defense" (unpublished, 1986).

91. Stolz, "Congress and Criminal Justice," p. 8.

92. See U.S. Congress, House of Representatives, Committee on Judiciary, *Hearings on H.R. 1280 and Related Bills before the Subcommittee on Criminal Justice*, 98th Cong., 1st sess. (1983); U.S. Congress, Senate, Committee on Judiciary, *Limiting the Insanity Defense: Hearings before the Subcommittee on Criminal Law*, 97th Cong., 2d sess. (1982); U.S. Congress, Senate, Committee on Judiciary, *Report on S. 1762, Comprehensive Crime Control Act of 1983*, 98th Cong., 1st sess. (1983); U.S. Congress, House of Representatives, Committee on Judiciary, *Report to House from Committee on Judiciary, H.R. 98-577*, 98th Cong., 2d sess. (1984); *Congressional Record*, 98th Cong., 2d sess., September 18, September 25, October 2, 4, 11, 1984.

93. Stolz, "Congress and Criminal Justice," pp. 9–10.

94. *Congressional Record*, September 25, 1984, pp. H10024–H10030, H10129–H10130.

95. *Congressional Record*, September 25, 1984, p. H10129.

96. *Congressional Record*, October 2, 1984, part 1:H10682–H10722, part 2:H10789–10824.

97. *Congressional Record*, October 4, 1984, pp. S13062–S13091.

98. *Congressional Record*, October 11, 1984, pp. S14266, H1228; Stolz, "Congress and Criminal Justice," p. 11.

99. Stolz, "Congress and Criminal Justice," pp. 16, 19–20.

100. 18 U.S.C., sec. 20(a) (1984).

101. In *United States v. Lyons*, 741 F.2d 243 (5th Cir. 1984), the Fifth Circuit judicially altered the standard for the insanity defense, making it similar to that enacted in 18 U.S.C., sec. 20(a) (1984).

102. S.R. 98-225, 98th Cong., 2d sess., reprinted in 4 *U.S. Code Cong. & Admin. News* 3407-8 (1984). Emphasis in original.

103. Ibid., pp. 3408-9 (statement of Richard J. Bonnie, Professor of Law and Director of the Institute of Law, Psychiatry, and Public Policy at the University of Virginia).

104. Board of Trustees of the American Psychiatric Association, *American Psychiatric Association Statement on the Insanity Defense* (December 1982), pp. 11–12, n. 16.

105. U.S. Congress, Senate, Committee on the Judiciary, Subcommittee on Criminal Law, *Hearings on S. 829* (May 1983), p. 526.

106. See Richard J. Bonnie, "The Moral Basis of the Insanity Defense," 69 *A.B.A.J.* 194, 196 (1983).

107. Governor's Task Force to Review the Defense of Insanity, Executive Department, State of Maryland, *Report to the Governor* (1984), p. 25.

108. See David E. Aaronson, "Maryland Responds to the *Hinckley* Case: Changes in the Insanity Defense," 85 *Maryland Bar Journal* 33 (1985).

109. Letter dated June 24, 1985, to David E. Aaronson from Elyce H. Zenoff, Professor of Law at the George Washington University.

110. LaFave and Scott, *Handbook*, pp. 281, 282, citing Herbert Wechsler, "The Criteria of Criminal Responsibility," 22 *U. Chi. L. Rev.* 367 (1955); Henry Weihofen, *Mental Disorder as a Criminal Defense* (Buffalo, N.Y.: Dennis, 1954), p. 84; Joseph Livermore and Paul Meehl, "The Virtues of *M'Naghten*," 51 *Minn. L. Rev.* 789, 794–95, 855 (1967).

111. LaFave and Scott, *Handbook*, p. 282.

112. U.S. Department of Justice, *Handbook on the Comprehensive Crime Control Act of 1984 and Other Criminal Statutes Enacted by the 98th Congress* (December 1984), pp. 59–60.

113. See *United States v. Freeman*, 357 F.2d 606, 623 (2d Cir. 1966). See also Chapter 1 for a discussion of the varying interpretations of the word "know" under the *M'Naghten* standard.

114. American Bar Association, *American Bar Association Policy on the Insanity Defense* (approved by the ABA House of Delegates, February 9, 1983), p. 4.

115. *McDonald v. United States*, 312 F.2d 847 (D.C. Cir. 1962). See earlier discussion in this chapter on the *Durham* rule.

116. S.R. 98-225, 98th Cong., 2d sess., reprinted in 4 *U.S. Code Cong. & Admin. News* 3411 (1984).

117. *United States v. Brawner*, 471 F.2d 969 (*en banc*, D.C. Cir. 1972).

118. Many commentators feel that abolishing the diminished capacity defense creates an anomaly, because the criminal law recognizes that even voluntary intoxication may be allowed as a defense to negate the required mental state of a specific intent crime, such as when a person became so drunk as to be unable to premeditate and deliberate killing another person. If a state of mind such as voluntary intoxication is allowed under these circumstances, it is argued that a reduction in mental capacity due to mental disease or defect should have the same result of reducing the grade or degree of the crime.

119. See S.R. 98-225, 98th Cong., 2d sess., p. 229, reprinted in 4 *U.S. Code Cong. & Admin. News* (1984); U.S. Department of Justice, *Handbook on the Comprehensive Crime Control Act*, p. 60.

120. Edward C. Cleary, gen. ed., *McCormick on Evidence* (3d ed., St. Paul, Mn.: West Publishing, 1984), ch. 35, pp. 946-1003; LaFave and Scott, *Handbook*, pp. 312-13.

121. See LaFave and Scott, *Handbook*, pp. 312-13, n. 116.

122. For citations to particular jurisdictions, see, for example, Annot., 17 A.L.R.3d 146, 159 (1968). See also Julian Eule, "The Presumption of Sanity: Bursting the Bubble," 25 *U.C.L.A. Rev.* 637 (1978); Abraham S. Goldstein, *The Insanity Defense* (New Haven: Yale University Press, 1967), ch. 8.

123. See generally Annot., 17 A.L.R.3d 146 (1968).

124. *In re Winship*, 397 U.S. 358 (1970).

125. See generally Annot., 17 A.L.R.3d 146 (1968).

126. *Davis v. United States*, 160 U.S. 469 (1895).

127. 18 U.S.C., sec. 20(b).

128. *ABA Policy on the Insanity Defense*, pp. 1-2.

129. Ibid., p. 7.

130. Ibid., pp. 6-7.

131. *APA Statement on the Insanity Defense*, pp. 12-13.

132. S.R. 98-225, 98th Cong., 2d sess., reprinted in 4 *U.S. Code Cong. & Admin. News* 3411-12 (1984).

133. U.S. Congress, Senate, Committee on the Judiciary, *Hearings on S. 818, S. 1106, S. 1558, S. 2669, S. 2672, S. 2678, S. 2745, and S. 2780* (July and August 1982), pp. 222-23 (statement of William J. Mertens on behalf of the National Legal Aid and Defender Association).

134. S.R. 98-225, 98th Cong., 2d sess., reprinted in 4 *U.S. Code Cong. & Admin. News* 3412 (1984).

135. Stolz, "Congress and Criminal Justice," p. 27.

136. See Sanford H. Kadish, Stephen J. Schulhofer, and Monrad G. Paulsen, *Criminal Law and Its Processes* (4th ed., Boston: Little, Brown, 1983), pp. 842-43; *Davis v. United States*, 160 U.S. 469 (1895); *Leland v. Oregon*, 343 U.S. 790, 799 (1952).

137. *Jones v. United States*, 463 U.S. 354, 356-61, 103 S. Ct. 3043, 77 L. Ed.2d 6914 (1983).

138. *Davis v. United States*, 160 U.S. 469 (1895).

139. Ibid., p. 475.

140. Ibid., pp. 476-77.

141. Ibid., p. 478.

142. Ibid., p. 488.

143. *Leland v. Oregon*, 342 U.S. 790 (1952).

144. Ibid., p. 792.

145. Ibid., p. 794.

146. Ibid., p. 793.

147. Ibid., p. 797.

148. Ibid., p. 799.

149. Ibid.

150. *In re Winship*, 397 U.S. 358 (1970).

151. *Mullaney v. Wilbur*, 421 U.S. 684 (1975).

152. *In re Winship*, 397 U.S. 358, 360 (1970).

153. Ibid., p. 368.

154. Ibid., p. 364.

155. Ibid., p. 363.

156. *United States ex rel. Tate v. Powell*, 325 F. Supp. 333 (E. D. Pa. 1971).

157. *Mullaney v. Wilbur*, 421 U.S. 684, 685–86 (1975).

158. Ibid., p. 702.

159. Ibid., p. 704.

160. See "The Burden of Proof and the Insanity Defense after *Mullaney v. Wilbur*," 28 *Me. L. Rev.* 435, 449–62 (1976).

161. Ibid., pp. 468–69.

162. *Rivera v. Delaware*, 429 U.S. 877 (1976).

163. *Rivera v. Delaware*, 351 A.2d 561, 562 (1976).

164. *Rivera v. Delaware*, 429 U.S. 877 (1976).

165. Ibid., p. 880 (Justices Brennan and Marshall dissenting).

166. *Patterson v. New York*, 432 U.S. 197 (1977).

167. Ibid., p. 198.

168. Ibid., pp. 199, 206.

169. Ibid., pp. 199–200.

170. Ibid., p. 207. Interestingly, the court observed that to find the New York statutory scheme violative of the due process clause would necessarily lead to overturning both *Leland* and *Rivera* (ibid., see notes 143 and 164 above).

171. Ibid., p. 213.

172. Ibid., p. 215.

173. Ibid., p. 216.

174. Ibid., pp. 215–16, n. 15.

175. *Jones v. United States*, 463 U.S. 354, 103 S. Ct. 3043, 77 L. Ed.2d 6914 (1983).

176. Ibid., pp. 356–61.

177. Ibid., pp. 366–68.

178. Ibid., p. 368, n. 17 (citing *Leland*—see note 143 above—as support).

179. Where the state is required to prove the defendant's sanity beyond a reasonable doubt and loses at trial, then—in order to justify commitment to a mental institution—the state is in the anomalous position of having to prove the same individual insane at a postverdict commitment hearing.

3

Expert Witnesses in Insanity Defense Trials
(with the assistance of Gloria Danziger and Nancy Streef)

INTRODUCTION

In any criminal trial where the defendant's sanity is at issue, expert testimony is a crucial factor in the outcome. Over the years, there has always been controversy as to what is the proper role for an expert witness when the insanity defense is raised. Some commentators have suggested doing away with expert testimony altogether. Those of an opposite viewpoint would admit a broad scope of opinion. Various reforms over the years, however, have attempted to control and limit the scope of this testimony. As recently as 1984, the Federal Rules of Evidence were amended to prevent expert testimony on the so-called ultimate issue. The debate still continues today about the appropriate role of mental health professionals in insanity defense trials and the nature and scope of their testimony.

This chapter discusses the role of expert witnesses in insanity defense trials. It begins with a section on historical background in order to give the reader a foundation for understanding the current debate over just what an expert should testify about. The discussion next addresses the debate over the role of the mental health professional in insanity defense trials, from the perspectives of both the legal and mental health communities. The chapter concludes with a discussion of proposals for change in the following areas: improving the quality of expert testimony; restricting the scope of expert testimony; improving jurors' understanding of their role in evaluating expert testimony; and court appointment of expert witnesses in appropriate cases.

HISTORICAL BACKGROUND

The first recorded instance of a forensic witness giving evidence at an insanity trial occurred in 1760 in England. Dr. John Munro—apothecary to Bethlehem Hospital—testified in the case of Earl Ferrers, who was on trial for murder.[1] Dr. Munro's testimony was introduced because of his familiarity with the insane. This knowledge—it was claimed—enabled him to distinguish the "true features" of madness.

An early U.S. case involving medical experts occurred in New York City in 1800. The state had charged the defendant, Levi Weeks, with the murder of his fiancée.[2] Although two brilliant attorneys—Alexander Hamilton and Aaron Burr—represented the defendant, the medical testimony in the case was of very low quality. One prominent physician simply testified as to the appearance of the body in the coffin.[3]

Between 1760 and 1815, medical witnesses' testimony remained remarkably free of technical jargon or allusions to physical explanations. Most often these witnesses served a legitimating function—that is, they provided a professional's affirmation of what the defendant's peers had already concluded.[4] In their role as the final—or "legitimating"—witnesses, medical experts focused on flightiness of conversation, lack of connections between the defendant's ideas, and the defendant's inability to follow a question with an appropriate answer, as indications of a defendant's insanity.[5]

In 1843, in the *M'Naghten* case,[6] an English court formed a test that focused on the cognitive capacity of the defendant. As discussed in Chapter 2, when the accused was laboring under such a defect of reason, from disease of the mind, as not to know the nature and quality of the act he was doing—or, if he did know it, then he did not know that he was doing what was wrong—then he could not be convicted for the criminal act.[7] The test's widespread adoption was based in part on the psychological theory under which the mind was divided into separate independent compartments, one of which could be diseased without affecting the others. The *M'Naghten* test purported to channel psychiatric testimony into a narrow issue of cognitive capacity.[8]

The psychiatrist called as a witness in a case relying on a strict application of the *M'Naghten* test was faced with a dilemma: Either he could restrict his testimony to the confines of the test, thereby depriving the trier of fact of a full presentation of the defendant's mental state; or he could give an opinion as to whether the defendant could tell right from wrong—which strategy would then allow the psychiatrist to present the reality of the defendant's mental condition.[9]

In 1954, Judge David Bazelon in *Durham v. United States*[10] attempted to bring the insanity defense test in line with current psychiatric thought. This case was the beginning of the U.S. Court of Appeals for the District of Columbia's pioneering decisions in the area of expert testimony.[11] In *Durham*, Judge Bazelon allowed psychiatrists the broadest latitude to explain the defendant's symptoms and to provide a detailed clinical history of the accused. It was hoped that this information would enable the jury to reach a composite conclusion that contained medical, legal, and moral components. The *Durham* test, however, led to "trial by label." Since no definition of "mental disease or defect" existed, medical experts defined the term with meanings drawn from their own discipline. This led to increased reliance on classifications in the American Psychiatric Association's diagnostic manual—terms developed to aid in understanding and treating mental disorders, not in assessing criminal responsibility. Administrative changes in a classification could have an effect on expert witnesses' testimony. For many expert witnesses, the diagnostic manual was and is the bible, on which great reliance is placed. For example, in a case cited earlier, doctors testified that the petitioner was a sociopath, and that a person with a sociopathic personality would not be suffering from mental disease. By the time court convened again, however, the psychiatrist's hospital had made a policy change, and had determined that—as an administrative matter—the state of a psychopathic or sociopathic personality did indeed constitute a mental disease. This type of testimony did not lend support to the cause of getting the *Durham* test adopted beyond the District of Columbia.

In 1957, the same court somewhat narrowed the *Durham* test in *Carter v. United States.*[12] The court emphasized that "the simple fact that a person has a mental disease or defect is not enough to relieve him of responsibility for a crime. There must be a relationship between the disease and the criminal act; and the relationship must be such as to justify a reasonable inference that the act would not have been committed if the person had not been suffering from the disease."[13] The decision in *Carter* clarified the *Durham* test by requiring that, in order for the criminal act to be "a product" of a mental disease or defect, the act would not have occurred "but for" the mental disease or defect.[14] Thus, as with *M'Naghten* and other formulations, the expert witness was required to address two different questions: (1) Was the defendant suffering from a mental disorder at the time of the alleged crime(s); and (2) if so, was there a causal nexus between the particular mental disorder and the alleged criminal conduct?

Over the years, Judge Bazelon became disillusioned with the psychiatrists' performances in his courtroom. In *Rollerson v. United States*,[15] he noted that "the frequent failure to adequately explain and support expert psychiatric opinion threatens the administration of the insanity defense in the District of Columbia."[16]

Bazelon's dissatisfaction continued; and, a few years later—in a landmark case—he appended an explanatory set of instructions to psychiatric witnesses, which was to accompany all orders requiring mental examinations. These instructions are still used in a modified form in the District of Columbia and in many other jurisdictions. They were also to be read aloud in court before the first expert testified.

> As an expert witness, you may, if you wish and if you feel you can, give your opinion about whether the defendant suffered from a mental disease or defect. You may then explain how the defendant's disease or defect related to his alleged offense, that is, how the development, adaptation and functioning of the defendant's behavioral processes may have influenced his conduct. This explanation should be so complete that the jury will have a basis for an informed judgment on whether the alleged crime was a "product" of his mental disease or defect. But it will not be necessary for you to express an opinion on whether the alleged crime was a "product" of a mental disease or defect and you will not be asked to do so.
>
> What is desired in the courtroom is the kind of opinion you would give a family which brought one of its members to your clinic and asked for your diagnosis of his mental condition and a description of how his condition would be likely to influence his conduct. Insofar as counsel's questions permit you should testify in this manner.[17]

Despite such efforts, Bazelon eventually gave up; he voted with the District of Columbia Appellate Court to discard the *Durham* standard. Jerome Hall commented on Bazelon's disillusionment as follows: "Psychiatry failed Judge Bazelon because like all of the social and behavioral sciences it lacks a concept of an evil-meaning mind as a cause, and I might add it also lacks a concept of what is good and right."[18] Yet, the medical expert—by giving testimony in terms of a nonmedical construct ("product")—expresses conclusions that, in essence, embody ethical and legal conclusions. It was an ironical situation: "[T]he *Durham* rule, which was adopted in large part to permit experts to testify in their own terms concerning matters within their domain which the jury should know, resulted in testimony by the experts in terms not their own, to reflect unexpressed judgments in a domain that is properly not theirs but the jury's."[19]

Dissatisfaction with the *M'Naghten* and *Durham* tests led to the American Law Institute's (ALI) adoption of the Model Penal Code's test for criminal responsibility in 1962. In section 4.01, the ALI formulated a test for the insanity defense, as discussed in Chapter 2.[20] The ALI test incorporated both cognitive and volitional tests.[21] It was hoped that the more explicit legal standards of this new test would remove some of the difficulties that jurors faced when deciding the weight to be given to expert testimony. The trier of fact could then more easily focus on the ultimate issues and, hopefully, be less likely to defer to expert witnesses.

Not everyone supported the ALI test. Judge Bazelon did not approve, and he remained dissatisfied with what he regarded as "encroachments by the experts" on the function of the jury.[22] Bazelon felt that the jury should be instructed to find a defendant not responsible "if at the time of his unlawful conduct his mental or emotional processes or behavior controls were impaired to such an extent that he cannot justly be held responsible for his act."[23] With such a test, the psychiatrist would be asked a single question: "What is the nature of the impairment of the defendant's mental and emotional processes and behavior controls?" It would leave to the jury the question of whether that impairment is sufficient to relieve the defendant of responsibility for the act charged.

Bazelon viewed the ALI test as useless in terms of making the "intertwining moral, legal, and medical" judgments necessary during an insanity defense trial. In fact, Bazelon wrote in his *Brawner* dissent that "because it describes the question as one of fact it may lull the jury into the mistaken assumption that the question of responsibility can best be resolved by experts, leaving the jury at the mercy of the witness who asserts most persuasively that, in his expert judgment, the defendant's capacity was or was not substantially impaired."[24]

Controversy over the use of expert witnesses in the insanity defense trial has not abated. Throughout the 1970s and into the 1980s, critics have contended that expert witnesses confuse the jury, hire themselves out to the highest bidder, fail to clarify the facts of a case, and generally dominate the proceedings to the detriment of an equitable resolution of the case. The following section discusses the various viewpoints surrounding this debate.

THE DEBATE ON THE ROLE OF
THE EXPERT WITNESS

The verdict in the *Hinckley* case ignited an intense national and congressional debate on the appropriateness of the insanity defense and the role of the expert witness. There was outrage that the jury had "freed" Hinckley to roam the streets again with a loaded gun. (In fact, Hinckley was immediately committed, and has been confined to St. Elizabeth's Hospital for more than five years; he is unlikely to be released in the near future.) According to popular opinion, the expensive expert witnesses hired by Hinckley's wealthy parents must have "duped" the jury into finding Hinckley not guilty by reason of insanity.

The *Hinckley* case illustrates the dominant role often played by expert witnesses in contested insanity defense trials and the difficulties that attorneys face in presenting expert witnesses to the jury. Hinckley's attempt to assassinate the president of the United States occurred in the late afternoon of March 30, 1981. The crux of the insanity defense's complexity is that it deals with a very elusive question: a person's mental condition not at the *present* time—which is more easily evaluated—but at a time in the *past*. During the five-month interval between arrest and indictment, Hinckley was confined at the Butner, North Carolina, Federal Correctional Institution—one of the most advanced and sophisticated facilities in the federal penal system for the diagnosis, review, and treatment of mental disorders among criminal defendants and persons facing charges for criminal offenses. Hinckley's order of commitment required the government officials at Butner to determine his mental condition and responsibility for the events of March 30.

While one might assume that all conceivable medical and psychiatric examinations and batteries of psychological tests were undertaken at Butner—and that Hinckley would be ready for trial immediately after his return—such was not the case. Both government and defense requested additional medical examinations and other evaluations. At any early stage in the pretrial proceedings, defense counsel and the prosecutors agreed to mutual access and exchange of relevant material—acquired independent of the other—having a bearing on the insanity issue. A feature of the Federal Rules of Criminal Procedure, Rule 16, is the provision for reciprocal discovery and reciprocal discovery agreements. In the *Hinckley* case—as in many other cases involving such agreements—differences arose as to the meaning and interpretation of the agreement. The trial judge was called on to resolve difficult questions relating to the attorney–client privilege and the "work-product" doctrine. Also, the trial judge in the *Hinckley* case granted an important—if not crucial—motion to suppress evidence. The matters suppressed included statements of Hinckley to District of Columbia police and Secret Service agents in a 30-minute interrogation following his arrest, and his personal diary, notes, and other writings seized from his cell at Butner (some of which were communications to his attorneys). The ruling was sustained on an expedited appeal to the U.S. Circuit Court for the District of Columbia.[25]

After screening and selection of the jury, the trial began. The first several trial days were devoted exclusively to the government's proof of the basic elements of the crime—which was completed with a minimum of effort and little, if any, cross-examination. The next five weeks of trial were confined to continuing rounds of expert testimony. The defense strategy was to present initial testimony through Hinckley's parents and siblings. This lay testimony was then followed by testimony from various expert witnesses including psychologists, psychiatrists, neuropsychiatrists and neuroradiologists. The testimony of these experts consumed the greater portion of the defense effort.

Hinckley's lawyers produced what has been commented on as an unusual and curious lineup of expert witnesses. For example, their principal witnesses—several psychiatrists—had excellent credentials as academicians, research specialists, and analysts—all highly recognized in their professions. Surprisingly, they and other defense experts were completely lacking in experience as forensic psychiatrists. They had no prior adversarial experience. None of them had ever been involved as a witness in a criminal trial proceeding. In sharp contrast, the government's expert witnesses (with one exception) were experienced and seasoned veterans of criminal trial proceedings—*all* were well versed in forensic medicine. The jurors listened for five weeks to a vast amount of conflicting, irreconcilable, and burdensome expert testimony.[26]

In another elusive and complex aspect of the *Hinckley* insanity defense, the jurors had to review this conflicting mass of expert testimony and relate it to an abstract concept of criminal responsibility: the insanity defense standard. The jurors were instructed on the prevailing law in the District of Columbia Circuit as related to the law of insanity, and its use in a criminal trial proceeding. They were told that, under the prevailing law (which has since been changed by an act of Congress, as discussed in Chapter 2), the government had to carry the burden of proof. The jury concluded that it did have a reasonable doubt as to the defendant's mental condition and his criminal responsibility for the events of March 30, 1981; and, as a result, it returned a not guilty by reason of insanity verdict.[27]

The *Hinckley* trial became a ready target for critics of the alleged excessive role of expert witnesses in insanity defense trials. The problem with expert witnesses on the insanity issue was described as follows:

1. The trial becomes a highly competitive intellectual contest between prosecution and defense experts.

2. Expert witnesses elaborate and overextend their opinions.

3. Expert witnesses pontificate and quibble about the relevance, significance, and applicability of various definitions and concepts found in the American Psychiatric Association diagnostic manual.

4. Expert witnesses labor over secondary and obscure meanings of highly technical terms. In short, psychodramas are sometimes acted out in the courtroom, and the primary concern—involving the defendant's culpability and responsibility—is often lost after the first intermission.[28]

The role of expert witnesses in insanity defense trials can be understood on two levels: scientific and legal. From a scientific perspective, expert opinion is—according to those who support the insanity defense—not mere conjecture, surmise, or speculation; it is the expert's judgment on a matter of fact. It differs from ordinary— or "lay witness"—testimony on matters of fact, in that it is not based on the use of unskilled senses or the observation of the average person, but on specialized training and/or theoretical information. Despite this professional view, there is continuing debate about the scientific validity of psychiatry, especially as applied to knowing what the state of mind of the defendant was at the time of the crime.[29] For example, Dr. Lee Steward Coleman—a psychiatrist in Berkeley, California—argues that psychiatrists are "widely unreliable as witnesses, capable of recording only subjective impressions." He maintains that "the courts would be better off" without psychiatric testimony.[30]

In response to the vigorous attacks from both within and outside the mental health profession on the reliability and validity of expert psychiatric testimony, others argue that—first of all—we should not compare the knowledge of mental health professionals with—for example—the knowledge of physicists about the laws of motion; but rather, with what the lay person knows about psychological aberration and criminal behavior. We should ask whether the observations, intuitions, and hypotheses of clinicians offer a useful and acceptable supplement to lay witness testimony. Second, the availability of cross-examination (characterized as the great engine of truth in the adversary system) provides the trier of fact with information about the limitations and deficiencies of the expert witness testimony.

Legal decision makers are also concerned that the incorporation of psychiatric concepts into the criminal law will impair the law's ability to achieve its policy objectives. Critics fear two developments: (1) that psychiatrists will have undue influence on ultimate legal determinations; and (2) that the law will become dependent on unproven concepts that belong to an outside discipline.[31] As Seymour Halleck points out, the psychiatrist has "no training, no science, and no theories"[32] to guide him on the question of legal responsibility. The law is concerned with establishing fault; it focuses on individual responsibility as a way of controlling behavior and articulating public morality. In contrast, psychiatrists and psychologists are concerned with identifying, diagnosing, and treating mental disorders, and in understanding the attitudes, actions, and environmental causes behind such disorders. The question long debated is whether these two goals are incompatible.

In a 1985 decision in *Ake v. Oklahoma*,[33] the U.S. Supreme Court may have ended the debate about whether psychiatrists and psychologists have a legitimate role in the courtroom when the insanity defense is raised. George Ake had been charged with first degree murder and shooting with intent to kill. At his arraignment, the trial court found his behavior so bizarre that a psychiatric evaluation was ordered to determine his competency to stand trial. He was found to be incompetent to stand trial and committed to a state hospital for six weeks, when he was found by a state psychiatrist to be competent so long as he remained on his medication. At a pretrial conference, Ake's attorney stated that the insanity defense would be raised; and he requested a psychiatric evaluation at the state's expense, because Ake was indigent. The trial court denied his motion, and its decision was affirmed by the Oklahoma Court of Criminal Appeals. Ake's only defense was insanity. There were no expert witnesses on either side to testify as to Ake's behavior at the time of the killings. He was found guilty by the jury, and sentenced to death.

In an 8-1 opinion, the U.S. Supreme Court reversed the Oklahoma Court of Criminal Appeals, for not granting the defendant access to a psychiatric evaluation. Justice Marshall—writing for the majority—concluded that "the government interest in denying Ake the assistance of a psychiatrist is not substantial, in light of the compelling interest of both the State and the individual in accurate dispositions."[34] Justice Marshall stated that, where the defendant's mental condition is critical to the issue of criminal responsibility, the assistance of a psychiatrist may well be crucial to the defendant's ability to marshal his defense. He concluded:

> [W]ithout the assistance of a psychiatrist to conduct a professional examination on issues relevant to the defense, to help determine whether the insanity defense is viable, to present testimony, and to assist in preparing the cross-examination of a State's psychiatric witnesses, the risk of an inaccurate resolution of sanity issues is extremely high. With such assistance, the defendant is fairly able to present at least enough information to the jury, in a meaningful manner, as to permit it to make a sensible determination.[35]

The Court limited its holding to one competent psychiatrist, and did not provide for a psychiatrist of the defendant's choice. The indigent defendant is not constitutionally entitled to have more than one evaluation. The Court said that the decision on how to implement the right to one competent psychiatrist is left to the states.

The controversy over the legitimacy and appropriate role of the expert witness in insanity defense cases has contributed to the refusal of a number of outstanding mental health professionals to testify at insanity defense trials. In 1960, Dr. Guttmacher reported the results of a survey of members of the American Psychiatric Association and of his own personal inquiries. Among those answering the survey and inquiry, 10 percent responded that they refuse to appear as expert witnesses under any circumstances; and 20 percent, that they refuse to appear as partisans. Guttmacher concluded that, in those 30 percent, one would find the best and the brightest of the profession.[36] He is not alone in this conclusion. One writer has commented that, "by our system of partisan expert witnesses we have alienated and deprived ourselves of the services of the best and accepted, and at the same time criticized and have been shocked by the performances of the worst."[37] It is open to question, however, whether Guttmacher had the statistical and evidential foundation to justify such a sweeping conclusion. Just because few full-time professors of psychiatry testify as expert witnesses in the United States does not mean that those that do testify are less qualified or are the bottom of the barrel.

As recently as 1982, Seymour Halleck has commented on psychiatrists who shun courtroom appearances: "It must be noted that a large number of psychiatrists avoid courtroom involvement like the plague," because—he reasoned—they are intolerant of the adversarial approach to truth finding.[38] Many feel that they have nothing to contribute in the determination of a person's guilt by reason of insanity. Some believe that the standards governing expert testimony require responses beyond their expertise. Others are troubled that expert testimony tends to be available primarily to the affluent.[39]

The psychiatrist who does testify—Halleck claims—"must be aware that he risks a certain amount of disapproval from the public and his colleagues. A battle of experts often ensues in which . . . there is no way psychiatrists can look or be scientific when they are debating moral concepts such as legal insanity."[40]

David Shapiro, a psychologist who has testified on forensic issues for both the defense and the prosecution during the past 18 years, agrees that his colleagues do shun courtroom appearances. He asserts that—often—the mental health experts who do agree to testify are "ignorant," and are primarily interested in selling their opinion to the "highest bidder."[41] Rather than learning about the case and the issues involved—or even about the standard for the insanity defense itself—these experts too often rely on the attorney to inform them about what is needed. Thus, part of the problem may not be so much the use of medical experts, but their lack of training and preparation for a courtroom appearance.

In psychiatry, it is uniquely hard to draw a line between matters of fact—on which expert testimony can be given—and matters of value—where evidence may involve the tacit conveyance of a decision on principle and policy. The jury may be incorrectly led to infer that the ultimate questions to be resolved are scientific, rather than moral. Consequently, experts are permitted to express opinions on issues which—if properly understood—are beyond clinical expertise. According to psychologists such as Shapiro, this misunderstanding is perpetuated by lawyers who are only interested in evidence supporting their side of the case.

The sweeping attack on the use of expert mental health testimony in insanity defense cases generally—and in the *Hinckley* case specifically—overlooks several points. First, as discussed in Chapter 1, most successful insanity defense pleas occur in cases where the prosecutors *agree* not to formally contest the defense. This results from the fact that the experts are in agreement, based on evidence that points overwhelmingly to a conclusion of insanity. As noted, in Maryland—for example—each year, only 2 or 3 defendants are actually found NGRI in contested trials, out of the 30–40 defendants (from among 150–200 cases each year in which the plea is entered) who are unanimously found by the experts to be insane. The contested cases, however, generally receive the most widespread media attention. Accordingly, the extent of disagreement among experts evaluating evidence in insanity defense cases is greatly exaggerated.

Second, the "battle of the experts" in contested insanity defense cases is partly a consequence of the adversary system. In a wide variety of civil and criminal cases, conflicting expert testimony is the norm—not the exception. Dr. Alan Stone, a Harvard Law School professor, observes:

> Every defendant in our legal system is entitled to an ardent advocate, even those like Hinckley whose violence has been filmed and shown on television. Ours is the adversary system, and that means if there is a possible insanity defense, the legal advocate has to get psychiatric testimony to make a case. The truth is that our adversary system demands that the lawyer try to find a psychiatric witness whose testimony will help the client. That is inherent in our adversarial system of justice; it is not confined to psychiatric witnesses. When IBM is sued in an anti-trust case, IBM's lawyers find an economist who will defend IBM's practices, using the very best economic arguments he or she can muster. The other side will hire an economist to attack, using the very best economic

counterarguments. If a bridge collapses, one side will bring in engineers who will offer scientific evidence and claim negligence; the other side will bring in engineers to offer scientific evidence on the other side. The same can be said for medical testimony in malpractice cases and a host of other situations involving expert testimony. It is the lawyer's job to find a witness to support his or her argument. This is the very basis of our adversarial system.[42]

In our system of criminal justice, a defendant is constitutionally entitled to adequate representation. Adequate representation means an ardent advocate. In both the civil and criminal justice systems, whenever an attorney is required to secure the services of an expert witness, it is inherent in our adversary system that this be done. It is the function of the trier of fact—be it judge or jury—to determine the ultimate facts of the case. Chapter 4 examines the role of the jury, and reviews available social science evidence of juror behavior in dealing with contested insanity defense cases.

Third, even before the 1984 congressional amendment to the Federal Rules of Evidence—which limited the testimony of expert witnesses on the so-called ultimate issues in insanity defense cases—common law rules of evidence, state evidence codes, and the Federal Rules of Evidence all gave broad discretion to the trial judge in regulating expert testimony. The trial judge must initially make a ruling—pursuant to Rule 702 of the Federal Rules of Evidence—on whether a person offered as an expert witness is sufficiently qualified to assist the jury. Rule 702 of the Federal Rules of Evidence provides:

> If scientific, technical, or other specialized knowledge will assist the trier of fact to understand the evidence or to determine a fact in issue, a witness qualified as an expert by knowledge, skill, experience, training, or education, may testify thereto in the form of an opinion or otherwise.

Also, Rule 403 authorizes a trial judge to exclude relevant evidence "if its probative value is substantially outweighed by the danger of unfair prejudice, confusion of the issues, or misleading the jury, or by considerations of undue delay, waste of time, or needless presentation of cumulative evidence." Finally, when the Federal Rules of Evidence were adopted in 1975, trial judges were given increased authority to appoint their own expert witnesses, as an alternative or supplement to the partisan presentation of expert witnesses.[43] These

and related evidentiary rules—when used discreetly by the trial judge—
can be an effective restraint on the tendency of psychiatric witnesses
to expand and go far beyond what is appropriate during the course
of testimony.

This discussion has reviewed the principal arguments in the debate
over the role of expert witnesses in insanity defense cases. Despite
vigorous attacks on the reliability of psychiatrists' and psychologists' methods and testimony, the prevailing attitude of the courts—
as reflected in the 1985 U.S. Supreme Court decision in *Ake v. Oklahoma*—suggests a general reliance on professional authority and
acceptance of the assumption that such testimony is useful. *Ake v.
Oklahoma* can be interpreted as a ruling on the legitimacy of admitting expert testimony in contested insanity defense cases. While
debate over the legitimacy of expert psychiatric testimony may continue, the debate in the future will probably focus primarily on sub-
sidiary questions. Most proposals for change in the presentation of
expert testimony respond to the following questions:

1. What steps can be taken to improve the availability of highly competent psychiatrists and psychologists who have training and experience in presenting expert testimony in insanity defense cases and
   who base their testimony on careful preparation, including adequate
   information about the facts of the case and the defendant's background?

2. Should the scope of expert testimony be restricted, preventing testimony in the form of opinions or conclusions on the ultimate issues?
   To state the question differently: are jurors helped or hindered in
   their role as the final independent fact-finders by the opinions of
   psychiatrists and psychologists on the so-called ultimate facts?

3. What steps can be taken by trial judges, attorneys, and expert witnesses to improve jurors' understanding of their role in evaluating
   expert testimony and to ensure that expert testimony will be of
   maximum assistance in jury deliberations?

4. Should there be greater reliance on the appointment of expert
   witnesses by the trial judge in insanity defense cases, as an alternative or supplement to the partisan presentation of expert testimony?

PROPOSALS FOR CHANGE IN THE PRESENTATION OF EXPERT TESTIMONY

Improving the Quality of Expert Testimony

Professor Stephen Morse proposes that trial judges should give greater scrutiny to the individual qualifications of expert witnesses. The courts should place greater attention on matching an expert's qualifications with the particular issues involved.[44] If mental health professionals are sufficiently trained and well informed about the facts of a particular case, mental health testimony will be of greater assistance to the jury.

Traditionally, in determining who qualifies as a mental health expert, the trial judge has merely inquired whether the professional meets minimum educational requirements. This results in a number of "experts" testifying in insanity defense trials who—many argue—are not qualified to do so. Professor Morse argues that trial judges should not assume expertise on the basis of degrees, license, or certification alone. If the testimony is to be observational and descriptive, "extensive clinical experience with crazy persons" is essential.[45]

Dr. David Shapiro—one of the prosecution's chief expert witnesses in the *Hinckley* trial—proposes even stricter requirements. In addition to board certification in forensic psychiatry or psychology, expert witnesses should have to demonstrate that "they understand the interface between psychiatry, psychology, and the legal system, and that they do a particular kind of examination that shows their appreciation of additional parameters."[46] He distinguishes forensic psychology from other types of psychology not only by virtue of subject matter, but also because it is a "whole different way of approaching the data, analyzing the data, and understanding what data sources to bring in."[47] Dr. Shapiro believes that adequate forensic testing is of crucial importance. Certain procedures should be an integral part of the formation of any forensic opinion: clinical interviews and history-taking; psychological testing; interviews with the defendant's family; interviews with witnesses; review of police reports; review of the defendant's school, employment, and hospital records; and examination of previous psychiatric treatment, if any. Finally, Dr. Shapiro argues that the psychological and psychiatric professionals have an independent duty to ensure that expert witnesses are adequately qualified.[48]

In a noteworthy article on the role of mental health professionals in the criminal process, Richard Bonnie and Christopher Slobogin argue that, to determine the defendant's veracity, the forensic evaluator often must discard the therapist's traditional role of inquiry in favor of a more probing, confrontational technique. They maintain that a clinician's "idiosyncracies" can be diminished by an interest in seeking additional information on the alleged offense and data on the subject's previous antisocial behavior and medical-psychiatric history. They propose interjecting additional observers into the interview process—"who can later add differing perspectives and reduce the effects of more obvious individual biases."[49]

Dr. Shapiro contrasts his approach to forensic evaluation with the approach of certain defense expert witnesses in the *Hinckley* trial:

> The defense team in *Hinckley* went out and hired some of the most prominent people in psychiatry and psychology. But most of them did not have the slightest idea of what a forensic evaluation consisted of. The chief defense psychiatrist, with a national reputation in schizophrenia, based his opinion on hours spent with Hinckley. But when Adelman cross-examined him, it came out that he had not talked to the arresting officer, he hadn't read the Secret Service report. He was rendering a conclusion on criminal responsibility based on his test results. He never did the investigatory work to see whether those test results and his diagnostic picture of Hinckley fit Hinckley's actual behavior at the time of the offense or his behavior in the days immediately preceding the offense.[50]

Barrington D. Parker, senior judge of the U.S. District Court for the District of Columbia—who presided over the *Hinckley* trial—has similarly observed that the defense expert witnesses were completely lacking in experience as forensic psychiatrists and had no prior experience as witnesses in criminal trial proceedings. Nevertheless, he observed that they had "impeccable and unassailable credentials as academicians, research specialists and analysts, highly recognized in their profession." Despite their lack of expertise and experience as forensic experts, Judge Parker has noted that—in contrast to Dr. Shapiro's view—"they measured up to experts proffered by the government—their performance was not lacking in any way."[51] Also, Roger Adelman—assistant U.S. attorney and chief prosecutor in the *Hinckley* case—disagrees that such formal requirements on expert testimony should be rigidly imposed by the trial judge. He states:

"All those things are desirable, but there may be people out there who have no formal training in forensic matters but who would be wonderful witnesses. Conversely, there may be people who have seven degrees in forensic psychiatry who may not be good witnesses."[52]

Few would disagree, however, with Dr. Shapiro's basic point. Assuming at least minimal qualifications, the quality of their testimony would be vastly improved if expert witnesses were to base their testimony on an exhaustive investigation of the relevant facts—which should go beyond psychological tests and interviews with the defendant. As discussed below, the jury should be clearly advised as to the place of expert testimony in the decision making process—advised both by the court and through skillful cross-examination. The attorneys should fully understand the psychiatric testimony, so that they can elucidate and draw out the appropriate testimony in a manner understandable to jurors. While explanatory clinical formulations given by mental health professionals are not a presentation of scientific facts, they usually do represent something more than idiosyncratic guesses. As Judge Bazelon writes: "The 'educated guess' that psychiatrists provide, and it is only an educated guess, is only as good as the investigation, the facts, and the reasoning that underlie it."[53] Such expert testimony can assist the fact finder by clarifying the alternative lines of explanation, identifying clinically reasonable possibilities that might not otherwise occur to lay jurors, and helping jurors to assess the significance—or lack thereof—of the defendant's claim of mental abnormality and its relationship to the alleged criminal behavior.

Restricting the Scope of Expert Testimony

Questions about the permissible scope of mental health expert testimony are among the most controversial raised in the debate on the insanity defense. The concern has been that psychiatrists and psychologists testifying in court have a tendency to dominate unduly or to usurp the function of the judge or the jury by offering conclusory opinions.[54]

The American Bar Association, the American Psychiatric Association, the National Mental Health Association, and most professionals and scholars agree that—as a general principle—expert mental health witnesses should restrict their testimony to the area of their specialized knowledge, and should not offer testimony on the ultimate legal issue of whether the defendant was *legally* insane at the time of the alleged crime(s). Yet, the crucial problem of how to apply this principle in practice remains. Whether formal restrictions—such as the 1984 congressional amendment to the Federal Rules of Evidence 704, and comparable amendments to state evidence codes—will make any real difference has not yet been determined.[55]

As part of the Insanity Defense Reform Act of 1984, Congress amended Rule 704 of the Federal Rules of Evidence in order to restrict mental health expert testimony, as follows:

> No expert witness testifying with respect to the mental state or condition of a defendant in a criminal case may state an opinion or inference as to whether the defendant did or did not have the mental state or condition constituting an element of the crime charged or a defense thereto. Such ultimate issues are matters for the trier of fact alone.[56]

This restriction was enacted as an exception to Rule 704(a), which had granted wide latitude to expert opinions. Rule 704(a) provides:

> Except as provided in subdivision (b), testimony in the form of an opinion or inference otherwise admissible is not objectionable because it embraces an ultimate issue to be decided by the trier of fact.

If there is no restriction that other experts should be limited in either their testimony or their role in the adversary process, then why should there be restrictions on judicial discretion to admit expert mental health opinions in criminal cases? Congress enacted the restriction as part of a broader effort—described in Chapter 2—to tighten the criteria by which defendants may be declared not responsible for their acts, in the aftermath of the *Hinckley* verdict. Congress sought to drive a wedge between the clinical or scientific testimony and the ultimate moral conclusions to be drawn by the trier of fact. The question of the degree of the defendant's grasp of the wrongfulness of his or her conduct may appear to be expressed in terms capable of expert assessment; but the standard actually poses a question as to whether it is just to hold the defendant responsible for the conduct, given his or her mental condition at the time. Congress was concerned that scientific credentials might persuade a jury that the issue before it is simply one of deciding which expert to believe.[57]

However, when Congress adopted the Federal Rules of Evidence in 1975—liberalizing the common law rules in many areas, including that involving expert testimony—it never intended to allow experts to testify in terms of mere conclusions of law. Both at common law and under the Federal Rules of Evidence—for example—an expert witness would not be allowed in a personal injury civil case to testify that a party was "negligent." Opinions that are only conclusions of law merely tell the jury what final result to reach. They somewhat resemble the manner of the oath-helpers of an earlier day. Such expressions of opinion are superfluous and unhelpful.

In liberalizing the rules of evidence in 1975, Congress did intend—however—to allow experts to testify on so-called mixed questions of law and fact, if such testimony was found by the trial judge under Rule 702—Testimony by Experts—to "assist the trier of fact to understand the evidence or to determine a fact in issue." An example used in the Advisory Committee's Note (which is part of the formal legislative history of the Federal Rules of Evidence) illustrates the difference between a mere conclusion of law in areas of "inadequately explored legal criteria" and more concrete opinions and inferences. The example involves mental health expert testimony in a civil case on an issue involving a contested will, as to whether the testator had the mental capacity to make a will. A question posed to a psychiatrist who had examined the testator at about the time the will was made—"Did T have the capacity to make a will?"—would be excluded both at common law and under Federal Rules of Evidence 704(a), as a mere legal conclusion. However, most jurisdictions define testamentary capacity in more technical and specific terms—as including a capacity to know the nature and extent of one's property, to identify the objects of one's bounty, and to understand the nature and effect of a will. The question "Did T have sufficient mental capacity to know the nature and extent of his property and the natural objects of his bounty and to formulate a rational scheme of distribution?" would—according to the Advisory Committee's Note— be allowed under Rule 704(a).[58]

The reason that Congress broadened the scope of opinions for expert witnesses in general when it adopted the Federal Rules of Evidence in 1975 was set forth in the official Advisory Committee's Note:

> The older cases often contained strictures against allowing witnesses to express opinions upon ultimate issues, as a particular aspect of the rule against opinions. The rule was unduly restrictive, difficult of application, and generally served only to deprive the trier of fact of useful

information. . . . The basis usually assigned for the rule, to prevent the witness from "usurping the province of the jury," is aptly characterized as "empty rhetoric." . . . Efforts to meet the felt needs of particular situations led to odd verbal circumlocutions which were said not to violate the rule. Thus a witness could express his estimate of the criminal responsibility of an accused in terms of sanity or insanity, but not in terms of ability to tell right from wrong or other more modern standards. And in cases of medical causation, witnesses were sometimes required to couch their opinions in cautious phrases of "might or could," rather than "did," though the result was to deprive many opinions of the positiveness to which they were entitled, accompanied by the hazard of a ruling of insufficiency to support a verdict. In other instances the rule was simply disregarded, and, as concessions to need, opinions were allowed upon such matters as intoxication, speed, handwriting, and value, although more precise coincidence with an ultimate issue would scarcely be possible.[59]

Under Rule 704(a), there is some uncertainty and latitude for interpretation as to when testimony constitutes a mere conclusion of law and when it is sufficiently detailed to be viewed by the trial judge as of assistance to the jury. The trial judge has discretion under Rule 702 to determine that such testimony will not be of assistance to the jury. Also, the trial judge has discretion under Rule 403—Exclusion of Relevant Evidence on Grounds of Prejudice, Confusion, or Waste of Time—to exclude testimony whose relevancy is substantially outweighed by the danger of unfair prejudice, confusion of the issues, midleading the jury, waste of time, or needless presentation of cumulative evidence.

The 1984 amendment to Rule 704 goes beyond the insanity defense to any ultimate mental state of a criminal defendant that would be relevant to an element of the crime charged or to any defense. The congressional intent was to reduce the discretion of trial judges in ruling on a case-by-case basis as to which opinions of mental health expert witnesses would be of assistance to the jury. As noted, the purpose of the amendment was to correct what Congress perceived as the problem of expert psychiatric witnesses giving conflicting testimony concerning the ultimate legal issues in a single trial. A congressional report stated that expert psychiatric witnesses should limit their testimony "to presenting and explaining their diagnoses, such as whether the defendant had a severe mental disease or defect and what the characteristics of such a disease or defect, if any, may have been."

The courts will now be called upon to clarify precisely what types of opinions may be presented by expert witnesses, under the restrictive Rule 704(b) set forth above. As discussed in Chapter 2, the present standard for determining the sanity of the defendant is whether "at the time of the commission of the acts constituting the offense, the defendant, as a result of a severe mental disease or defect, was unable to appreciate the nature and quality or the wrongfulness of his acts."[60] The expert will probably *not* be allowed to express opinions on the following questions: (1) Was the defendant insane? (2) Could the defendant tell right from wrong? (3) Could the defendant appreciate the wrongfulness of his conduct? It is much less clear whether the expert will be allowed to answer a question as to whether the defendant possessed a "severe mental disease or defect" at the time of the crime. The congressional report mentioned above suggests that an expert witness might be permitted to address this question.

The American Bar Association, through its Standing Committee on Association Standards for Criminal Justice—which supported placing restrictions on the scope of expert testimony in insanity defense cases—recognized the difficulties in applying a ban against so-called ultimate issue testimony. It noted—for example—that terms such as "appreciate" also have clinical context, because they refer to mental and emotional phenomena. The ABA report stated: "If the expert is barred from using such terms, it can be predicted that the experts will merely paraphrase the test language to convey the same conclusion—by using the term 'understanding,' for example."[61] The ABA also raised a question of whether expert testimony would be permitted as to the term "mental disease or defect." If the term is given a legal rather than a medical meaning by the courts, the case for excluding expert opinions phrased in such terms is much stronger. Again, the ABA did recognize that expert witnesses have the ability to say pretty much what they want to say, without using these terms: "Such a bar would not have an unduly restrictive effect on the expression of clinical opinion because the expert remains free to use the concept of 'mental disorder' as well as the specific nomenclature on which the expert relies."[62]

The American Bar Association concluded that restrictions on ultimate issue testimony cannot be fully determined in the abstract. The ABA would leave specific types of "penultimate testimony" to resolution on an individual basis. As to the term "appreciation," it concludes:

> The two main factors which should be taken into account by the courts of each jurisdiction in determining whether expert testimony on "appreciation" should be admissible are (i) the specificity of the jurisdiction's definition of "appreciate" (the more technical and specific the meaning of the term, the stronger the argument for barring its use by experts); and, (ii) the general practice in the jurisdiction regarding ultimate issue testimony by experts (if ordinary practice is to admit such testimony, as under Federal Rule 704, the greater the difficulty of administering an exception).[63]

Given the above discussion, it seems fairly predictable that adoption by the states of restrictive provisions comparable to Rule 704(b) is likely to stimulate much appellate court litigation as its application is tested on a case-by-case basis.

Indeed, there have already been appellate decisions on the federal-level ruling on Rule 704(b). In *United States v. Mest*,[64] the defense counsel attempted to ask its expert witness if she had an opinion regarding whether, at the time of the alleged act, the defendant had the capacity to realize the wrongfulness of his behavior and to conform his behavior to the legal requirements. The prosecution objected to this question, on the basis of Rule 704(b). The court sustained the objection. However, the court was of the opinion that Rule 704(b) has only the effect of changing "the style of question and answer that can be used to establish both the offense and the defense in each particular case."[65] The court stated that every "actual fact" pertaining to the mental condition of the defendant—as presented by the expert witnesses from both sides—was still admissible.[66] After the amendment, the experts could not take the additional step of giving the trier of fact their opinion as to the probable relationship between the medical concepts and the legal issues that the trier of fact must decide. In another recent decision—*United States v. Freeman*—the U.S. Court of Appeals for the Eleventh Circuit upheld Rule 704(b) against a Fifth Amendment challenge.[67]

It is too early to predict what impact, if any, Rule 704(b) and similar state evidence-code provisions will have in the presentation of expert testimony in insanity defense cases. Some experts in criminal trial litigation have questioned whether these provisions will have any major impact in limiting the scope of expert testimony. It may be that expert witnesses will simply paraphrase the legal terms, and convey the same conclusory opinions. For example, Roger Adelman—the chief prose-cutor in the *Hinckley* case—observes: "The District of Columbia had a similar rule from 1967 to 1972 and during that time the testimony was pretty much the same as it has been since then. In other words, psychiatrists can say pretty much what they want to say without reaching the ultimate issue. They can give descriptive testimony in such a way that it will in effect convey their conclusion anyway."[68]

Improving Jurors' Understanding of Their Role in Evaluating Expert Testimony

It is generally acknowledged that jurors need to be clearly in-formed about the nature and limitation of expert mental health testimony. A standard for jury instructions has been developed by the American Bar Association's Standing Committee on Association Standards for Criminal Justice:

> The court should instruct the jury concerning the functions and limita-tions of mental health and mental retardation profession expert testi-mony. . . . [T]hese instructions may be given prior to the introduction of the expert testimony. The jury should be informed that the purpose of such testimony is to identify for the trier of fact the clinical factors relevant to the issues of past, present, and future mental condition or behavior that are under consideration.
>
> Jurors also should be informed that they are not asked or expected to become experts in psychology or other sciences, and that their task is to decide whether the explanation offered by a mental health or mental retardation professional is persuasive. In evaluating the weight to be given an expert's opinion, the jury should consider the qualifica-tions of the witness, the theoretical and factual basis for the expert's opinion, and the reasoning process by which the information available to the expert was utilized to formulate the opinion. In reaching its decision on the ultimate questions in the trial, the jury is not bound by the opinions of expert witnesses. The testimony of each witness should be considered in connection with the other evidence in the case and given such weight as the jury believes it is fairly entitled to receive.[69]

A useful starting point for formulating language for the jury is Judge David L. Bazelon's famous appendix to his opinion in *Wash-ington v. United States*, set forth earlier in this chapter.[70] Thus, the trial judge has an important educational role: to give understandable jury instructions, both prior to the introduction of expert testimony and at the close of the trial.

The attorneys can also do much to improve jurors' ability to perform their independent fact-finding role in evaluating expert testimony. It is the attorney's responsibility to translate sophisticated psychiatric testimony into lay person's terms, through questioning in direct- and cross-examination. As Roger Adelman states: "I think the trial lawyer has the responsibility to make the case clear to the jury, and secondarily it is the psychiatrist's responsibility to explain that, for example, a certain disorder with a long Greek name is really nothing more than what we call depression, without losing the meaning of the term."[71]

Adelman—among others—also looks to other areas of courtroom procedure for better assisting jurors in performing their independent fact-finding function:

> Based on my experience in a lot of cases—not only the insanity cases—one thing we have to look for is ways of presenting the evidence to the jury in a way that the jury can understand it and in a way that the jury can participate in the trial. In complicated cases, we should start thinking about things such as jurors taking notes, jurors asking questions under the supervision of the court, jurors getting interim summations throughout the trial, jurors being permitted to hear supplemental arguments at the end of the case, the court sending its instructions to the jurors in writing rather than just orally relating to them what the law is at the end of a long trial, etc. In other words, there are procedural devices within our system that can help cut through some of the confusion.[72]

Finally, as mentioned earlier, cross-examination can be a powerful tool for informing the jury of the limitations and weaknesses of expert opinion. Martin Orne—Professor of Psychiatry at the University of Pennsylvania and director of the Unit for Experimental Psychiatry—has participated as an expert witness in some 30 criminal trials. He observes: "Most of the problems which have come up about the insanity defense [are caused by attorneys who] do not properly cross-examine the underlying assumptions of the expert who says this person is insane." Orne recommends that the questions to be asked include: "Would you explain what you mean by insanity? What are the objective symptoms? Could this individual have been faking? Have you seen anybody who has made this up?" Instead—says Orne—too often, lawyers allow the credentials of experts to be placed into the record and then urge them to draw conclusions, without properly explaining the basis of these conclusions to the less knowledgeable lay jurors.[73] Also, if the expert has performed a less than thorough investigation of the defendant and his or her background, the lack of a quality psychiatric evaluation can be brought home to the jury.

Court Appointment of Expert Witnesses in Appropriate Cases

When the Federal Rules of Evidence was adopted in 1975, the power of the trial judge to appoint expert witnesses was affirmed, and procedures were devised to facilitate the use of this authority. Many state evidence codes—modeled on the Federal Rules of Evidence—have adopted similar procedures. Rule 706 provides:

Rule 706. Court Appointed Experts

(a) Appointment. The court may on its own motion or on the motion of any party enter an order to show cause why expert witnesses should not be appointed, and may request the parties to submit nominations. The court may appoint any expert witnesses agreed upon by the parties, and may appoint expert witnesses of its own selection. An expert witness shall not be appointed by the court unless he consents to act. A witness so appointed shall be informed of his duties by the court in writing, a copy of which shall be filed with the clerk, or at a conference in which the parties shall have opportunity to participate. A witness so appointed shall advise the parties of his findings, if any; his deposition may be taken by any party; and he may be called to testify by the court or any party. He shall be subject to cross-examination by each party, including a party calling him as a witness.

(b) Compensation. Expert witnesses so appointed are entitled to reasonable compensation in whatever sum the court may allow. The compensation thus fixed is payable from funds which may be provided by law in criminal cases and civil actions and proceedings involving just compensation under the fifth amendment. In other civil actions and proceedings the compensation shall be paid by the parties in such proportion and at such time as the court directs, and thereafter charged in like manner as other costs.

(c) Disclosure of appointment. In the exercise of its discretion, the court may authorize disclosure to the jury of the fact that the court appointed the expert witness.

(d) Parties' experts of own selection. Nothing in this rule limits the parties in calling expert witnesses of their own selection.

Some persons argue that the adversary system itself—with its partisan reliance on the selection of expert witnesses—has been partly responsible for the fact that many of the best and brightest mental health professionals refuse to participate as expert witnesses in insanity defense trials. Others argue that partisan selection and presentation of expert witnesses—often resulting in a battle of the experts—has contributed to juror confusion and misunderstanding. Finally, some see Rule 706 as a potential vehicle for implementing the mandate of *Ake v. Oklahoma*[74]—that an indigent accused be afforded at least one competent psychiatrist to provide an evaluation of his mental condition, when there is an indication of possible insanity defense. In appropriate cases, court appointment may be a useful tool in responding to the concern that the insanity defense is a rich person's defense. Rule 706 can be used either as a supplement to or an alternative to partisan selection of expert witnesses.

In the authors' national survey of expert opinion on significant issues relating to the insanity defense—the findings of which are presented in Chapter 5—we included a question on the desirability of the court appointment of expert witnesses, as follows:

> During the trial, should each side (the defense and the prosecution) retain the practice of calling its own expert witnesses; or should the court select the expert witnesses?[75]

The responses to this question are set forth in detail in Table 5.5. Not surprisingly, forensic psychiatrists and psychologists and state mental health directors—more than the legal actors—favored the use of court appointment of expert witnesses. Interestingly, the psychologists and mental health directors are more likely than the psychiatrists to favor court appointment of expert witnesses. Among the legal actors, the defense attorneys were the strongest supporters of the status quo. Sixty-seven percent of them wanted to retain the practice of each side calling its own experts. A significant finding was the willingness of many judges—both federal and state—to agree to the appropriateness of court appointment of expert witnesses, either as an alternative or as a supplement to selection of expert witnesses by the parties: 46.9 percent of federal judges, district and appellate; 45.4 percent of state appellate judges; and 38.8 percent of state trial court judges.

CONCLUSION

Despite vigorous attacks on the extensive reliance on and dominance of mental health testimony in contested insanity defense trials, the prevailing attitude of the courts, as reflected in the U.S. Supreme Court decision in 1985 in *Ake v. Oklahoma*, is general approval of the use of expert testimony as a useful supplement to lay witness testimony.

A major problem with the use of psychiatrists and psychologists in the courtroom is the lack of adequate training and specific preparation for the courtroom appearance. Trial judges should give greater scrutiny to the individual qualifications of expert witnesses. Unfortunately, many of the most competent mental health professionals are unwilling to participate as expert witnesses in insanity defense cases. One remedy, in appropriate cases, is greater reliance on appointment of expert witnesses by the trial judge as an alternative or supplement to the partisan presentation of expert testimony.

Trial judges need to more clearly inform jurors, through understandable jury instructions and preliminary remarks, of the nature and limitations of expert mental health testimony and how they should perform their independent fact finding function. Attorneys need to better assist jurors in evaluating expert testimony through well prepared questions that translate sophisticated psychiatric testimony and jargon into understandable language.

A trend in the post-*Hinckley* era is to attempt to restrict the scope of mental health testimony by forbidding opinions to be expressed on so-called "ultimate factual issues." The crucial problem is how to apply these restrictions. It is too early to predict what impact, if any, the amendment to Rule 704 of the Federal Rules of Evidence and similar provisions in state evidence codes will have in practice on the presentation of expert testimony in insanity defense cases.

NOTES

1. Joel Peter Eigen, "Historical Developments in Psychiatric Forensic Evidence: The British Experience," 6 *International Journal of Law and Psychiatry* 423–29 (1983).

2. Manfred Guttmacher, *The Mind of the Murderer* (New York: Farrar, Straus, and Cudahy, 1960), p. 115.

3. Ibid.

4. Eigen, "Historical Developments," p. 426.

5. Ibid.

6. *Regina v. M'Naghten*, 10 Cl. and F. 200, 8 Eng. Rep. 718 (1843).

7. Ibid.

8. *People v. Drew*, 22 Cal. 3d 333, 583 P.2d 1318 (1978), in which the court adopted the ALI test because it takes account of advances in psychological knowledge and changes in legal thought.

9. Ibid.

10. *Durham v. United States*, 94 U.S. Appl D.C. 228, 214 F.2d 862 (1954).

11. The *Durham* test states that an accused is not criminally responsible if his unlawful act was the product of mental disease or mental defect. There must be, however, a causal connection between such mental abnormality and the act. See Chapter 2 for a detailed discussion of the *Durham* test.

12. *Carter v. United States*, 252 F.2d 608, 615-16 (1957).

13. Ibid.

14. See *United States v. Brawner*, 471 F.2d 969 (*en banc*, D.C. Cir. 1972), in which the court said that exculpation is established only if, as a result of the mental disease, defendant lacks the substantial capacity required for responsibility.

15. *Rollerson v. United States*, 343 F.2d 269 (D.C. Cir. 1964).

16. Ibid., p. 271.

17. *Washington v. United States*, 129 U.S. App. D.C. 29, 390 F.2d 444 (D.C. Cir. 1967).

18. Alan Stone, *Mental Health and Law: A System in Transition* (Rockville, Md.: NIMH, 1975), p. 226.

19. *United States v. Brawner*, 471 F.2d 969, 983 (*en banc*, D.C. Cir. 1972).

20. Section 4.01 states that:

(1) A person is not responsible for criminal conduct if at the time of such conduct as a result of mental disease or defect he lacks substantial capacity either to appreciate the criminality (wrongfulness) of his conduct or to conform his conduct to the requirements of law.

(2) As used in this Article, the terms "mental disease or defect" do not include an abnormality manifested only by repeated criminal or otherwise anti-social behavior.

21. The cognitive aspect deals with the mental process of judgment, memory and reasoning, as opposed to emotional and volitional processes.

22. See *United States v. Brawner*, 471 F.2d 969, 1031 (*en banc*, D.C. Cir. 1972) (Judge Bazelon concurring in part and dissenting in part).

23. Ibid., p. 1032.

24. Ibid., p. 1034.

25. Barrington D. Parker, senior judge of the U.S. District Court for the District of Columbia, "*Hinckley* and Its Aftermath," presentation before the

9th Annual Dinner of the Association of Black Lawyers of Westchester County (mimeograph; May 22, 1987), pp. 2-4.

26. Ibid., pp. 8-9.

27. Ibid., p. 13.

28. Ibid., p. 10.

29. For writings bearing on this issue, see, for example, Allen Bartholomew and Kerry Milte, "The Reliability and Validity of Psychiatric Diagnoses in Courts of Law," 50 *Australia L.J.* 450 (1976); Bernard Diamond, "Criminal Responsibility of the Mentally Ill," 14 *Stan. L. Rev.* 59 (1967); Bernard Diamond, "The Psychiatrist as Advocate," 1 *J. Psychiatry & L.* 18 (1973); Bruce Ennis and Thomas Litwack, "Psychiatry and the Presumption of Expertise: Flipping Coins in the Courtroom," 62 *Calif. L. Rev.* 693 (1974); Seymour Halpern, "The Fiction of Legal Insanity and the Misuse of Psychiatry," 2 *J. Legal Medicine* 19 (1980); Karl Menninger, *The Crime of Punishment* (New York: Viking Compass, 1968); Stephen Morse, "Crazy Behavior, Morals, and Science: An Analysis of Mental Health Law," 51 *S. Cal. L. Rev.* 527 (1978); J. Ziskin, *Coping with Psychiatric and Psychological Testimony* (3d ed., Venice: Law and Psychology Press, 1981). See also T. S. Szasz, *Law, Liberty, and Psychiatry: An Inquiry into the Social Uses of Mental Health Practices* (New York: Collier Books, 1963); and A. Watson, "On the Preparation and Use of Psychiatric Expert Testimony: Some Suggestions in an Ongoing Controversy," 6 *A. A. P. L. Bul.* 226 (1978). The debate over the value of psychiatric testimony has been even more prevalent and vociferous in the area of psychiatrists' ability to predict dangerousness. See Laura Haddad, "Predicting the Supreme Court's Response to the Criticism of Psychiatric Predictions of Dangerousness in Civil Commitment Proceedings," 64 *Neb. L. Rev.* 215 (1985).

30. Irving Kaufman, "The Insanity Plea on Trial," *New York Times Magazine*, August 8, 1982, pp. 16, 18.

31. See, for example, Peter Dahl, "Legal and Psychiatric Concepts and the Use of Psychiatric Evidence in Criminal Trials," 73 *Calif. L. Rev.* 411 (1985).

32. Seymour Halleck, *Law in the Practice of Psychiatry* (New York: Plenum Press, 1980).

33. *Ake v. Oklahoma*, 470 U.S. 68, 105 S. Ct. 1087 (1985).

34. Ibid.

35. Ibid.

36. Guttmacher, *Mind of the Murderer*, p. 119.

37. Niles, "Impartial Medical Testimony," 45 *Ill. Bar J.* 282 (1957), as quoted in Halleck, *Law and Psychiatry.*

38. Ibid.

39. In *Ake v. Oklahoma*, 470 U.S. 68, 105 S. Ct. 1087 (1985), the U.S. Supreme Court held that, when a defendant has made a preliminary showing that his sanity at the time of the offense is likely to be a significant factor at trial, the Constitution requires that the state provide access to a psychiatrist's assistance

on this issue, if the defendant cannot otherwise afford one. Further, the overwhelming percentage of insanity defense pleas that result in a verdict of not guilty by reason of insanity are actually uncontested cases—in which the state and the defense agree to the verdict, based on unanimous findings of the examining psychiatrists. Thus, expensive in-court psychiatric testimony is the exception rather than the rule. For these reasons, the argument that the insanity defense is a rich person's defense needs to be qualified. See the discussion in Chapter 1.

40. Halleck, *Law and Psychiatry*, p. 219.

41. Personal conversation with Dr. David Shapiro.

42. Alan Stone, "The Insanity Defense on Trial," *Harvard Law School Bulletin* 17 (Fall 1982).

43. *Federal Rules of Evidence for United States Courts and Magistrates*, Rule 706 (St. Paul, Minn.: West Publishing, 1984). The text of this rule is set forth in the last section of this chapter.

44. Morse, "Crazy Behavior," pp. 527, 640-45, as quoted in Richard Bonnie and Christopher Slobogin, "The Role of Mental Health Professionals in the Criminal Process: The Case for Informed Speculation," 66 *Va. L. Rev.* 427, 454-55 (1980).

45. Ibid.

46. Personal conversation with Dr. David Shapiro.

47. Ibid.

48. Ibid.

49. Bonnie and Slobogin, "Mental Health Professionals in the Criminal Process," pp. 505-7.

50. Ibid.

51. Parker, "*Hinckley* Aftermath," pp. 8-9.

52. Personal conversation with Roger Adelman.

53. David Bazelon, "A Jurist's View of Psychiatry," 3 *Journal of Psychology and Law* 175, 181 (1975).

54. I. Keilitz and J. Fulton, *The Insanity Defense and Its Alternatives: A Guide for Policymakers* (Washington, D.C.: National Center for State Courts, 1984), p. 18.

55. Ibid., p. 51.

56. *Federal Rules of Evidence*, Rule 704(b). This provision was enacted in the Comprehensive Crime Control Act of 1984 (Pub. L. No. 98-473, tit. II, 98 Stat. 1837, 1976), enacted October 12, 1984.

57. American Bar Association, Standing Committee on Association Standards for Criminal Justice, *Standards for Criminal Justice: First Tentative Draft Criminal Justice Mental Health Standards* (commentary to Standard 7-6.6; July 1983), p. 283.

58. "Advisory Committee's Note to Rule 704(a)," *Federal Rules of Evidence*, p. 95.

59. S.R. 98-225, 98th Cong., 2d sess., pp. 230–31, reprinted in *U.S. Code Cong. & Admin. News* 3404, 3412 (1984). Citations omitted.

60. 18 U.S.C., sec. 20(a) (1984).

61. ABA, *Standards for Criminal Justice: First Tentative Draft*, p. 285.

62. Ibid., p. 286.

63. Ibid., pp. 285–86.

64. *United States v. Mest*, 789 F.2d 1069 (4th Cir. 1986).

65. Ibid., p. 1071.

66. Ibid., pp. 1071–72.

67. *United States v. Freeman*, 804 F.2d 1574 (11th Cir. 1986). The defendant had argued that Rule 704(b) restricted the presentation of his defense. The court disagreed, finding no such restriction in violation of the Constitution. The court went on to note that the amendment applied to the government's expert witnesses as well as to the defendant's expert witnesses.

68. Personal conversation.

69. *ABA Standards for Criminal Justice*, Standard 7-3.13, p. 134.

70. *Washington v. United States*, 129 U.S. App. D.C. 29, 390 F.2d 444 (D.C. Cir. 1967). See discussion in text accompanying note 17.

71. Personal conversation with Roger Adelman.

72. Ibid.

73. This discussion of Dr. Orne's views is set forth in D. Kiesel, "Spotting Fake Insanity," 70 *A. B. A. J.* 33 (December 1984).

74. *Ake v. Oklahoma*, 470 U.S. 60, 105 S. Ct. 1087 (1985). See discussion in text accompanying note 33.

75. Rita J. Simon and David E. Aaronson, "Survey of Opinion about the Defense of Insanity," (see Chapter 5 for a report on the authors' findings).

4

The Jury and the Insanity Defense

Whenever a jury returns a verdict of not guilty by reason of insanity after a defendant has committed a heinous, violent act against a public figure or a person of prominence, the reactions are always the same. The jurors are labeled incompetent; it is said that they have failed to understand the issues involved in the insanity plea, and that they are incapable of rendering a verdict consistent with the rules of law and the evidence. The value of the jury as an institution is questioned, and proposals for its abolition gain considerable support. On the other hand, little attention is paid to the jury that finds a defendant guilty in defense of insanity trials. Thus, for example—even though every assassin or would-be assassin of a U.S. president or presidential aspirant who pleaded not guilty by reason of insanity has been found guilty except for Richard Lawrence who shot at but missed Andrew Jackson, and before John Hinckley shot and wounded Ronald Reagan—the verdict in the *Hinckley* trial became another major occasion for attacking the integrity of the jury system, on grounds of incompetence and ignorance.

The intensity and tone of the media's and the public's reactions to the *Hinckley* trial is reminiscent of the British reaction to the jury's verdict in the trial of Daniel M'Naghten. As in the United States, the British public—from Queen Victoria to the ordinary citizens—believed that the jury had participated in a travesty of justice when it found Daniel M'Naghten not guilty by reason of insanity after he shot and killed Edward Drummond, secretary to Prime Minister Robert Peel, in the mistaken belief that Drummond was Peel.

They were also outraged that the consequences of M'Naghten's act should result in his being committed to Broadmoor, a mental institution, which the newspapers referred to as a "retreat for idlers."

We did not assess all of the juries' verdicts in trials involving an insanity defense after an attempt had been made on the life of a president or presidential aspirant, but a review of many of those events has placed the jury's performance in the *Hinckley* trial in a more realistic light. Let us briefly consider the jury's record in such cases.

The first reported jury trial involving a defense of insanity after an attempt had been made on the life of a president occurred in 1835. Richard Lawrence fired at President Jackson from a range of about 13 feet as he was walking through the rotunda of the capitol.

> The cap went off with a loud report, but the powder did not ignite and the pistol did not fire. Lawrence dropped the first pistol and transferred the other to his right hand. Meanwhile, Jackson rushed at Lawrence with his cane upraised. Lawrence fired the second pistol into Jackson's chest at pointblank range. It also misfired. Subsequent examination of the pistols showed that they were properly loaded. Their misfiring was attributed to humidity and near-miraculous good fortune.[1]

Lawrence pleaded not guilty by reason of insanity. The prosecutor—Francis Scott Key—cooperated with the defense in establishing a liberal test for insanity.

> Lawrence was to be found not guilty by reason of insanity for the deed was the "immediate, unqualified offspring of the disease,"—even if at the time of the attack he comprehended the nature of the act and knew the difference between right and wrong.[2]

The jury found Lawrence not guilty by reason of insanity, and he spent the rest of his life in mental institutions.

Forty-six years later, in July 1881, Charles Guiteau shot and killed President James Garfield, four months after Garfield had assumed office. Prior to his successful assassination of the president of the United States, Guiteau had engaged in many bizarre activities, and his life demonstrated instability and lack of control over his behavior. There was a history of mental illness in the family. One of Guiteau's uncles died insane; the sanity of two of his sisters was questioned; and Guiteau's two first cousins were committed to asylums. Shortly

before the assassinations, Guiteau received a message that God
wanted him to save the country from ruin by eliminating Garfield.

> Guiteau bought a forty-four caliber pistol with borrowed money. He
> paid an extra dollar in order to get a fancier handle, because he thought
> it would look better in a museum. The owner of the gunshop showed
> Guiteau how to load the revolver and suggested a spot where Guiteau
> could practice.[3]

During the trial Guiteau claimed that he had acted as an agent of
God and was thus guiltless. It took a jury one hour and five minutes
to find him guilty and sane, and he was hanged in front of a large
crowd. Reports indicate that the spectators in the court applauded
when the jurors announced their verdict, and the newspapers and
public officials commended their act. An autopsy done after Guiteau's
death found syphilitic lesions on his brain.

Forty years later, in October 1921, John Schrank shot and
wounded in the chest the then presidential aspirant, Theodore
Roosevelt.

> Standing about six feet from Roosevelt, Schrank would most likely
> have killed Roosevelt, had the bullet not spent much of its force pass-
> ing through Roosevelt's metal glass case and the fifty-page manuscript
> of a speech he was to give, which was folded double in the breast pocket.

As early as 1901, McKinley's ghost had appeared to Schrank in a
dream, and accused Roosevelt of the (McKinley) assassination.

> On the eleventh anniversary of President McKinley's death, while Roose-
> velt was campaigning on the Bull Moose platform, the ghost of McKin-
> ley again appeared to Schrank, touched him on the shoulder, and told
> him not to let a murderer become president.[4]

This apparently confirmed Schrank's conviction that he must be the
agent of God to see that Roosevelt did not live to win what Schrank
construed to be a third term—although, of course, it would not be a
full third term, since Roosevelt had only been elected once in his
own right.

Having determined to kill Roosevelt, Schrank set out to stalk him
on his campaign tours. In more than 2,000 miles and 24 days of travel

in eight states, Schrank managed to be in the same city at the same time as Roosevelt in only three instances: Chattanooga, Chicago, and Milwaukee. Schrank said his nerve momentarily failed him in Chattanooga. He refrained from shooting Roosevelt in Chicago for fear of damaging the reputation of that city. He finally acted in Milwaukee.

After Schrank's arrest, the court appointed five psychiatrists to examine him. They unanimously reported that he was not competent to stand trial. Schrank spent the rest of his life in Wisconsin mental institutions.[5]

On February 15, 1933, Guisseppe Zangara attempted to assassinate president-elect Franklin Roosevelt. Following World War I, Zangara had served for five years in the Italian army. Sometime during this period he had bought a pistol in order to assassinate the king of Italy, but was discouraged by the guards and crowds surrounding the king. At the age of 23—shortly after his discharge from the Italian army—he emigrated to the United States.[6]

In the winter of 1932–33, Zangara was apparently determined to kill President Hoover, but the cold weather in Washington deterred him. When he learned that president-elect Roosevelt planned to be in Miami, Zangara went to Miami. The shot that he presumably fired at Roosevelt hit and killed Mayor Anton Cermak of Chicago, who was sitting next to Roosevelt. Zangar was found to be sane, and he was electrocuted.

In November 1963, Jack Ruby pleaded insanity after he fatally shot Lee Harvey Oswald—the presumed assassin of President John F. Kennedy—before millions of television witnesses. A jury found Ruby guilty, and he was sentenced to life imprisonment.[7]

In 1968, attorneys for Sirhan Sirhan—the assassin of presidential aspirant Robert Kennedy—pleaded "diminished responsibility" for their client, claiming that he was "not capable of mature consideration when the act was committed."[8] After 17 hours of deliberation, the jury found Sirhan guilty of first degree murder. The same jury also deliberated on Sirhan's sentence. It took the jurors nearly 12 hours to decide that Sirhan should be condemned to death in the gas chamber.

In 1972, when Arthur Bremen introduced a plea of insanity after he shot and paralyzed George C. Wallace—the governor of Alabama and a presidential candidate—it took a jury 90 minutes to determine that Bremen was sane and guilty.[9] He was sentenced to 63 years in prison.

In the staff report to the National Commission on the Causes and Prevention of Violence (1968), the authors quoted psychiatrist Donald Hasting as concluding that all of the presidential assassins (those who were successful, and those who failed)—with the exception of the Puerto Rican nationalists who attempted to kill Truman—were "mentally disturbed persons who did not kill to advance any national political plan."[10] Dr. Hasting—the report claimed—"goes so far as to diagnose their mental illness as schizophrenia, in most instances a paranoid type."

But in every trial with the exception of Lawrence's, the juries found the defendants guilty as charged. There were no public outcries in response to any of these verdicts; no media denouncement of the failure of the jury system; no official demands for changes in the rule of law. The public, the press, and the officials supported the juries' verdicts. Their silence indicated that justice had been done in the eyes of the public, the media, and the government.

Was the jury in the *Hinckley* case less competent, less wise, and more ignorant of the law than the juries who found Guiteau, Zangara, Bremen, Ruby, and Sirhan guilty of their heinous acts? We do not know firsthand what happened in the deliberating rooms of any of these trials. We know what the final verdict was; and, in recent trials, we also know how individual jurors reacted to their experiences, after the fact. But questions remain about the jury's competence to decide the complex issues involved after a defense of insanity has been raised. We know that the jury did not fare well in the court of public opinion after its verdict was announced in the *Hinckley* trial.

This chapter introduces another form of evidence about the jury's behavior in defense of insanity trials. It is evidence gleaned from juries' behavior and verdicts in field experiments. Beginning in the early 1950s—and for more than a decade thereafter—research on the jury system was conducted at the Law School of the University of Chicago. What has since become known as the "Chicago Jury Project" involved a wide range of studies on various aspects of the jury's performance. The research was conducted by lawyers and social scientists. Such diverse research methods as experiments, surveys, observations, and case studies were included in the overall research program.

The data referred to in this chapter are taken primarily from experimental jury studies, and most particularly from Simon's study of *The Jury and the Defense of Insanity*.[11] The major purposes of

that study—conducted between 1957 and 1961—were to examine the
jury's reactions to alternative legal criteria for determining criminal
responsibility; to ascertain how—and how well—the jury understood
and evaluated expert psychiatric testimony; and to determine whether
the jury understood the consequences of a not guilty by reason of
insanity verdict.

The research was conducted in the trial courts in Chicago, Minneapolis, and St. Louis. The subjects were real jurors who had been
called for their regular period of jury duty, and had then been assigned
by the judge to serve on one of the experimental trials.

The experimental procedure consisted of the following steps:

1. A transcript was obtained of an actual case. The transcript was edited
and condensed from a trial that lasted between two to three days to
one that could be heard in about 60 to 90 minutes. The experimental
transcript contained the lawyers' opening and closing statements and
the judge's instructions to the jury, as well as the testimony of all the
witnesses.

2. The "experimental" trial was then recorded, with the parts of the
attorneys, witnesses, principals in the case, and the judge performed by
persons associated with the University of Chicago, largely members of
the law school faculty.

3. With the cooperation of local bar associations and presiding judges
in three jurisdictions, Chicago, St. Louis, and Minneapolis, subjects for
the experiment were drawn by lot from the local jury pools. The jurors
were assigned to the recorded trials by the court. A judge instructed
them as to their duties by explaining the court's interest in this comprehensive study of the judicial process. He also told them that while their
verdicts in the case could have no immediate practical consequences,
the judges of this court were very much interested in the results of the
study. A juror's service was not voluntary; it was part of his regular
period of jury duty.

4. Before listening to the trial, each juror filled out a questionnaire.
The questionnaire asked for much of the same kind of information that
the trial lawyer seeks during an extensive voir dire or pretrial examination of prospective jurors, in order to decide which jurors to challenge
and which to accept. Questions as to the juror's age, occupation, marital
status, ethnicity, religion, education, income, and other characteristics
were included along with a series of general attitude items.

5. The jurors then listened to the recorded trial. The trial was inter-
rupted once for lunch. Before leaving the court the jurors were instructed not to discuss the case among themselves. After lunch the
jurors reported back to the jury room and the trial was resumed.

6. After the trial, but before the deliberation, each juror was asked to fill out a brief questionnaire in which he/she was asked to state how he would decide the case at this time.

7. The jurors were then ready to deliberate. They had been told before the trial began that their deliberations would be recorded. Everyone (the bailiff, the experimenters, etc.) left the jury room except the twelve jurors, who had been instructed to select one of their members as foreman.

8. When the jury reached a verdict, the foreman reported it to the experimenter. The jurors were given a final questionnaire in which they were asked about their reactions to the trial and to the deliberation. They were also asked if, sitting as a one-person jury, each of them would have found as the group did.

9. The jury was then taken in front of the judge to report its verdict. The judge thanked the jurors for their service and either dismissed them or sent them back to the jury pool for further duty.[12]

Concerning the validity and generalizability of the data to real jurors, Simon wrote in 1967:

One of the major advantages of the technique described is that it legitimately opens the doors to the inner sanctum of the jury room, and permits systematic observations of the jury's deliberations. But that there are weaknesses and difficulties in the procedure is apparent not only to critics of the approach but to its authors as well. The first and most obvious weakness is that the verdicts have no practical significance. The jurors are told at the onset of the experiment that their verdicts will not affect the defendant's fate. What evidence do we have that the verdicts from the experimental juries are comparable to the verdicts that real juries would have reached in similar situations?

Our strongest evidence is indirect. It comes from the deliberations themselves. In the opening minutes of their discussion, many of the experimental juries sound as if they, too, were doubtful about the meaningfulness of the whole experience; but then something quite dramatic occurs. The jurors become so involved in defending their own interpretation of the case and in convincing others of the correctness of their views that they forget that their verdicts will have no practical significance.

The length of the deliberations is another indirect measure of the realism of the experience. The discussions lasted for many hours, usually long past the time when the court would normally recess for the day. On several occasions the jurors continued through the dinner hour until late in the evening, and once a jury was "locked up" and continued its discussion the next day before it finally reported that it was hope-lessly hung. We found that the average experimental jury's deliberation lasted as long as the average deliberation for a trial that takes two to three days.

The recorded deliberations also proved to be very similar to those provided by interviews with individual jurors who sat on real cases, when each juror was asked to re-create the deliberation as he perceived it.[13]

In total, information was collected on 98 juries that had been exposed to two trials. One of the trials was adapted from the 1954 *Durham* case, discussed at length in Chapter 2. The other was also adapted from a District of Columbia trial. It involved a charge of incest. Each of the experimental trials had six different versions, which are described graphically below.

VERSIONS OF THE HOUSEBREAKING TRIAL

Commitment Instruction	Rules of Law		
	M'Naghten	*Durham*	No Instruction on Responsibility
	(number of juries)		
Present	5	5	5
Absent	5	5	5

VERSIONS OF THE INCEST TRIAL

Psychiatric Testimony	Rules of Law		
	M'Naghten	*Durham*	No Instruction on Responsibility
	(number of juries)		
Model	9	13	11
Typical	11	13	11

In the housebreaking design, five juries heard a trial in which they were instructed using the *M'Naghten* criteria; they were told that, if they found the defendant not guilty by reason of insanity, he would be automatically committed to a mental institution until—in the opinion of the psychiatrists—he was cured. Each group of five juries heard one of the other five versions (for example: the *Durham* rule and no information about what would happen to the defendant if they found him not guilty by reason of insanity; or a version in which no criterion on the matter of responsibility was provided, and no information about commitment).

The same procedure was followed in the incest trial, except that—instead of varying the commitment instruction—almost half of the juries heard what some of the leading forensic psychiatrists (Manfred Guttmacher, then chief medical officer of the Supreme Bench of Baltimore; and Winfred Overholser, then director of St. Elizabeth's Hospital in Washington, D.C.) considered to be "model" psychiatric testimony, while the other 35 juries heard "typical" psychiatric testimony (which, in fact, was the testimony heard during the original trial). More specifically, the typical testimony described the defendant's current symptoms and gave psychiatric labels to the juries, but offered almost no historical or developmental account of the origins of the defendant's behavior.

In the model testimony, the psychiatrists offered a longer and more detailed clinical history of the defendant's illness, from his infancy until his indictment. When medical labels were applied, they were defined in language that should have been understandable to the average layman. In the model version, the psychiatrists made more of an effort to tie together the defendant's clinical history and symptoms with his current behavior. The model testimony lasted almost twice as long as the typical testimony.

In both versions, the jury was instructed in the following manner by the court on how it should treat expert testimony:

> The important point of all this discussion of expert witnesses and opinion testimony is that you are not bound as jurors to accept the testimony of expert witnesses. You should certainly consider carefully the qualifications of the witnesses, their experiences, their observations of the defendant, their opportunity to observe, and all of the factors that they told you about in their lengthy testimony today. Then you are to give to their testimony as experts such weight as in your judgment it is fairly entitled to receive with full recognition of the fact that while you shouldn't arbitrarily disregard the testimony of any witness, yet, if you are satisfied that you don't accept the testimony of the expert witnesses you are not bound to do so.[14]

The research design described above produced verdicts for 98 juries and 1,176 individual jurors, each of whom reported verdicts before and after the juries deliberated. Having described the research design, we are now prepared to present the information derived from that design in some detail, because the data provide a rare opportunity to find out what goes on behind the closed doors of the jury deliberating room and because such access should allow us to answer important questions about juries' competence and motivation in tackling the complicated legal and moral issues that are raised by a defense of insanity. Furthermore, how these juries performed should provide insight into the performance of the *Hinckley* jury, and should tell us more about the wisdom of having juries make the crucial determination as to the guilt or innocence of defendants who plead insanity as a defense.

First of all, what were the jurors' perceptions of mental illness and of a defendant who introduces a plea of insanity? We found that most jurors perceive mental illness as complex and multifaceted. They do not assume that low IQ is a proxy for determining that a person is mentally ill, nor do they believe that bizarre or violent behavior is a necessary characteristic of all mentally ill people. One juror deliberating on a version of the incest case put it this way:

> [I] don't think being able to pass a test has anything to do with insanity. As far as his mental knowledge is concerned, he can have all kinds of knowledge about certain subjects, but it does not make him sane. Did you ever see any of these patients in mental hospitals? There are lots of them that are pretty well. If you saw them anywhere else, you would not think they were insane. And they are not dumb either. Lots of them are not dumb. You can really teach them something like anyone else, and boy, they can be pretty smart at it. They are not a bit dumb.[15]

Another juror who also deliberated on the incest case confessed that his first reaction on hearing that the charge was incest was: "The man must be crazy." But after he listened to the details of the case—which described the number of times the acts were committed, the defendant's use of contraceptives, the facts about his employment record and the steady advances he made in his position—the juror began to doubt his initial reaction. The same juror went on to analogize:

The point is you can have a quirk and still be a member of society as long as you have the mental sense not to allow your quirk to break the law. But, if you break the law, because you have this quirk and still have the mental capacity to know what you are doing and go ahead and do it deliberately, then you are not insane. Then it is no excuse or alibi that you have a quirk. The judge's instructions say that if you think he has a mental illness then you should judge this man insane. If I cut my finger am I ill? I have damage to my body, but is that an illness? I mean is it to the degree that we are trying to judge here?[16]

It was not unusual for the jurors to supply personal experiences. In exposing their own experience to the scrutiny of others, jurors not only provided the group with more concrete information about mental illness; but, in many instances, they obtained therapy for themselves. The opportunity to describe one's own involvement with someone who is mentally ill—in an atmosphere that was both impersonal and supportive—permitted expressions of ambivalence about one's own participation.

Such expressions often served two functions. They relieved some of the jurors' guilt about their own behavior vis-à-vis the spouse or parent whose commitment they were responsible for, and they reduced some of the jurors' negative affect toward the defendant. One juror supplied this analogy:

He had a mental disorder, but was it of such a magnitude that the man was not responsible for his acts? Can a man have a mental disorder and still have enough free will to make up his mind whether to commit an act or not? You follow me? I mean suppose I like to go out and get drunk on Saturday nights and I love to and I do it lots of Saturday nights. But as long as I make a mental decision ahead of time that that is what I am going to do, and make it, say, in a reasonably sound mind, then I am responsible for going out and getting drunk on Saturday night. I mean, I make the decision of my own free will, I use what is normally deemed as a normal mind to make the decision, because after I am drunk I no longer have a normal mind. But did this man have free will? What I am trying to differentiate is whether this mental disorder or emotional disorder, depending on which man you want to listen to, was such that it denied this man free will in making a decision. If the mental disorder denied him the free will, then he cannot act like an average person on making a decision. See what I am trying to say? Is the act of having a neurosis, and the psychiatrists can tell if there is

neurosis, a type of mental disorder that takes away your free will? As
long as a person can make a rational decision then the neurosis is not
sufficient to say that a man is not guilty of a crime.[17.]

In essence, many of the jurors were saying that, when all aspects
of the defendant's life were examined, his behavior appeared no less
rational than their own—except for his incestuous relations with his
daughters. They found no evidence that would support exempting
the defendant from responsibility, unless commission of the act itself
was sufficient grounds for declaring him mentally incompetent—and
that criterion they were unwilling to accept.

In the housebreaking trial based on the *Durham* case, the jurors
heard about a defendant who had a long history of mental illness,
had made several suicide attempts, and had prior commitments to a
mental hospital. In that case, a frequent argument used by the jurors
who believed that the defendant's behavior manifested insanity was
the nature of the items he attempted to steal. The fact that the items
were small and of little value indicated that he was not robbing for
profit—that is, there was no rational purpose behind his behavior. As
one juror said:

> Look at it this way. If you were going to go out and break into some-
> one's house, would you take the chance of breaking into somebody's
> house and getting caught and spending a couple of years in jail just to
> steal a cigarette lighter or a pair of cuff-links?[18]

The second fact most frequently cited by jurors who thought the
defendant was insane was the defendant's position when he was
caught by the police.

> The defendant was hiding in such a childish way, in a corner holding
> something over his face like an ostrich. His failure to resist arrest by
> fighting or running away was not the behavior in their opinion of the
> normal criminal, who would have been aware of his situation and the
> consequences of being caught.[19]

Jurors who argued in favor of finding the defendant sane emphasized essentially the same facts as the jurors who favored a not guilty
by reason of insanity verdict—namely: the defendant's behavior at
the scene of the crime, and the items he attempted to steal. The fact
that the defendant committed a crime against property indicated

sanity. The implication is that, when the insane commit antisocial acts, they commit acts of violence—not those in which personal gain might be a factor. In this case, not only did the defendant commit a crime for which personal gain was involved, but he carried it out in a typically criminal fashion.

As one juror observed:

> If in broad daylight, with people watching him, he had thrown a brick through the window and then tried to enter the house, that would have indicated insanity (i.e., uncontrollable, compulsive behavior). But here we have a case in which the defendant broke into an empty house in the middle of the night by fiddling with the lock.[20]

These actions indicated the defendant's ability to plan and carry out purposive behavior: He must have been watching the house for some time, and knew that it would be unoccupied.

Another juror commented:

> When he entered, he did so quietly and at a time when any ordinary burglar would think it safe to break in. Once he was in the house, he didn't turn on any lights, which again is normal for a burglar; and he was selective in the articles he stole; that is, he took small pieces that were easy to carry and negotiable. Later, when confronted by the police, the defendant acted like a normal criminal. Hiding, cowering, playing dumb when you know you're caught is what they all do. In addition, the fact that he was hiding indicated shame, and if you're ashamed, it means that you are aware that you have done wrong.[21]

For jurors who deliberated on the housebreaking case, sane behavior was most often differentiated from insane behavior by the defendant's ability to act rationally and to commit legally punishable acts in which personal gain was a consideration.

A second major question in this early study of jury behavior was whether the experimental variables (rules of law, commitment instructions, and psychiatric testimony) made a difference in the juries' verdicts. We had expected that juries who were instructed under the *M'Naghten* right-wrong criterion would be more likely to find the defendants (in both trials) guilty than would juries who were instructed using the *Durham* criterion, which is concerned with whether the defendant was suffering from a mental disease and whether the criminal act was a product of that disease. Juries that were not instructed about commitment procedures were expected to find the defendant guilty more often than juries who were provided with such information. Juries exposed to the model psychiatric testimony were expected to find the defendant not guilty by reason of insanity more often than juries who heard the typical testimony.

As shown by the figures presented below, most of these expectations were not realized. Why they were not is what much of *The Jury and the Defense of Insanity* is all about. In this chapter, we present some of the explanations in briefer form. First, we report the juries' verdicts categorized by the given rules of law.

HOUSEBREAKING TRIAL

Juries Instructed under:

Verdicts	M'Naghten	Durham	No Instruction
NGRI	7	4	6
Guilty	2	3	1
Hung	1	3	3
Total	10	10	10

INCEST TRIAL

Juries Instructed under:

Verdicts	M'Naghten	Durham	No Instruction
NGRI	–	5	4
Guilty	19	15	14
Hung	1	6	4
Total	20	26	22

In analyzing the pattern reported above, Simon wrote this in regard to the housebreaking case:

> [T]he *M'Naghten* juries behaved more like the *Uninstructed* jurors than the juries who were instructed under the *Durham* formula. But with

only ten replications in each category, the numbers of jurors that the 60 or 70 percent represent is too small to be given much significance.[22]

This is how she analyzed the verdict pattern in the incest experiment:

The findings in the incest experiment demonstrate that under the *M'Naghten* rule, jurors are less likely to acquit the defendant on grounds of insanity than they are under *Durham* and *Uninstructed* versions. When jurors are permitted to deliberate in the absence of a court-defined criterion of responsibility, they are more likely to find in favor of the defendant, but no more likely than when they are instructed under the *Durham* formula. Juries' verdicts in the *Uninstructed* and *Durham* versions are almost identical. The *Durham* rule produces a powerful difference in jurors' verdicts, but it must be noted that it does not produce a monolithic response. Not all the juries that deliberated under *Durham* found the defendant not guilty by reason of insanity. Indeed most of them found the defendant guilty.[23]

As shown in the chart below, there was no difference in verdicts between those juries who were instructed before they began their deliberations that the defendant would be committed to a mental institution should they find him not guilty by reason of insanity and those who received no information concerning the defendant's fate should they determine that he was insane at the time of the crime.

HOUSEBREAKING TRIAL

Commitment Instruction	Juries' Verdict		
	NGRI	Hung	Guilty
Given	9	4	2
Not given	8	4	3

Simon commented about those results as follows:

There may be some puzzle as to how to interpret the lack of differences between the two treatments. Perhaps the jury is after all not concerned with the defendant's disposition? Or perhaps the jury somehow determines by itself, in the absence of specific information, that the court will provide for some period of commitment before it allows the defendant to go free?[24]

We did have information bearing on both hypotheses. In the house-breaking trial, the jurors were asked:

> In a criminal case like this one, what do you think happens to the defendant when the jury returns a verdict of not guilty by reason of insanity?

The alternatives were the following:

1. Put in a mental institution for a period of time set by the court
2. Put in a mental institution until, in the opinion of the psychiatrists, the defendant is cured
3. Put in prison
4. Placed on probation
5. Set free

This question was put to all jurors—those who were given the commitment instruction, and those who were not. Ideally, all jurors who were exposed to the commitment instruction version should have checked alternative 2. In any case, we expected different

Table 4.1
Juror's Expectations about the Court's Disposition of the Defendant,
by Commitment Instruction (in percent)

Commitment Instruction	Mental Institution*	Prison	Probation or Free	Combined
Given	93	3	4	100 (N = 180)
Not given	91	3	6	100 (N = 180)

*Of those respondents who checked "mental institution," 20 percent (in both treatments) indicated that they believed the length of time the defendant remained in the institution was designated by the court. The remaining 71 or 73 percent of the jurors indicated that they believed the defendant "is put in a mental institution until, in the opinion of the psychiatrists, he is cured."

Source: Rita J. Simon, *The Jury and the Defense of Insanity* (Boston: Little, Brown, 1967), p. 94.

responses to this question, depending on the commitment instruction that jurors received. But Table 4.1 shows that 93 percent of the jurors who received the commitment information checked the correct answer, and 91 percent who did not receive the information also checked the "commitment to mental institution" alternative. Thus, jurors who did not receive the commitment instruction correctly assumed that the defendant would be committed.

We had two expectations about the effects of the psychiatric testimony on the juries' verdicts. We thought that the model version would result in a greater proportion of NGRI verdicts, and that the *Durham* rule—in contrast to the *M'Naghten* rule—would have a greater impact on the jury under the model version. Neither expectation was realized. Four juries who heard model testimony found the defendant not guilty by reason of insanity, as opposed to five juries who heard the typical testimony; and 23 juries who heard the model testimony found the defendant guilty, as opposed to 25 juries who heard the typical testimony and found the defendant guilty.

Access to the deliberations provided further insights into how the jurors reacted to the experts' testimony. In listening to the tapes, it was not only clear that the jurors understood the technical vocabulary as well as the essence of the testimony, but that they took upon themselves the difficult task of distinguishing how their role in the proceedings differed from or complemented that of the psychiatrists. During the deliberations, the jurors discussed over and over again, "Who should have the final say about what happens to the defendant—a jury of laymen or a group of medical experts?" Most of the time, the jury resolved its dilemma by spelling out for itself the separate tasks that the law expected each to perform. In essence, the jury concluded that the experts' testimony emphasized only one aspect of the problem—the clinical part—and that their testimony contributed little to the major dilemma that confronted the jury—that of placing the clinical or purely medical facts about the defendant into a moral-legal context. The jurors reminded each other of the court's instruction that the presence of a mental illness or aberration should not by itself excuse the defendant, and that it was the jury's task to decide whether the particular manifestation of mental illness exhibited by the defendant met the norm of nonresponsibility specified by the rule of law.

The following comment taken from one of the deliberations captures the jurors' reactions to the psychiatrists' testimony.

Just because these doctors are educated and they are way up over our heads, it doesn't mean that we have to accept what they say as truth and that's it. In other words they would be deciding for us. We would not be deciding for ourselves what is right in this particular case. If that were so, then this case should never have gone to a jury. I mean, then we would have to depend upon men specialized in the field of psychiatry to judge this man. The judge said that we could disregard their testimony, if we wanted to. After all, you can't base your whole opinion on the fact that these people have degrees.[25]

Let us go back now to the matter of the jury's understanding about rules of law, and—more specifically—consider the issue of whether juries distinguish among criteria of responsibility. After the jurors had completed their deliberations, they were asked a series of questions about the rule of law. For example, they were asked which rule of law they would recommend that the courts adopt for future usage in defense of insanity trials. The question was posed to them in the following manner.

In the case you just heard, the judge gave you instructions along these lines:
I. If you believe the defendant was unable to tell right from wrong at the time he committed the crime and the criminal act *was the result of his not being able to tell right from wrong*, you must find the accused not guilty by reason of insanity.
It has been proposed that juries be instructed along these lines:
II. If you believe the defendant was suffering from a mental illness at the time he committed the crime and the criminal act *was the product of the mental illness*, you must find the accused not guilty by reason of insanity.[26]

For jurors who heard the *Durham* rule, the instructions under I and II were reversed. For all jurors, the question that followed was:

Which instruction do you think the court should use in the future?
  —The instruction that I heard.
  —The proposed alternative.
  —It wouldn't make any difference.

Jurors were also asked to choose the rule of law that they would request the judge to read to the jury, if "[y]ou were the defendant's attorney, and wanted to obtain a verdict of not guilty by reason of

Table 4.2
Instruction Recommended for Future Usage, by Prior Exposure to Instruction (in percent)

Prior Exposure	Instruction Recommended			Total (*N*)
	M'Naghten	*Durham*	No Difference	
M'Naghten	37	26	37	100(270)
Durham	28	45	27	100(319)

insanity."[27] The jurors were given the same alternatives as those listed under the future usage question.

We examined jurors' recommendations about which instructions the courts should use in the future by holding constant the rule of law to which they had been exposed. The data in Table 4.2 describe the responses.

As expected, Table 4.2 shows that the jurors who were instructed under *M'Naghten* were more likely to recommend *M'Naghten*, and that the jurors who were instructed under *Durham* were more likely to recommend *Durham*. But the margin of preference was slightly larger for *Durham* (45 percent who heard and recommended *Durham* minus 28 percent who heard *Durham* but recommended *M'Naghten* equals 17 percent) than it was for *M'Naghten* (37 – 26 = 11 percent). And the proportion of jurors who had no opinion concerning future usage was more heavily represented in the *M'Naghten* category than in the *Durham* category—37 percent, compared to 27 percent.

As to which rule of law they would want the judge to apply if they were representing the defendant, the results were unequivocal:

Instruction That Jurors Believe to Be Favorable to the Defendant

Rule of Law	Percent (*N*)
M'Naghten	19 (112)
Durham	49 (293)
No difference	32 (184)

Table 4.3
Instruction Believed Favorable to the Defendant, by Instruction
Recommended for Future Usage (in percent)

Instruction Believed Favorable to Defendant	Instruction Recommended			
	M'Naghten	*Durham*	No Difference	Total (*N*)
M'Naghten	69	20	11	100 (112)
Durham	31	58	11	100 (293)
No difference	13	13	74	100 (184)

The *Durham* rule received a clear advantage. Almost half of the jurors believed that it would be more favorable to the defendant. In contrast, only 19 percent believed that it would be more advantageous to argue the defendant's case under the *M'Naghten* rule. Like the responses to the future usage question, slightly less than one-third of the jurors saw no difference between the two instructions.

We know that prior exposure did not significantly influence the jurors' choices in this matter, because the jurors were exposed to the different instructions in approximately equal numbers; and the 49 to 19 percent is a sizable difference. Thus, this finding strongly suggests that jurors really do perceive differences between rules.

To what degree are jurors' policy recommendations affected by their desire to have a rule favorable to the defendant? Table 4.3 describes the relationship between their belief that a rule favors the defendant and their recommendations for future usage.

Table 4.3 shows that 69 percent of the jurors who believed the *M'Naghten* rule to be more favorable to the defendant recommended it for future usage, and 58 percent of the jurors who believed the *Durham* rule to be more favorable to the defendant recommended it for future usage. In this matter, the margin of preference was larger for the *M'Naghten* rule (69 – 20 = 49 percent) than it was for the *Durham* rule (58 – 31 = 27 percent). Seventy-four percent of the jurors who reported no difference in response to one item reported no difference in response to the other.

Finally, we also examined the jurors' individual verdicts by the rule of law that they recommended the courts use in the future.

Recommendations for Future Usage, by Verdicts (in percent)

Verdict	*M'Naghten*	*Durham*	No Difference	Total (*N*)
NGI	22	55	23	100 (183)
Guilty	37	28	35	100 (406)

The data show that 22 percent of the jurors who found the defendant not guilty by reason of insanity recommended *M'Naghten*, and 55 percent recommended *Durham*. Among the jurors who voted guilty, 37 percent recommended *M'Naghten*, and 28 percent recommended *Durham*. Among the NGRI verdict jurors, the margin of preference was (55 – 22 =) 33 percent in favor of *Durham*. Among the guilty verdict jurors, the margin of preference was (37 – 28 =) 9 percent in favor of *M'Naghten*.

To summarize what we have learned about juries' sensitivity and understanding of the rules of law in defense of insanity trials, we found that jurors tended to recommend that the rule they used in reaching their decision be adopted for future usage by the court. But when asked which rule they would like to have the court use if they were the defendant's attorney, the *Durham* rule was favored by more than 2–1 over *M'Naghten*; and a higher percentage of jurors who found the defendant not guilty by reason of insanity were more likely to recommend adoption of the *Durham* rule than were jurors who found the defendant guilty and recommended the *M'Naghten* rule.

One final consideration about the jury's performance on defense of insanity cases goes to the matter of the jurors' willingness to make the decision in such cases. For example, would the jury prefer that medical experts have the final say on the sanity or insanity of the defendant? Do jurors favor abdicating their jurisdiction over the fate of defendants who have introduced a defense of insanity?

Following the completion of their deliberation in both the housebreaking and incest trials, we asked the jurors:

> Which do you believe is the best way of deciding what should be done with a person who has committed a crime and pleads that he is insane?
> —He should be tried before a jury just like anyone else.
> —He should be tried before a judge.
> —He should be turned over by the court to a group of psychiatrists and they should determine what is to be done with him.[28]

The data shown below describe the percentage of jurors who favored decision by psychiatrists.

Jurors Favoring Decision by Psychiatrists

	Percent (*N*)
Housebreaking trial	66 (360)
Incest trial	33 (816)

These percentages—66 in the housebreaking trial, and 33 in the incest trial—suggest that jurors are more willing to delegate responsibility to medical experts when the case involves a relatively minor crime and/or when the defendant is psychotic or patently insane.

The data below show that jurors who voted for acquittal on grounds of insanity on the predeliberation ·questionnaire favored decision by psychiatrists more heavily.

Percent of Jurors Favoring Decision by Psychiatrists, by Verdict

	NGI (*N*)	Guilty (*N*)
Housebreaking trial	71 (238)	65 (122)
Incest trial	41 (269)	30 (547)

The jurors' responses about who should make the final decision in defense of insanity trials tells us something about how jurors perceive the division of labor between themselves and psychiatrists. The jurors are much more concerned about exercising their responsibility when a defendant has committed a heinous crime and is not patently insane than they are when the defendant has committed a relatively mild offense and is patently insane.

To conclude, we return to our initial question: Is the jury capable, competent, and motivated to make—and to make wisely—the difficult decisions in defense of insanity trials. We think a review of its performance in real cases—and even more careful scutiny of its performance in the Chicago Jury Project studies—reveals that the jury understands its role and responsibilities in such trials, adheres to the division of labor between it and the expert witnesses, and reaches decisions consistent with the rule of law and the evidence it heard

during the trials. We would apply those conclusions to the performance of the jury in the John Hinckley trial.

NOTES

1. Rita J. Simon, "Assassination Attempts Directed at the Office of the
President of the United States," in James F. Kirkham, Sheldon Levy, and William
Crotty (eds.), *Assassination and Political Violence*, vol. 8: *Report of the National
Commission on the Causes and Prevention of Violence* (Washington, D.C.: U.S.
Government Printing Office, 1969), pp. 49–50.

2. Ibid., p. 50.

3. Ibid., p. 53.

4. Ibid., p. 56.

5. Ibid., p. 57.

6. Ibid.

7. Ibid., p. 61.

8. Ibid., p. 62.

9. Valerie P. Hans and Neil Widmar, *Judging the Jury* (New York: Plenum
Press, 1986), p. 190.

10. Simon, "Assassination Attempts," p. 62.

11. Rita J. Simon, *The Jury and the Defense of Insanity* (Boston: Little,
Brown, 1967).

12. Ibid., pp. 36–37.

13. Ibid., pp. 37–38.

14. Ibid., p. 81.

15. Ibid., p. 154.

16. Ibid., p. 147.

17. Ibid., p. 149.

18. Ibid., p. 140.

19. Ibid.

20. Ibid., p. 141.

21. Ibid.

22. Ibid., p. 68.

23. Ibid., p. 73.

24. Ibid., p. 93.

25. Ibid., p. 164.

26. Ibid., p. 192.

27. Ibid., p. 188. Emphasis in original.

28. Ibid., p. 86.

5

Survey of Judges, Prosecutors, Defense Attorneys, and Mental Health Professionals

This chapter describes the results of a 1984 survey of experts' opinions about the most salient issues involving the defense of insanity. The thrust of the survey was to find out how various types of experts perceived and evaluated the major issues surrounding the defense of insanity and to compare responses among the experts, each of whom perform different roles in defense of insanity proceedings. How much consensus is there about the legal criteria that ought to be applied; the burden of proof (should it be on the defense or the prosecution, and with what degree of certainty?); the verdict form; and the division of labor between trial judge and jury, and between expert and lay witnesses—and what should happen to defendants who are found not responsible for the acts they committed?

The target population is the principals involved in the debate on issues concerning the insanity defense and the architects who are likely to introduce changes in the law. They are the judges who hear the cases; the attorneys who argue them; the psychiatrists, psychologists and other mental health officials who testify in them; and the lawmakers and appellate bench who revise the rules and formulate new ones.[1]

Of the 2,278 questionnaires that were sent out at two different times, we received 928 back, for a 40.9 percent rate of return. While this rate is below the desired 50 percent for a mail survey, given the target population (judges are especially notorious about participating in surveys, and lawyers are almost as bad) and the fact that the response patterns on the survey for the two separate time periods were practically identical, we believe that the results are worth reporting.[2] Before doing so, a brief account of the personal and social characteristics of the participants needs to be presented.

The large majority of respondents in every category were male: judges—86 percent; lawyers—87 percent; and mental health experts—78 percent. The average age of the judges was 56; lawyers, 41; and mental health officials, 46. All of the judges and attorneys had at least an LL.B. or a J.D. degree. About 10 percent of the judges also had an LL.M. or a doctor of laws degree. All of the psychiatrists were M.D.s; 68 percent of the psychologists had at least a Ph.D., and 30 percent also had a law degree. Most of the mental health directors held either M.D. or Ph.D. degrees; 12 percent held an M.A. or M.S. as his or her highest degree.

Forty-one percent of the federal judges graduated from Ivy League law schools or top-ranked state schools, in contrast to 24 and 19 percent of the state appellate and trial court judges. Among the attorneys, 23 percent of the prosecutors received their law degrees from Ivy League or top-ranked state schools, as opposed to 14 percent of the public defenders and 8 percent of the private practice members of the National Association of Criminal Defense Lawyers (NACDL). Within the mental health professions, 37 percent of the psychiatrists graduated from Ivy League or top-ranked state universities, as opposed to 15 percent of the psychologists and 8 percent of the mental health directors.

The federal judges and the state appellate judges had been on the bench an average of 15.5 years; the state trial court judges averaged 10.6 years on the bench. The attorneys were in practice for an average of 15 years. The psychiatrists reported an average of 26.3 years of practice; the psychologists and mental health directors, 15.5 years. Between 67 and 79 percent of the state judges (trial-level and appellate) had tried or presided over at least one defense of insanity trial; so had 63 percent of the federal judges. Sixty-nine percent of the prosecutors and 78 percent of the defense attorneys had tried at least one defense of insanity case. Ninety-five percent of the psychiatrists had examined at least one defendant, and had testified in at least one defense of insanity trial. So had 80 percent of the psychologists and 69 percent of the mental health directors.

SURVEY FINDINGS

The survey began by asking respondents which criterion the courts ought to apply in defense of insanity trials. Their choices were: the

Table 5.1

Criterion Courts Ought to Apply in Defense of Insanity Trials, by Respondent Category (in percent)

Criteria	1	2	3	4	5	6	7	8	9	Combined
American Law Institute	53.1	41.9	49.2	37.4	70.5	70.1	57.4	63.4	53.9	53.5
M'Naghten	18.4	38.2	37.2	44.3	11.5	9.6	27.8	7.3	19.3	28.3
Combination M'Naghten/Irresistible	8.2	10.9	5.5	0.7	16.4	18.0	3.7	4.9	3.8	8.0
Other	6.1	3.6	5.1	6.8	1.6	1.8	11.1	24.4	15.4	6.0
None/Abolish	4.1	3.6	0.3	4.7	—	—	—	—	3.8	1.4
No answer	10.1	1.8	2.7	6.1	—	0.5	—	—	3.8	2.8
Total	100	100	100	100	100	100	100	100	100	100
(N)	(49)	(55)	(328)	(147)	(61)	(167)	(54)	(41)	(26)	(928)

Legend: 1 = district and appellate federal judges; 2 = state appellate judges; 3 = state trial court judges; 4 = prosecuting attorneys; 5 = public defenders; 6 = private attorneys; 7 = forensic psychiatrists; 8 = forensic psychologists; 9 = state mental health directors

American Law Institute's formulation; *M'Naghten*; a combination of *M'Naghten* and irresistible impulse; or some other, which they were asked to supply.[3] Table 5.1 describes the results for the nine groups of experts.

Note that the lawyers' responses are at the extremes. As a group, the prosecutors are most opposed to the ALI rule and most favorable to the *M'Naghten* criterion. The public defenders and the NACDL respondents are most favorable to the ALI criterion and most opposed to *M'Naghten*. The federal (district and appellate) judges and the state trial judges—along with the psychiatrists and mental health officials—hold similar views: Slightly more than 50 percent of them favor the ALI rule. The state appellate judges are closer to the prosecutors, in their lack of support for the ALI rule and their endorsement of *M'Naghten* or a combination of *M'Naghten* and irresistible impulse; and the psychologists are closer to the defense attorneys, in their support for the ALI rule and lack of support for *M'Naghten*. More psychologists and mental health officials prefer "other" criteria such as the New Hampshire Rule, *Durham*, or the rule proposed by the British Royal Commission on Capital Punishment in 1953 ("[A person is not responsible for his unlawful act if] at the time of the act the accused was suffering from disease of the mind [or mental deficiency] to such a degree that he ought not to be held responsible").

When we further examined the experts' responses according to the states in which they practiced (for example: judges who presided in states in which the ALI rule had been adopted, as opposed to judges who presided in states in which the *M'Naghten* rule applied), we found that the majority of the state judges (trial court and appellate) and the prosecutors preferred the rule of law applied in their state. Thus—as Table 5.2 indicates—among prosecutors in states that used ALI, 57 percent preferred that rule over *M'Naghten* (25 percent). Among the prosecutors who came from states that used *M'Naghten*, 62 percent preferred *M'Naghten*, as opposed to ALI (18 percent). The responses of the state judges were similar to those of the prosecutors.[4] But the responses of the defense attorneys and the mental health officials did not exhibit the same pattern. The large majority of respondents in those categories preferred the ALI rule, irrespective of the criterion used in their state.

As shown by Table 5.3, on the matter of which side should have the burden of proof and with what degree of certainty, the majority of respondents in all of the categories (save for the defense attorneys)

Table 5.2
Criteria That the Court Ought to Apply

Respondent's Preference	Rules of Law Applied in Respondent's State		
	ALI	*M'Naghten*	Other
State Judges*			
ALI	60.6	25.9	73.9
M'Naghten	28.6	54.4	8.7
Other	8.5	17.0	13.1
No answer	2.3	2.7	4.3
Prosecuting Attorneys			
ALI	57.1	17.8	54.5
M'Naghten	25.4	61.6	36.4
Other	12.7	12.4	9.1
No answer	4.8	8.2	—
Public Defenders and NACDL			
ALI	73.9	71.7	37.5
M'Naghten	5.4	13.3	12.5
Other	19.6	15.0	50.0
No answer	1.1	—	—
Mental Health Officials			
ALI	68.2	46.5	50.0
M'Naghten	9.6	27.9	33.0
Other	22.2	23.3	16.7
No answer	—	2.3	—

*Federal judges are not included, because the ALI formula was used in all of the federal circuits.

favored shifting the burden from the prosecution (to prove sanity beyond a reasonable doubt) to the defense (to prove insanity). Most of them also favored having the defense prove insanity beyond a reasonable doubt. On this issue, the federal and state benches (at the trial and appellate levels) and the mental health professionals lined up with the prosecutors, and were even more likely than the prosecutors to favor shifting the burden from the prosecution to the defense, with a higher degree of certainty. The public defenders and NACDL respondents gained little support from any of the other

Table 5.3
Burden of Proof: Which Side Should Have It and to What Degree, by Respondent Category (in percent)

Burden of Proof	1	2	3	4	5	6	7	8	9	Combined
Prosecution, beyond reasonable doubt	14.3	16.4	11.3	4.8	72.2	55.7	5.6	4.9	3.9	21.9
Prosecution, preponderance of evidence	2.0	3.6	3.7	0.7	9.8	6.0	3.7	7.3	3.9	4.1
Defense, beyond reasonable doubt	57.2	63.7	54.6	47.6	16.4	29.9	53.7	43.9	53.9	46.7
Defense, preponderance of evidence	16.3	12.7	25.3	43.5	–	4.2	24.1	36.7	26.9	22.0
Other	4.1	3.6	3.9	3.5	1.6	3.6	13.0	4.8	7.6	4.3
No answer	6.1	–	1.2	–	–	0.6	–	2.4	3.8	1.0
Total	100	100	100	100	100	100	100	100	100	100
(N)	(49)	(55)	(328)	(147)	(61)	(167)	(54)	(41)	(26)	(928)

Legend: 1 = district and appellate federal judges; 2 = state appellate judges; 3 = state trial court judges; 4 = prosecuting attorneys; 5 = public defenders; 6 = private attorneys; 7 = forensic psychiatrists; 8 = forensic psychologists; 9 = state mental health directors

groups in their desire to retain the burden of proof on the prosecution, and at the beyond a reasonable doubt level of certainty.

Verdict forms are another area of experimentation and debate within the larger controversy over the defense of insanity. Table 5.4 describes how the various groups of respondents aligned themselves on that issue. This time, the defense attorneys and the mental health professionals were on one side, and members of the judiciary (state and federal, trial-level and appellate) and the prosecutors were on the other. The majority in the latter groups favored adoption of the "guilty but insane" or "guilty but mentally ill" verdict forms over the older and more widely used "not guilty by reason of insanity" version, because the new versions state explicitly that the defendant is guilty of having committed a criminal act. Between the two new versions, the guilty but insane form was favored by judges and prosecutors over the guilty but mentally ill version, because it implies a tougher standard for exemption than the latter. A large majority of the defense attorneys and the mental health professionals favored the more traditional verdict form of not guilty by reason of insanity over either of the guilty-but versions.

Comparing the types of alignments and preferences that have been expressed on the three major issues surrounding the insanity debate—legal criterion, burden of proof, and verdict form—we note that, on the first issue, the defense attorneys were the strongest supporters of the American Law Institute's criterion and the prosecutors the strongest supporters of the *M'Naghten* rule. The mental health professionals were closer to the defense attorneys; and the judges—especially the state judges—were closer to the prosecutors in their support of *M'Naghten*.

On burden of proof, the majority of respondents in all of the categories (save for the defense attorneys) favored a shift from current practice—whereby the prosecution has to prove sanity beyond a reasonable doubt—to the defense having to prove insanity beyond a reasonable doubt. Concerning the verdict form, members of the judiciary—along with the prosecutors—favored the more recently adopted verdict form that includes the label "guilty" over the more traditional and widely used *not* guilty by reason of insanity, which was supported by the mental health professionals as well as the defense attorneys.

The attorneys' responses were more consistent than were those of the judges or the mental health professionals. The prosecutors want

Table 5.4
Verdict Forms, by Respondent Category (in percent)

Verdict Forms	1	2	3	4	5	6	7	8	9	Combined
Not guilty by reason of insanity	28.6	30.9	26.2	21.8	72.1	64.1	57.4	53.7	61.7	39.8
Guilty but insane	32.7	36.4	35.4	45.6	6.6	11.4	16.7	9.8	3.8	27.6
Guilty but mentally ill	28.6	25.5	25.9	27.2	14.8	18.5	9.3	24.4	23.1	23.1
Other	4.1	7.3	11.3	4.8	4.9	6.0	16.6	9.7	7.6	8.3
No answer	6.0	–	1.2	0.6	1.6	–	–	2.4	3.8	1.2
Total	100	100	100	100	100	100	100	100	100	100
(N)	(49)	(55)	(328)	(147)	(61)	(167)	(54)	(41)	(26)	(928)

Legend: 1 = district and appellate federal judges; 2 = state appellate judges; 3 = state trial court judges; 4 = prosecuting attorneys; 5 = public defenders; 6 = private attorneys; 7 = forensic psychiatrists; 8 = forensic psychologists; 9 = state mental health directors

to retain the traditional *M'Naghten* right–wrong criterion; they want the burden of proof shifted to the defense; and they believe the verdict form ought to include the label "guilty." Roughly the same proportion of defense attorneys favor the ALI criterion, want to maintain the burden of proving sanity on the prosecution, and support the not guilty by reason of insanity verdict form.

Chapter 3 discussed the role and function of expert witnesses in defense of insanity trials, and explained that they are often topics of controversy. Much of the controversy has centered on who should select the experts (the court or the adversaries in the trial); on what issues the experts should be allowed to express an opinion (for example: the defendant's mental state, or the defendant's condition vis-à-vis the legal criteria—be it right from wrong, or capacity to conform his or her conduct to the requirements of the law); and on the competence of the experts to determine whether the defendant is legally insane. Now we compare how judges, attorneys, and the potential expert witnesses themselves evaluate the experts' role.

The responses in Table 5.5 show that the mental health professionals differ among themselves about whether each side should call its own experts, or whether the court should do the selecting. The psychologists and the mental health directors are more likely than the psychiatrists to favor having the court call the experts, and less likely to support the practice most common in the courts today—that of having each side call its own experts. The psychiatrists' views are closer to the judges and the prosecutors, in that about half in each category preferred the existing practice. The defense attorneys are the strongest supporters of the status quo. Sixty-seven and 70 percent of them wanted to retain the practice of each side calling its own experts. Less than 10 percent favored turning the responsibility over to the courts.

On the matter of how much responsibility the experts ought to have—whether their testimony should be limited to clinical-medical issues (for example: the defendant's mental state at the time he or she committed the illegal act, and relevant prior history), or whether they should be allowed to express their opinion on the ultimate question in an insanity defense—we found that the defense attorneys (public defenders and NACDL) were the strongest proponents of allowing the mental health experts the broadest mandate for their testimony. Table 5.6 shows that more than 90 percent favored allowing the experts to testify on the moral-legal issues, and not limiting

Table 5.5

Who Should Select the Expert Witnesses, by Respondent Category
(in percent)

Selected by	1	2	3	4	5	6	7	8	9	Combined
Each side	40.9	52.8	57.0	49.0	67.3	70.1	48.1	31.8	26.9	55.2
Court	12.2	10.9	16.2	22.4	8.2	4.2	20.4	34.1	42.4	15.7
Both	34.7	34.5	22.6	21.8	21.3	23.4	29.6	24.4	23.1	24.4
Other	6.1	1.8	3.0	6.2	1.6	2.3	1.9	9.7	3.8	3.6
No answer	6.1	–	1.2	0.6	1.6	–	–	–	3.8	1.1
Total	100	100	100	100	100	100	100	100	100	100
(N)	(49)	(55)	(328)	(147)	(61)	(167)	(54)	(41)	(26)	(928)

Legend: 1 = district and appellate federal judges; 2 = state appellate judges; 3 = state trial court judges; 4 = prosecuting attorneys; 5 = public defenders; 6 = private attorneys; 7 = forensic psychiatrists; 8 = forensic psychologists; 9 = state mental health directors

Table 5.6
Range of Expert Testimony, by Respondent Category (in percent)

Testify on Ultimate Question	1	2	3	4	5	6	7	8	9	Combined
Yes	79.7	67.3	80.9	65.3	91.8	94.0	59.2	65.9	57.7	78.0
No	12.2	29.1	15.2	31.3	6.6	5.4	38.9	34.1	34.6	18.9
Other	2.0	1.8	2.7	2.1	—	—	1.9	—	—	1.6
No answer	6.1	1.8	1.2	1.4	1.6	0.6	—	—	7.7	1.5
Total	100	100	100	100	100	100	100	100	100	100
(N)	(49)	(55)	(328)	(147)	(61)	(167)	(54)	(41)	(26)	(928)

Legend: 1 = district and appellate federal judges; 2 = state appellate judges; 3 = state trial court judges; 4 = prosecuting attorneys; 5 = public defenders; 6 = private attorneys; 7 = forensic psychiatrists; 8 = forensic psychologists; 9 = state mental health directors

Table 5.7
Extent to Which Psychiatrists Can Determine Whether Defendant Is Legally Insane, by Respondent Category (in percent)

Psychiatrists Can Determine	1	2	3	4	5	6	7	8	9	Combined
All of the time	—	—	0.3	—	1.6	—	—	—	—	0.2
Most of the time	34.8	32.8	38.1	17.0	45.9	43.7	72.2	31.7	61.7	38.2
Some of the time	49.9	63.6	46.1	42.9	42.7	46.1	22.2	36.6	19.2	43.9
Once in a while	15.3	3.6	10.7	27.9	8.2	7.2	—	2.4	3.8	11.2
Never	—	—	2.4	10.9	1.6	1.8	5.6	22.0	11.5	4.6
Other	—	—	1.2	0.7	—	0.6	—	2.4	—	0.7
No answer	—	—	1.2	0.6	—	0.6	—	4.9	3.8	1.4
Total	100	100	100	100	100	100	100	100	100	100
(N)	(49)	(55)	(328)	(147)	(61)	(167)	(54)	(41)	(26)	(928)

Legend: 1 = district and appellate federal judges; 2 = state appellate judges; 3 = state trial court judges; 4 = prosecuting attorneys; 5 = public defenders; 6 = private attorneys; 7 = forensic psychiatrists; 8 = forensic psychologists; 9 = state mental health directors

them to a clinical-medical diagnosis. The mental health professionals and the prosecuting attorneys were more likely to favor limiting the experts to their own do. ain. The judges' views were in between the defense attorneys and the prosecuting attorneys and mental health professionals.

As to the likelihood that psychiatrists would be able to determine whether the defendant was legally insane, here again—as shown in Table 5.7—we found disagreements among the mental health professionals.

The psychiatrists were their own strongest supporters. Seventy-two percent of them believed that they could make the crucial determination about whether the defendant was legally insane. The mental health directors—many of whom are themselves psychiatrists—are the next largest category of believers in the psychiatrists' competence and skill. But note that the psychologists were most likely to believe that their fellow clinicians are never able to make such a determination. Even the defense attorneys—who are anxious to have the experts testify as to the relationship between a defendant's mental state and the legal criterion under which he or she is being tried—were not willing to support the psychiatrists as strongly as the psychiatrists support their own expertise. Comparing all of the groups' responses, we note that more of the psychologists and prosecutors were skeptical of the psychiatrists than any of the other respondents.

Most trials involving a defense of insanity are heard before a jury. Chapter 4 assessed various aspects of the jury's performance by examining the jury's competence for understanding the rule of law, the experts' testimony, and the procedures following a not guilty by reason of insanity verdict. In this chapter, we describe how the experts evaluate the jury's performance. We asked first: "Who is more likely to find a defendant not guilty by reason of insanity—a judge or a jury?" Table 5.8 shows that there was no consistent pattern among the various groups of experts.

The psychiatrists were least likely—and members of the NACDL were most likely—to believe that a jury more often than a judge would find a defendant not guilty by reason of insanity. More so than in responses to most of the other items on this survey, we found that, on this issue, there was a lack of consensus among experts in the same profession or among those who play similar roles in defense of insanity trials. The data in Table 5.8 show that the psychologists and mental health directors disagreed with the psychiatrists, and that

Table 5.8
More Likely to Find a Defendant NGRI: Judge or Jury, by Respondent Category (in percent)

More Likely to Find NGRI	1	2	3	4	5	6	7	8	9	Combined
Judge	30.6	25.5	32.0	26.5	34.4	22.8	57.3	34.2	38.5	30.9
Jury	30.6	49.1	38.8	44.9	41.0	54.4	24.1	29.3	38.5	41.6
No difference	26.5	21.8	25.6	26.5	16.4	16.2	9.3	26.8	11.5	22.0
Other	4.1	1.8	2.7	1.4	6.6	6.0	9.3	7.3	7.7	4.1
No answer	8.2	1.8	0.9	0.7	1.6	0.6	–	2.4	3.8	1.4
Total	100	100	100	100	100	100	100	100	100	100
(N)	(49)	(55)	(328)	(147)	(61)	(167)	(54)	(41)	(26)	(928)

Legend: 1 = district and appellate federal judges; 2 = state appellate judges; 3 = state trial court judges; 4 = prosecuting attorneys; 5 = public defenders; 6 = private attorneys; 7 = forensic psychiatrists; 8 = forensic psychologists; 9 = state mental health directors

the public defenders' views were closer to those of the prosecutors than they were to the private defense attorneys (NACDL) in believing that a jury would find a defendant not guilty by reason of insanity more often than a judge.

When asked "Does the jury understand the judge's instructions as to the legal criterion it is to employ?" the judges (both state and federal, appellate and trial-level) are most likely to believe that the jurors understand what the judge tells them concerning the rule of law they are to apply. As the responses in Table 5.9 show, the mental health professionals and the different categories of attorneys are less likely than the judges to believe that the jury understands the legal criterion it is to apply.

There is greater consensus among the experts on whether the legal criterion affects the jury's decision. As shown by Table 5.10, the psychiatrists are least likely to believe that the jurors are influenced by the rules of law. But between 46 and 56 percent of the other respondents in all of the other categories believe that the legal criteria affect the jury's verdict always or most of the time. In response, then, to the three items on the jury's performance in defense of insanity trials, the psychiatrists emerge as the respondents most skeptical of the jury's competence to carry out the tasks assigned to it.

Much of the debate about the legitimacy of the defense of insanity has focused on these issues: what should happen to a defendant who is declared not guilty by reason of insanity, and who should make that determination. Since such a defendant is found not guilty, should that person go free, or should he or she be incarcerated in a mental institution—and, if so, for how long; and how and by whom should the determination be made? Should the defendant's fate following a verdict of not guilty by reason of insanity be determined at a separate hearing before a judge, or before a panel of medical and/or legal experts? Should the commitment be automatic, or subject to medical-psychiatric examination? There has also been debate about how to treat a defendant who has introduced a defense of insanity but is found guilty. Should the determination of his or her punishment take a different form from that usually followed in criminal trials in which the issue was never raised and the defendant was declared guilty?

On the matter of how and by whom the fate of a defendant found not guilty by reason of insanity should be determined, between 51 and 67 percent of the respondents in all of the categories favored

Table 5.9
Jury Understands Legal Criterion, By Respondent Category (in percent)

Jury Understands	1	2	3	4	5	6	7	8	9	Combined
Always	2.0	1.8	4.6	2.7	—	2.4	—	—	—	2.7
Most of the time	65.3	67.3	55.8	38.1	26.2	37.1	35.2	26.8	30.8	45.7
Some of the time	20.4	27.3	28.4	36.1	50.9	46.7	55.5	51.3	53.9	37.2
Hardly ever	—	1.8	7.9	18.4	19.7	10.2	9.3	17.1	3.8	10.3
Never	—	—	0.3	2.7	—	0.6	—	—	—	0.6
Other	4.1	—	2.1	1.4	1.6	3.0	—	—	3.8	2.2
No answer	8.2	1.8	0.9	0.6	1.6	—	—	4.8	7.7	1.3
Total	100	100	100	100	100	100	100	100	100	100
(N)	(49)	(55)	(328)	(147)	(61)	(167)	(54)	(41)	(26)	(928)

Legend: 1 = district and appellate federal judges; 2 = state appellate judges; 3 = state trial court judges; 4 = prosecuting attorneys; 5 = public defenders; 6 = private attorneys; 7 = forensic psychiatrists; 8 = forensic psychologists; 9 = state mental health directors

Table 5.10
Rules of Law Affect Jury's Decision, by Respondent Category (in percent)

Rules of Law Affect Jury's Decision	1	2	3	4	5	6	7	8	9	Combined
Always	6.1	9.1	11.0	15.0	13.1	14.4	5.6	14.6	3.8	11.6
Most of the time	44.9	43.7	44.9	34.0	32.8	35.9	27.8	39.1	42.4	39.4
Some of the time	18.4	29.1	27.4	30.6	34.4	41.9	50.0	26.8	38.5	32.2
Hardly ever	16.3	14.5	12.2	15.0	14.8	6.0	14.8	19.5	7.7	12.4
Never	–	1.8	–	0.7	3.3	–	–	–	–	0.4
Other	4.1	–	2.4	2.7	1.6	0.6	1.8	–	3.8	2.0
No answer	10.2	1.8	2.1	2.0	–	1.2	–	–	3.8	2.0
Total	100	100	100	100	100	100	100	100	100	100
(N)	(49)	(55)	(328)	(147)	(61)	(167)	(54)	(41)	(26)	(928)

Legend: 1 = district and appellate federal judges; 2 = state appellate judges; 3 = state trial court judges; 4 = prosecuting attorneys; 5 = public defenders; 6 = private attorneys; 7 = forensic psychiatrists; 8 = forensic psychologists; 9 = state mental health directors

Table 5.11
Who Should Determine Fate of Defendant Found Not Guilty
by Reason of Insanity, by Respondent Category (in percent)

Who Should Determine	1	2	3	4	5	6	7	8	9	Combined
Jury	2.0	1.8	3.4	5.4	6.6	2.4	3.7	2.4	–	3.4
Presiding judge	61.4	52.7	67.1	60.6	60.7	60.5	66.7	51.4	65.6	62.5
Panel: medical-clinical experts	2.0	5.5	3.7	2.0	19.7	17.4	7.4	14.6	7.7	7.8
Legislation	14.3	29.1	19.2	26.5	11.5	7.2	13.0	19.5	11.5	17.5
Other	14.2	9.1	5.8	5.8	1.5	12.0	9.2	12.1	11.4	7.7
No answer	6.1	1.8	0.8	0.7	–	0.5	–	–	3.8	1.1
Total	100	100	100	100	100	100	100	100	100	100
(N)	(49)	(55)	(328)	(147)	(61)	(167)	(54)	(41)	(26)	(928)

Legend: 1 = district and appellate federal judges; 2 = state appellate judges; 3 = state trial court judges; 4 = prosecuting attorneys; 5 = public defenders; 6 = private attorneys; 7 = forensic psychiatrists; 8 = forensic psychologists; 9 = state mental health directors

having the presiding judge make that determination, as shown in Table 5.11. Less than 7 percent of any of the respondents favored turning over the responsibility to a jury. The state legislature was the second most popular choice of all the respondents—save for the public defenders and the NACDL, who prefer that the decision be made by a panel of medical or clinical experts.

Practically none of the experts (1 percent of all the respondents) advocate the automatic release of a defendant who has been found not guilty by reason of insanity.[5] The desired procedure among respondents in every category (save for the prosecuting attorneys) is to have the defendant examined by medical experts who would report their findings to a judge, who would then make the final decision. The modal response among the prosecuting attorneys was "automatic commitment to a mental institution."

There was greater disagreement among the experts on the matter of how a defendant who had introduced a defense of insanity but was found guilty should be treated. The majority of the defense attorneys (public defenders and NACDL) believed that the court should require a medical examination before deciding on punishment. Interestingly, as the responses in Table 5.12 demonstrate, most of the mental health professionals did not share that view; they agreed with the prosecuting attorneys and the judges that such a defendant should not be treated any differently than someone who had not introduced an insanity defense.

Respondents in all categories differentiated between whether defendants who committed violent acts—as opposed to those who committed property offenses—and were found not guilty by reason of insanity are released too soon. As the percentages in Tables 5.13 and 5.14 describe, taken as a whole, about twice as many respondents believe that offenders who committed violent offenses are released too soon, as opposed to being committed for the right length of time; while, for the property offenders, the responses are divided almost evenly between "too soon" and "the right length of time." Note that the respondents in the mental health professions (especially the directors of mental health facilities) and the public defenders were much less likely to believe that violent offenders are released too soon than were the prosecuting attorneys and the judges.

There is more consensus about the correct length of incarceration for property offenders; only a bare majority of the prosecuting attorneys believe that NGRI property offenders are released too soon.

Table 5.12
Should an Insanity Defense Defendant Who Is Found Guilty Be Treated Differently From Other Guilty Defendants, by Respondent Category
(in percent)

Treatment of Guilty Defendant	1	2	3	4	5	6	7	8	9	Combined
Same	57.3	65.5	79.0	76.9	31.1	38.9	63.0	51.2	77.1	64.1
Different; court should order medical examination	30.6	25.5	14.3	17.7	67.3	53.3	27.8	36.6	11.5	28.6
Other	6.0	7.2	5.8	4.2	1.6	7.2	9.2	12.2	7.6	6.0
No answer	6.1	1.8	0.9	1.2	–	0.6	–	–	3.8	1.2
Total	100	100	100	100	100	100	100	100	100	100
(N)	(49)	(55)	(328)	(147)	(61)	(167)	(54)	(41)	(26)	(928)

Legend: 1 = district and appellate federal judges; 2 = state appellate judges; 3 = state trial court judges; 4 = prosecuting attorneys; 5 = public defenders; 6 = private attorneys; 7 = forensic psychiatrists; 8 = forensic psychologists; 9 = state mental health directors

Table 5.13
Are NGRI Defendants Who Committed Violent Offenses Released Too Soon, by Respondent Category (in percent)

Released	1	2	3	4	5	6	7	8	9	Combined
Too soon	46.9	56.5	61.6	74.2	14.8	23.4	20.4	24.4	3.8	46.9
About right length of time	20.5	12.7	19.8	13.6	26.2	25.1	38.8	36.7	38.5	22.2
Too long	6.1	5.4	6.4	2.0	34.4	23.4	27.8	29.2	42.4	13.8
Other	16.3	23.6	11.0	8.8	21.3	25.1	13.0	7.3	11.5	14.9
No answer	10.2	1.8	1.2	1.4	3.3	3.0	–	3.3	3.8	2.2
Total	100	100	100	100	100	100	100	100	100	100
(N)	(49)	(55)	(328)	(147)	(61)	(167)	(54)	(41)	(26)	(928)

Legend: 1 = district and appellate federal judges; 2 = state appellate judges; 3 = state trial court judges; 4 = prosecuting attorneys; 5 = public defenders; 6 = private attorneys; 7 = forensic psychiatrists; 8 = forensic psychologists; 9 = state mental health directors

157

Table 5.14
Are NGRI Defendants Who Committed Property Offenses Released Too Soon, by Respondent Category (in percent)

Released	1	2	3	4	5	6	7	8	9	Combined
Too soon	20.4	30.9	34.5	50.3	4.9	11.4	14.5	19.5	3.8	27.3
About right length of time	34.8	32.7	36.6	25.9	26.2	27.5	27.9	19.5	46.3	31.3
Too long	6.1	5.5	3.7	2.0	39.4	21.0	33.5	36.7	23.1	12.8
Other	28.5	29.1	23.5	18.4	26.2	37.1	24.1	21.9	23.0	25.8
No answer	10.2	1.8	1.7	3.4	3.3	3.0	—	2.4	3.8	2.8
Total	100	100	100	100	100	100	100	100	100	100
(N)	(49)	(55)	(328)	(147)	(61)	(167)	(54)	(41)	(26)	(928)

Legend: 1 = district and appellate federal judges; 2 = state appellate judges; 3 = state trial court judges; 4 = prosecuting attorneys; 5 = public defenders; 6 = private attorneys; 7 = forensic psychiatrists; 8 = forensic psychologists; 9 = state mental health directors

The prosecuting attorneys' responses deviated from the others even more dramatically on the issue of whether society is adequately protected by having defendants who are found not guilty by reason of insanity released on medical-clinical authority. As shown in Table 5.15, only 22 percent of the prosecutors believe that society is adequately protected in such circumstances—as opposed to 80 and 76 percent of the public defenders and the NACDL, and 46 percent of all the judges.

It is interesting that a smaller percentage of the mental health professionals believe society is adequately protected by their decisions than do the defense attorneys.

Toward the end of the survey, we asked respondents for their views on such general issues as whether the insanity defense is a loophole that allows too many guilty defendants to go free; whether it is a defense used mainly by the rich; whether, in their view, the insanity defense has been introduced more frequently in the past 15 or so years than in earlier times; and whether it has been used effectively by the defense. Finally, we polled the respondents for their views on whether the courts ought to retain or abolish the defense of insanity.

As reported in Table 5.16, more than 90 percent of the defense attorneys and more than 80 percent of the psychiatrists and psychologists disagreed—the majority of them strongly—that the insanity defense is a loophole that allows too many guilty defendants to go free. The prosecuting attorneys' responses were much more evenly distributed on this issue than were those of the defense attorneys; and the judges' views were closer to those of the prosecuting attorneys than they were to the defense attorneys or the psychiatrists and psychologists.

The one question on the entire survey about which the prosecuting and defense attorneys expressed similar views is the belief that the insanity defense is a rich person's defense. It may not be surprising that almost half of the prosecuting attorneys hold that view; but it is startling that 60 and 55 percent of the public defenders and the NACDL believe it as well. As shown in Table 5.17, a majority of the judges and mental health professionals neither agreed nor disagreed with the observation.

Most of the experts in every category believe that there has been no change in the frequency with which the defense of insanity has been raised during the past 15 or so years.[6] Among the few who did

Table 5.15
Society Regarded to Be Adequately Protected by Having Clinicians Decide When NGRI Defendants Should Be Released, by Respondent Category (in percent)

Adequately Protected	1	2	3	4	5	6	7	8	9	Combined
Yes	55.2	32.7	48.6	22.4	80.3	76.2	68.5	51.2	69.3	52.7
No, minimum term should be imposed	26.5	30.9	33.5	58.6	6.6	7.2	5.6	22.0	15.4	27.8
Other	12.2	34.6	15.2	17.0	11.5	15.0	25.9	24.4	11.5	17.4
No answer	6.1	1.8	2.7	2.0	1.6	1.6	–	2.4	3.8	2.1
Total	100	100	100	100	100	100	100	100	100	100
(N)	(49)	(55)	(328)	(147)	(61)	(167)	(54)	(41)	(26)	(928)

Legend: 1 = district and appellate federal judges; 2 = state appellate judges; 3 = state trial court judges; 4 = prosecuting attorneys; 5 = public defenders; 6 = private attorneys; 7 = forensic psychiatrists; 8 = forensic psychologists; 9 = state mental health directors

Table 5.16
Insanity Defense Regarded as Loophole, by Respondent Category (in percent)

Insanity Defense Is a Loophole	1	2	3	4	5	6	7	8	9	Combined
Strongly agree	6.1	5.5	8.2	19.0	–	1.8	–	–	3.8	7.0
Agree	18.4	12.7	16.5	28.6	3.3	–	9.3	2.4	7.7	13.1
Neither agree nor disagree	18.4	18.2	22.0	20.4	1.6	5.4	9.3	12.2	7.7	15.4
Disagree	32.7	38.2	38.4	25.9	24.6	25.1	22.2	29.3	30.8	31.3
Strongly disagree	16.3	23.6	14.0	5.4	68.9	67.7	59.2	56.1	42.3	31.9
Other	2.0	–	–	–	–	–	–	–	3.0	0.1
No answer	6.1	1.8	0.9	0.7	1.6	–	–	–	4.7	1.2
Total	100	100	100	100	100	100	100	100	100	100
(N)	(49)	(55)	(328)	(147)	(61)	(167)	(54)	(41)	(26)	(928)

Legend: 1 = district and appellate federal judges; 2 = state appellate judges; 3 = state trial court judges; 4 = prosecuting attorneys; 5 = public defenders; 6 = private attorneys; 7 = forensic psychiatrists; 8 = forensic psychologists; 9 = state mental health directors

Table 5.17

Insanity Defense Regarded as a Rich Person's Defense, by Respondent Category (in percent)

Insanity Defense Is a Rich Person's Defense	1	2	3	4	5	6	7	8	9	Combined
Strongly agree	4.1	3.6	6.1	20.4	21.3	16.8	1.9	12.2	3.8	11.0
Agree	32.7	25.5	23.5	27.9	39.3	38.3	29.6	22.0	30.9	29.0
Neither agree nor disagree	20.4	18.2	24.1	17.7	13.1	13.2	9.3	12.2	26.9	18.5
Disagree	30.6	32.7	31.7	25.9	11.5	17.4	27.8	31.7	11.5	26.1
Strongly disagree	2.0	20.0	11.0	5.4	3.3	6.0	22.2	19.5	15.4	9.9
Other	2.0	–	2.7	2.0	8.2	7.2	9.3	–	7.7	4.0
No answer	8.2	–	0.9	0.7	3.3	1.1	–	2.4	3.8	1.5
Total	100	100	100	100	100	100	100	100	100	100
(N)	(49)	(55)	(328)	(147)	(61)	(167)	(54)	(41)	(26)	(928)

Legend: 1 = district and appellate federal judges; 2 = state appellate judges; 3 = state trial court judges; 4 = prosecuting attorneys; 5 = public defenders; 6 = private attorneys; 7 = forensic psychiatrists; 8 = forensic psychologists; 9 = state mental health directors

Table 5.18

Success of Insanity Defense during the Past 15 Years, by Respondent Category (in percent)

Opinion on Success of Defense	1	2	3	4	5	6	7	8	9	Combined
More successful	4.1	20.0	18.0	25.9	—	7.8	20.4	2.4	23.1	15.2
No change in verdict	61.2	65.5	63.8	53.7	41.0	47.3	50.0	51.2	61.6	56.3
Less successful	14.3	12.7	13.1	14.3	55.7	38.9	29.6	39.0	11.5	22.8
Other	10.2	1.8	3.6	2.0	3.3	3.6	—	4.9	—	3.3
No answer	10.2	—	1.5	4.1	—	2.4	—	2.4	3.8	2.4
Total	100	100	100	100	100	100	100	100	100	100
(N)	(49)	(55)	(328)	(147)	(61)	(167)	(54)	(41)	(26)	(928)

Legend: 1 = district and appellate federal judges; 2 = state appellate judges; 3 = state trial court judges; 4 = prosecuting attorneys; 5 = public defenders; 6 = private attorneys; 7 = forensic psychiatrists; 8 = forensic psychologists; 9 = state mental health directors

Table 5.19
Courts Should Retain Insanity Defense, by Respondent Category (in percent)

Favor Retention	1	2	3	4	5	6	7	8	9	Combined
No, abolish	6.1	5.5	8.2	21.8	1.6	0.6	1.9	—	3.8	7.4
Yes, retain	63.3	76.6	70.7	42.2	90.2	89.8	87.0	73.1	69.3	72.6
Yes, retain, but with limitations	22.4	16.4	16.5	34.6	6.6	7.8	11.1	22.0	19.2	16.8
No answer	8.2	1.5	4.6	1.4	1.6	1.8	—	4.9	7.7	3.2
Total	100	100	100	100	100	100	100	100	100	100
(N)	(49)	(55)	(328)	(147)	(61)	(167)	(54)	(41)	(26)	(928)

Legend: 1 = district and appellate federal judges; 2 = state appellate judges; 3 = state trial court judges; 4 = prosecuting attorneys; 5 = public defenders; 6 = private attorneys; 7 = forensic psychiatrists; 8 = forensic psychologists; 9 = state mental health directors

think so, a higher percentage believe it has been raised more rather than less frequently, as reported in Table 5.18. Most of them also believe that there has been no change in how successful the defense has been, during the past 15 years. By professional status, there was considerable disagreement among those who did perceive a difference. Less than 10 percent of the defense attorneys—for example—believe that the insanity defense has been used with greater success during the past 15 years, as opposed to 50 percent who believe it has been used less successfully. Almost twice as many prosecuting attorneys perceive the defense as having been more rather than less successful. It appears as if each side is acknowledging its adversary's greater effectiveness.

Like the defense attorneys, more psychiatrists and psychologists also perceive the defense as becoming less rather than more successful. Across the categories of judges, responses are divided almost evenly. Slightly more federal judges see the defense as having been less rather than more successful, while the appellate and state trial judges are somewhat more likely to see the defense of insanity as having had greater success.

Finally, on the ultimate question—"Should the court retain or abolish the defense of insanity?"—most of the respondents in every category (even the prosecutors) favor retention. Table 5.19 shows that less than 10 percent of the judges, mental health professionals, and defense attorneys advocate abolishing the defense of insanity. Only 17 percent of the respondents as a whole would place restrictions on its use. The prosecutors are the deviant group. Thirty-five percent favor restrictions, and 22 percent advocate abolishing it completely.

THE PUBLIC'S VS. THE EXPERTS' OPINIONS

This section compares our 1984 survey of experts' responses against a 1982 public opinion poll conducted in Delaware (and—in regard to abolition—against a 1982 national public opinion survey, as well).

In response to the question:

How strongly do you agree or disagree with the following statement? The insanity defense is a loophole that allows too many guilty people to go free. Do you strongly agree, agree, disagree, strongly disagree, or neither agree nor disagree with that statement?[7]

Results from the two sets of respondents (Delaware public and expert) are shown below.

The Insanity Defense Is a Loophole

Response	Delaware	Expert
	(in percent)	
Strongly agree, and agree	87.1	7.0
		13.1
Neither agree nor disagree	6.1	15.4
Disagree, and strongly disagree	6.8	31.3
		31.9
No answer	—	1.3

The public expressed strong consensus that the insanity defense is a loophole that allows persons who are guilty to go free. Only one in five of the experts perceive the defense in that way. Even the prosecuting attorneys—who are most skeptical about the insanity defense—did not share the public's evaluation. Forty-eight percent of them—compared to 87 percent of the general public—viewed the insanity defense as a loophole (see Table 5.16).

The experts and the public are in much closer agreement on the matter of whether the insanity defense is a rich person's defense, whose outcome may vary depending on the resources available to the defendant to hire expert witnesses and to prepare his or her defense.

The Insanity Defense Is a Rich Person's Defense

Response	Delaware	Expert
	(in percent)	
Strongly agree	5.4	11.0
Agree	33.5	29.0
Neither agree nor disagree	—	18.5
Disagree	58.5	26.1
Strongly disagree	2.5	9.9
Other	—	4.0
No answer	—	1.5

Forty percent of the experts[8] and 39 percent of the Delaware public believe that rich people have an advantage in being able to implement a defense of insanity, because they have the resources to support it. We noted earlier with some surprise that more of the defense attorneys than the prosecutors agreed with that observation.

Public opinion in Delaware demonstrated less confidence in psychiatrists' ability to determine legal insanity than did most of experts. As shown by the percentages below, twice as many respondents in the Delaware survey believed that psychiatrists could *not* (save for once in a while) determine legal insanity as those who thought they could (all or most of the time).

Extent to Which Psychiatrists Can Determine Whether Defendant is Legally Insane

Response	Delaware	Expert
	(in percent)	
All of the time	1.0	0.2
Most of the time	17.1	38.2
Some of the time	47.0	43.9
Once in a while	23.5	11.2
Never	11.4	4.6
No answer, and other	—	2.1

The prosecutors' reactions matched the public's beliefs about psychiatrists' ability almost exactly. Note in Table 5.7 that 17 percent of the prosecutors thought that, most of the time, psychiatrists could determine whether the defendant was legally insane.

Finally, on the issue of whether the plea of insanity ought to be abolished, we were able to compare the experts' opinions against a national public opinion survey[8] and the Delaware survey. The data show that the experts were much more disposed toward retaining the defense of insanity than were either the Delaware or national samples. On balance, even the prosecutors—who favored abolition more than any of the other experts—were more favorable toward retention of the defense than the public was (see Table 5.19).

Should the Insanity Defense Be Abolished?

Response	Experts	National	Delaware
		(in percent)	
Abolish	7.4	66.0	49.9
Limit	16.8	–	–
Retain	72.6	24.0	51.1
No answer or no opinion	3.2	10.0	–

Remember, however, that the public was polled shortly after the *Hinckley* case had been decided; and, as shown by the responses below, the public largely felt that John Hinckley should have been found guilty.

As you know, the jury decided yesterday that Hinckley was insane and therefore not legally responsible for having wounded Reagan and three other men back in March of 1981. Do you think that justice was done in the trial of John Hinckley or not?

	Percent
Justice was done	16
Justice was not done	76
Unsure	8

Unfortunately, the legitimacy of the defense of insanity is often questioned only after a horrendous event followed by a sensational trial has occurred. At those times, most people are anxious to abolish it, in the fantasy that—by so doing—they will also do away with the heinous act that has been committed in its name. It may well be that the public's reactions to the defense of insanity would have been closer to those of the experts if they had been asked to consider the issue in the absence of a dramatic trial and a horrendous event.

NOTES

1. Specifically, the categories of respondents are state trial court judges, state appellate judges, federal district judges, federal appellate judges, prose-

cuting attorneys, public defenders, members of the National Association of Criminal Defense Lawyers (NACDL), forensic psychiatrists, psychologists, and state mental health program directors.

2. The rate of return for each category of respondents was as follows: federal judges (district and appellate), 39.5 percent; state trial judges, 38.7 percent; state appellate judges, 38.9 percent; NACDL, 44.6 percent; public defenders, 42.1 percent; prosecutors, 39.3 percent; forensic psychiatrists, 37.5 percent; forensic psychologists, 56.2 percent; and state mental health directors, 52 percent.

3. The survey was conducted before the passage of the Insanity Defense Reform Act. Therefore, that standard was not included as one of the options.

4. We subsequently examined all of the responses according to the rule of law applicable in the jurisdiction in which they practiced; and, therefore, we know that there were no differences on any of the other issues posed in the survey.

5. Data are not presented in tabular form.

6. Data are not presented in tabular form.

7. The same question with the same response choices appeared in the survey conducted in 1982 by Valerie Hans and Dan Slater in New Castle County, Delaware, and in the 1984 survey of experts conducted by the authors.

8. The national public survey was conducted by a national polling organization, Audits and Surveys, on July 13, 1982.

6

Alternatives: The Movement to Abolish the Defense, and the Guilty But Mentally Ill Verdict
(with the assistance of Paul Schneiderman and David Frankel)

This chapter begins with an examination of the history of the movement to abolish the insanity defense. In the first section the focus is on early legislative reform efforts and judicial opposition to the special defense. The next sections contain a review of the major arguments against the insanity defense—in which both the ideological and procedural objections are discussed—and conclude with an analysis of the new proposals for reform and modern attempts at abolition. The chapter then introduces the guilty but mentally ill statutes, and examines their effectiveness and impact on posttrial commitment procedures.

THE ABOLITION MOVEMENT

Early History

The movement to abolish the defense of insanity was part of the larger penal reform movement of the late nineteenth century, which virtually ended the long prevailing institutions of corporal and capital punishment. In fact, Norval Morris argues that "[h]istorically the defense of insanity made good sense. The executioner infused it with meaning. And in a larger sense, all criminal sanctions did so too, since they made no pretense of being rehabilitative."[1]

The first significant attempt to abolish the defense did not occur until the first quarter of the twentieth century. In 1909, the State of Washington enacted legislation that, in effect, not only abolished insanity as a separate defense, but also excluded all evidence of mental abnormality from the trial of guilt. The 1909 statute states:

> It shall be no defense to a person charged with the commission of a
> crime, that at the time of its commission, he was unable by reason of
> insanity, idiocy, or imbecility to comprehend the nature and quality of
> the act committed, or to understand that it was wrong; or that he was
> affected with a morbid propensity to commit prohibited acts, nor shall
> any testimony or other proof thereof be admitted into evidence.[2]

Instead, the legislature mandated that the issue of insanity was to be decided by the trial court, without a jury: "[I]f it found the accused insane at the time of the offense, [it] was to order him committed to a mental institution."[3]

Likewise, in 1911, Dr. William White proposed that the duty of the jury should be limited to determining whether the defendant was the true assailant. In essence, Dr. White's proposal and the Washington statute would have placed the determination of type and length of confinement solely in the hands of the presiding judge and psychiatrist at sentencing.[4]

The Washington statute was challenged a year after its passage, in *State v. Strasbury.*[5] The state supreme court held the statute to be unconstitutional. It stated:

> That since the mental responsibility of a defendant was a fact bearing
> on guilt, it was an issue to be tried by the jury. The court reasoned that
> the right of trial by jury must mean that "the accused has the right to
> have the jury pass upon every substantive fact going to the question of
> his guilt or innocence."[6]

The overruling of the Washington statute did not mark the end of the movement to abolish the insanity defense. In 1922, California's Chief Justice Curtis D. Wilbur called for its abolition and the exclusion of all evidence of mental illness from the trial of guilt. In an article featured in the *American Bar Association Journal*, Wilbur maintained that "the defense of insanity is a trap for the insane, and a way of escape for the sane."[7] He explained that the truly insane are usually convicted because of the utter barbarity of their crimes. The sane defendant—he argued—is often acquitted by reason of insanity because he or she acted no differently than the jurors would have acted under the same circumstances.

Six years later, in 1928, U.S. Supreme Court Justice Benjamin Cardozo attacked the formulation of the defense for its hypocrisy. He asserted that "if insanity is not to be a defense, let us say so frankly and even brutally, but let us not mock ourselves with a definition that palters with reality. Such a method is neither good science nor good law."[8]

Also in 1928, Mississippi enacted legislation stipulating that:

> insanity of the defendant at the time of the commission of the crime shall not be a defense against indictments for murder and the courts shall so instruct the jury in trials for murder.[9]

Upon conviction, the offender was to be imprisoned for life, unless the governor--through gubernatorial authority alone--ordered the offender to be transferred to a mental institution. Commenting on the Mississippi statute, Sheldon Glueck argued that the objective of the legislation was to "minimize the well known evil resulting from the all too frequent interposition of the defense in homicide cases where no other defense is available."[10]

In 1931, the constitutionality of the Mississippi statute was considered by the state supreme court in *Sinclair v. State.*[11] Writing for the majority, Justice Elderidge observed that, along with being cruel and unusual, the punishment of an insane individual does not serve the goal of deterrence. The court concluded that a defendant should not be precluded from introducing all relevant evidence into the trial.

Additionally, a 1928 Louisiana statute provided that, when the issue of insanity was raised, "the defendant was to be tried before a lunacy commission which could commit if the defendant was found insane, or order a trial if he was found sane, at which trial the defendant would be precluded from raising the insanity defense."[12] This statute--like the Washington and Mississippi statutes before it--was held unconstitutional in that it violated due process and the right to a trial by jury.

Philosophical Doubts

Supporters of the insanity plea argue that its purpose is to distinguish between those who can be held responsible for their criminal conduct and those who cannot be held justly responsible for

such behavior because of mental illness. The law must make a distinction between those who *would* not and those who *could* not conform
their conduct to the requirements of law. In this manner, the criminal justice system can reassure itself that only those who freely
choose their criminal behavior are the ones who are punished.

Yet, abolitionists point out that, even if the supporters' assertion
is correct, the insanity plea—as a tool for discriminating between
those who could not and those who would not—is highly ineffective.
Barbara Wooton—for example—has noted that

> [t]he distinction between illness and evil is anything but clear cut. . . .
> The worst feature of all the formulae that have been tried is their insist-
> ence on a hard and fast and totally unrealistic line between the sheep
> and the goats.[13]

In her view, such tests have only served to create a false dichotomy
between the responsible and the nonresponsible. Those who support
abolition have argued that, within crime itself, there exists a great
scope of human capacity for evilness, as well as for self-control.[14]

Some abolitionists maintain that the distinction between "mad"
and "bad" *cannot* be made. They argue that no objective criteria to
do so have yet been formulated. In their view, there is still "no accurate scientific basis for measuring one's capacity for self control or
for calibrating the impairment of such a capacity."[15] It is relatively
impossible—they claim—to discriminate between an irresistible impulse and one that was simply not resisted. In short, we cannot objec-
tively determine whether an offender was undeterrable or merely
undeterred. On this point, Dr. Stanton Samenow attests: "I can't
even tell you what I was thinking about a week ago, or a year ago, let
alone what someone else was thinking."[16]

Thomas Szasz, a leading abolitionist, argues that the insane are
no different from anybody else, and cannot be separated out from
the rest of society. He maintains that it is absurd to assume "that just
as human beings can be divided into two classes by gender, one male
and the other female, they can be divided into classes by psychiatric
criteria, one sane, the other insane."[17]

Most abolitionists believe that the distinction between the mad
and the bad *should not* be made. They argue that no matter how
helpful such a categorization may be in the treatment of the mentally disordered, it is irrelevant to the criminal process. Such categori-

zations—in their view—serve to soothe the public conscience, and to detract attention from the serious failings of the criminal justice system. Norval Morris observes that "the special defense [is] a tribute to our capacity to pretend to a moral position while pursuing profoundly different practices."[18]

By furnishing a select group with an excuse, the system appears merciful and just. But critics maintain that, by providing the opportunity for exculpation and treatment to the few, it denies such considerations to the many. The number of those acquitted by reason of insanity—let alone the number of those who invoke the defense—bears scant resemblance to the actual number of mentally ill offenders caught up in the system.[19] Abolitionists further assert that the elimination of the insanity defense would actually call our attention to the pervasiveness of the problem, and help us to develop effective measures for dealing with the mentally ill offender.

Thomas Szasz also argues that—in effect—the assignment of the label "mad" to the criminal offender robs him of his human dignity. Szasz believes that the criminal justice system should regard all offenders as responsible human beings capable of appreciating and controlling their own actions. Commenting on Szasz's views, William Raspberry of the *Washington Post* points out:

> [I]n all but the rarest of cases, we ought to assume that people—even people with mental problems—are responsible for what they intentionally do. For example, John Hinckley, Jr. obviously intended to kill the President. He understood what he was doing, desired its outcome, and knew that it was prohibited. It is simply not the case that Hinckley, and those like him, are any less guilty than other criminals.[20]

Herbert Goldstein, coauthor of "Abolish the Insanity Defense—Why Not?," has also argued that the mad offender should not be separated from the bad offender. He contends that "there are remarkably few persons who have committed seriously harmful acts whose condemnation will not serve *some* function of the criminal law."[21]

Supporters and opponents of the defense of insanity find themselves on opposite sides on the deterrence issue. Abolitionists believe that the conviction and punishment of the mentally ill offender serves both specific and general deterrence. An offender is specifically deterred insofar as incapacitation renders him incapable of committing socially harmful acts while incarcerated. Moreover, utilitarians reason that the offender becomes reluctant to commit any subsequent offenses, because the threat of future punishment weighs heavy on his mind. However, supporters of the insanity defense have questioned the validity of that contention. They argue that persons who are severely mentally ill cannot be deterred through threats of punishment.

Abolitionists counter by pointing out that the mentally ill do—in fact—respond to threats of sanction, and can be controlled through orders and threats.[22] Furthermore, they maintain that general deterrence is best served when insane offenders are included among those penalized for criminal behavior. H. L. A. Hart has pointed out that, with the elimination of the insanity defense, "many people who now take a chance in the hope that they will bring themselves, if discovered, within these exampling provisions would in fact be deterred."[23]

The punishment of all criminals—regardless of any incapacitating conditions—would send a distinct message to all potential offenders that their chances of avoiding the punitive arm of the law are slim. As Baruch Brody has noted, "the more criminals that we punish, the more seriously the threat of punishment will be taken."[24] Herbert Morris believes that all human beings who engage in criminal conduct have the inalienable right to be punished. Denial of such punishment is an abridgment of the fundamental right to be treated as a human being.[25] In the same vein, Szasz has maintained that those exonerated of their crimes by reason of insanity face a harsher penalty than if they had been judged sane, because then—at least—their humanity would have been acknowledged. An example of Szasz's convictions may be observed in his testimony at the trial of a young woman accused of infanticide. Without having examined the defendant, Szasz testified that she was "simply stupid, evil, and bad," not insane.[26]

Assessing the problem from the perspective of the victim, Jonathan Rowe has noted that "you don't have to believe that retribution is the whole purpose of the law to acknowledge that something very basic in us requires that when someone causes serious harm to someone else, he should pay."[27] Obviously, crimes committed by persons who are mentally ill are no less damaging to their victims than crimes committed by "evil" perpetrators.

Still others who advocate abolition of the defense of insanity assert that the law should not discriminate between the "mad" and the "bad" insofar as distinctions between the "addicted" and the "bad," the "stupid" and the "bad," and the "deprived" and the "bad" are not recognized under the law in decisions regarding the assignment of blame and responsibility. In providing a special defense for insanity—they argue—the law unduly emphasizes the psychological over the social.

Even Judge David Bazelon—once a strong supporter of the defense—has noted the bias. He contends that "[t]here is little difference between a compulsion to commit crimes because of psychological reasons . . . and an equally strong compulsion grounded in socioeconomic conditions."[28] If this is indeed the case, Norval Morris wonders why a defense of living in a black ghetto is not permitted. He has argued that such adverse social conditions are statistically more criminogenic than psychosis and that they just as much limit an individual's freedom of choice.[29]

Consequently, Morris reasons, any system that refuses to recognize adverse social conditions as an affirmative defense should also refuse to recognize insanity as a separate defense. In support of Morris's contention, Joseph Goldstein has asserted that "the factors which move a man to crime are too various and unfathomable. It no longer serves the needs of society because too many other factors are at work—economic, social and political—to take seriously any longer the occasional criminal trial involving the insanity defense."[30]

Procedural Concerns

The operation and administration of the insanity defense have also been the subject of criticism and attack at various levels. Within the abolitionist camp, there are those who have refused to accept any substitute proposals and who shun all revamping schemes. They contend that the defense must be completely removed from the criminal law. In support of their position, Judge Leventhal in *United States v. Brawner*[31] argued: "[W]hat should by now be clear is that the problems of the responsibility defense cannot be resolved by adopting for the standard or for the jury instructions any new formulation of words."[32]

The insanity defense has also been criticized for its arbitrary and discriminatory operation. Opponents point out that decisions to raise the plea may depend more on the seriousness of the charges, evidentiary considerations, and the social status of the accused than on the defendant's psychological state at the time of the alleged offense. The insanity plea is rarely invoked as a defense to relatively minor offenses. The *Report of the President's Commission on Crime in the District of Columbia* notes that those misdemeanants adjudged not guilty by reason of insanity in the District of Columbia between 1958 and 1965 spent an average of 15.8 months confined to St. Elizabeth's Mental Hospital.[33] Had those same offenders pleaded guilty to the charges against them, the maximum penalty they could have received is 12 months in jail.

In addition, the prosecution may raise the insanity plea in many jurisdictions in cases where evidence strong enough to convict is lacking. Jonathan Rowe cites a study finding that the prosecutors in several jurisdictions invoked the insanity plea more often than the defense. Abolitionists argue that the state thus gains indefinite control over the mentally disordered offender, without having to prove his or her guilt beyond a reasonable doubt.[34]

Many of those in favor of abolition contend that the defense is discriminatory insofar as it benefits the rich more than the poor and the white more than the black. Seymour Halleck has pointed out that the defense is disproportionately invoked by those who can afford favorable psychiatric testimony, while the "fate of the indigent defendant is determined by the report of the court appointed psychiatrist."[35] Rowe explains that an upper class defendant who commits an atrocious act is more likely to be seen as crazy than is the lower class defendant for whom that type of crime is considered closer to the norm.[36] In the same vein, Abraham Halpern has noted that, although whites make up only 31 percent of the prison population in the state that he studied, they account for more than 64 percent of those found not guilty on grounds of insanity.[37] Opponents of the plea argue that these statistics clearly represent a racial bias in successful insanity pleas.

Psychiatry and the Mental Health System

Still another source of dissatisfaction with the insanity defense has been its reliance on the testimony of psychiatrists. Abolitionists charge that the disciplines of law and psychiatry are incompatible: the differences between the free will precepts of the law and the determinist ideology of psychiatry cannot be reconciled. Moreover, they assert that the criminal trial is already a highly complicated and intricate process. There is no need to further burden the court with testimony from individuals who neither believe in the essential tenets of the criminal law nor can agree on the meaning of the key operational terms of their discipline.

Difficulties with psychiatric testimony were noted as early as 1904 by Judge Edge. He felt that he could have "no faith in expert evidence called by the parties. They might be the best of experts but their statements are as wide as the poles asunder."[38] A half century or so later, Thomas Szasz wrote that psychiatric testimony is simply psychiatric opinion. Psychiatric fact does not exist.[39] And most recently—in the 1980s—the lack of faith in expert testimony was cited as one of the chief factors leading to abolition of the defense of insanity by the Montana legislature.

We noted in Chapter 3 that, while some mental health professionals make their living out of courtroom appearances, the majority would rather stay out of the courtroom. The majority claim that the criminal process puts them in an "unnatural adversarial role" and that their usefulness is usurped by the overriding goals of the criminal justice system. The language of the legal responsibility tests—for example—artificially constrains their testimony, by not allowing them to present the full picture concerning the mental condition of the accused. John Palimore contends that "an adversarial system is an appropriate method for ascertaining whether the accused committed the act or not, but such a system is not suited to make determinations regarding an individual's mental condition."[40]

Some have also objected to the language of the special verdict. They argue that the verdict of "not guilty by reason of insanity" gives the appearance of complete forgiveness. The verdict—they believe—is countertherapeutic, because it frees the mentally disordered offender from taking full responsibility for his actions. The court—they note—imparts a clear message to the mentally disordered acquittee: "Although you have committed a heinous crime, it was not your fault. You are excused." In effect, this allows the offender to ignore the seriousness of his conduct and to believe that he is beyond the domain of the law.

If the goal of therapy is to get the individual to take responsibility for his or her actions and gain control of his or her life, then—as Richard Allen recommended to the National Commission on Reform of Federal Criminal Laws—mentally ill offenders must be treated "as responsible for their conduct rather than as helpless victims of the 'sickness.'"[41]

Still another "mental health" source of dissatisfaction with the insanity defense is that it places excessive burdens on psychiatric resources and hospital space. Under the automatic commitment provisions, hospitals must provide space for a number of acquittees who are unresponsive to therapy yet require incarceration. This practice—they claim—has resulted in "a fundamental unfairness not only to the offender but to the other patients and staff as well."[42]

David F. Leroy, a leading Idaho abolitionist, has argued that, when the insanity defense was available in Idaho, it took up an inordinate amount of time and money in relation to its actual usefulness. Leroy claims that, of the 250,000 criminal cases recorded in Idaho between 1978 and 1981, an average of only 245 defendants per year served notice of their intention to use the defense. These defendants were given psychiatric evaluations by the Idaho Department of Health and Welfare—a procedure that was expensive and time consuming. In the end, no more than 12 of all those examined were acquitted each year by reason of insanity.[43]

A survey conducted in 1973 by a U.S. Senate committee investigating criminal reform legislation found that, of those surveyed, 62 percent of the state departments of mental health favored abolition of the insanity defense. As reasoning for their support of abolition, many stressed the heavy burden that the defense placed on their staffs, as well as the valuable time it took away from treatment.[44]

Seymour Halleck has noted that—regardless of its intentions—the administration of the insanity defense "accomplishes little insofar as it usually results in offenders being institutionalized anyway."[45] Those in favor of this practice believe that a postacquittal commitment is necessary, insofar as it provides treatment for the mentally ill. But Norval Morris has stressed that it is erroneous "to assume benevolence, to assume that there are more psychiatric resources, better physical conditions, and earlier release practices pursuant to a finding of not guilty on grounds of insanity than pursuant to a conviction."[46] Moreover, the dissenting opinion in *Sinclair v. State*[47] observed that a place of confinement—regardless of what it may be called—remains a prison, and is intended as such for all those held there.[48]

Finally, many abolitionists have expressed concern over the double stigma produced when an insane acquittee is committed to a mental institution. They maintain that, while responsible offenders are solely stigmatized as "bad," the nonresponsible offender is labeled as both "bad" and "mad." In fact, Morris documents that authorities in mental hospitals "regard their patients who have been arrested and charged with a crime as both insane and criminal, 'mad' and 'bad.'"[49] In addition, he believes that these patients have also come to identify themselves as both mad and bad. In short, abolitionists argue that the insanity defense is actually a means of affecting indefinite control and harsh stigmatization on those who suffer from the wrath of our ambivalence.

Modern Attempts and New Proposals

Although early attempts to abolish the insanity defense failed, advocates continue to press for abolition. Three schools of thought have emerged. All three maintain that the separate defense of insanity should be abolished. However, the groups diverge over the issue of mental illness and its relationship to the legal concept of "mens rea" (the state of mind component of crimes).

The first group advocates a strict mens rea approach, whereby all evidence of mental illness would be restricted from entering into the determination of the accused's state of mind at the time of the alleged misconduct. They argue that the issue of mental disease or defect is simply irrelevant to the legal inquiry. Mental illness should only be considered at the dispositional stage of the trial.

The second group believes in a liberal interpretation of the mens rea doctrine. Unlike the first group, they maintain that every substantive fact should be considered relevant to the establishment of the defendant's guilt or innocence. Clearly, mental illness would constitute an important consideration in this context.

The third group argues that the legal concept of mens rea should be wholly abandoned. As such, the presentation of mental illness would be considered immaterial to the determination of whether the accused was the true transgressor or not.

Those who follow the first school of thought maintain that the defense of insanity should be eliminated from the trial of guilt. However, mens rea would still remain a necessary condition for the establishment of criminal responsibility. According to Norval Morris— a leading advocate of this strict mens rea approach—"[T]he accused's mental condition should be relevant to the question of whether he did or did not, at the time of the act, have the prohibited mens rea of the crime of which he is charged."[50]

Issues regarding mental disorder would only be relevant to the postconviction disposition. Abolitionists argue that, after the issue of guilt has been settled, then mental health professionals can make their greatest contribution to the legal system. In the 1972 *Brawner* case, an amicus curiae brief filed by the American Psychiatric Association called for the removal of the psychiatrist from any participation in the determination of criminal responsibility.[51]

The Swedish system works under a similar strict mens rea approach. In Sweden, the "responsible/nonresponsible" dichotomy has been eliminated. Instead, the Swedish system holds all offenders— sane or insane—subject to the administration of justice: "[E]ven if it is determined that a crime was committed as a result of 'mental disease, feeble mindedness or [comparable mental malady],' the mentally ill offender nevertheless is subject to a sanction."[52] Accordingly, evidence of mental illness is prohibited from entering the trial of guilt.

This position is similar to those adopted by the Washington, Mississippi, and Louisiana legislatures, as described at the beginning of this chapter. Those statutes were all held unconstitutional. Nevertheless, proponents of this strict mens rea approach do not fear for its constitutionality. In defense of this position, Morris has pointed to the 1968 Supreme Court decision in *Powell v. Texas*[53]—in which the Court found that the statute in question did not violate the Eighth Amendment, since it punished an act, not the mere status of the person committing the act. By analogy—Morris has argued—it would be cruel and unusual punishment to convict a criminal defendant of being mentally ill, but it would not be cruel and unusual punishment to convict a mentally ill person of a crime he committed, as long as the state proves the requisite mens rea of the crime.[54] Still others who defend the constitutionality of the strict mens rea approach point to the U.S. Supreme Court decisions in *Leland v. Oregon*[55] and *Patterson v. New York*,[56] where the Court indicated that insanity is *not* the negation of mens rea. In other words, guilt can be established regardless of the defendant's mental illness at the time he committed the crime.

The second school of thought takes a more liberal mens rea approach. Its proponents argue that a separate defense of insanity is superfluous. For example, Goldstein and Katz maintain that the "insanity defense may not be needed at all, since lay evidence and psychiatric testimony as to mental disorder could have come into evidence on the *mens rea* issue."[57] Accordingly, all issues relevant to mens rea should be presented in the trial of guilt. In fact, Raymond Spring has pointed out that Section 4.02 of the American Law Institute's Model Penal Code holds that the evidence of a mental disease or defect is admissible whenever it is relevant to prove that the defendant did or did not have the state of mind that is an element of the offense.[58] Proponents of this approach argue that this formulation avoids the constitutional difficulties of earlier state efforts to abolish the insanity defense.

Many who are opposed to this approach argue that the liberal mens rea proposal would effectively expand—rather than limit—the role of the mental health expert in the courtroom. Yet, the American Medical Association—in its decision to advocate abolition of the insanity defense—has contended that, under the liberal mens rea approach,

> expert testimony regarding the defendant's mental impairment . . . would be relevant to the extent that it negates the minimal functional capacity required to form the requisite intent. Psychiatric testimony describing the defendant's impaired capacity to appreciate the gravity of the act, or to control his behavior, would merely explain rather than negate the existence of his conscious intent, and thus would not constitute admissible evidence. Nor would expert evidence be admissible to show that an actor's consciously entertained *mens rea* was the product of an unconscious disease process.[59]

Consequently, supporters of this position argue that the main source of contradictory and befuddling expert testimony would be eliminated from the courtroom. And, more importantly—they believe—since the issue of mens rea would be defined in terms of the cognitive functioning of the conscious mind, its determination should be well within the wisdom of the community.[60] Thus, the jury should have little or no need for expert testimony to help it reach a fair decision.

Under this liberal mens rea approach, evidence of mental disease or defect strong enough to raise a reasonable doubt in the minds of jurors would—in essence—result in an outright acquittal. The result—they claim—would be positive, since it would avoid the hypocrisy of automatic commitment. Abolitionists argue that many of those who are hospitalized are clearly not there for treatment, but are kept solely for the protection of the community. Under the liberal mens rea proposal, this would no longer be the case. Richard Singer sees it as providing "a double gain for the defendant: he can both avoid incarceration and demonstrate that he did not have the mental state necessary for conviction."[61]

But, what if the evidence of the accused's mental disorder is not strong enough to negate mens rea? Then—advocates of the second school of thought maintain—such evidence presented in the trial of guilt would be considered as mitigating circumstances, to be reflected in the sentencing disposition. If the court finds that the guilty defendant is so mentally disordered—or was, at the time of his unlawful conduct—it may choose to authorize treatment, rather than imprisonment. Moreover—the American Medical Association points out—in such cases, it is wise to forgo retribution in favor of treatment for the offender and protection to the public.[62]

There have been several attempts to replace the defense of insanity with the liberal mens rea model. In 1973, the Nixon administration proposed such a move as part of its War on Crime. The proposal stated:

> It is a defense to a prosecution under any federal statute that the defendant, as a result of mental disease or defect, lacked the state of mind required as an element of the offense charged. Mental disease or defect does not otherwise constitute a defense.[63]

Nixon believed that the insanity defense allowed criminals to escape punishment. He expressed his disagreement and anger over many of the successful insanity pleas of the early 1970s, such as the murderer acquitted because he was unable to control his "black rage," and the tax evader acquitted because he suffered from the "American Dream Syndrome." However, Nixon appears to have been most heavily influenced by the story of Gary Trapnell—an accused aircraft hijacker—"who boasted about the way he manipulated the insanity defense by feigning mental illness."[64] Consequently, Nixon argued that the liberal mens rea approach was needed to combat such "'unconscionable abuse' of the insanity defense by criminals."[65]

In 1982, a similar proposal was endorsed by the Reagan administration. The 1982 proposal would have allowed a special verdict of "not guilty *only* by reason of insanity" to be added to the established guilty and not guilty verdicts. The special verdict would be returned in a case where the defense was able to negate the requisite mens rea through presentation of the accused's mental disorder. Under the Nixon proposal, such an individual would have received a not guilty verdict and would have been set free. Under the Reagan proposal, such an individual would have been committed under the not guilty only by reason of insanity verdict.

Neither the Nixon nor the 1982 Reagan proposal passed in Congress. In fact—as noted in Chapters 1 and 2—the federal insanity defense remained unchanged until passage of the Comprehensive Crime Control Act of 1984, which restricted—but did not abolish—the affirmative defense of insanity.

More recently, however, two states have been successful in substituting the liberal mens rea proposal for the separate affirmative insanity defense. In 1979, the Montana legislature promulgated an Act to Abolish the Defense of Mental Disease or Defect in Criminal Actions and to Provide an Alternative Sentencing Procedure.[66]

The 1979 statute reads as follows:

Evidence that the defendant suffered from a mental disease or defect is admissible whenever it is relevant to prove that the defendant did or did not have the state of mind which is an element of the offense.[67]

Additionally, in 1982, Idaho enacted legislation that provided for abolition of the insanity defense. It held, however, that "[n]othing herein is intended to prevent the admission of expert evidence on the issue of *mens rea* or any state of mind which is an element of the offense, subject to the rules of evidence."[68]

Critics of the liberal mens rea approach claim that, although constitutional issues have been avoided, the liberal mens rea test has not lived up to expectation. For example, the American Medical Association contends that the role of the expert would be limited, if not totally eliminated. In Montana, however, this has not been the case. Bender reports that the "elimination of the affirmative defense of mental illness or defect has not . . . eliminated expert testimony."[69] Moreover—she argues—abolition of the insanity defense has left the courts without the appropriate guidelines necessary to constrain expert testimony. Although it is clear that experts may not make conclusive statements on the question of whether the accused possessed the requisite mens rea, they may give their opinion as to the ability of the defendant to possess a particular state of mind.[70]

Guidelines for such testimony still have not been formulated. Opponents of this position are also fearful that expert opinion has been having too great an influence on jury decisions.

As noted above, the mentally disordered defendants who present evidence strong enough to raise a reasonable doubt to negate mens rea are free under the liberal mens rea approach. But in Montana, acquitted defendants believed to present a danger to themselves or to the community are subject to the risk of indefinite civil commitment. On the other hand, convicted mentally ill offenders may receive treatment if the sentencing court finds—by clear and convincing evidence— that their mental disorders prevented them from appreciating the wrongfulness of their conduct or from conforming their conduct to the requirements of the law.[71] The terms of commitment imposed, however, may not exceed the maximum penalty prescribed for the offense. Consequently, many of those exonerated from guilt and currently committed may face harsher sentences than those found guilty.

Nevertheless, many believe that the adoption of the liberal mens rea approach to insanity in Montana and Idaho has eliminated much of the confusion and uncertainty over the issue of criminal responsibility. Supporters argue that the legislation is constitutional and adequately protects the rights of the community and the accused, and, in doing so, it has restored confidence in the criminal justice and mental health systems.

Finally, we reach the third school of thought. Its supporters are by far the most radical group among the abolitionists. Unlike Morris's strict mens rea approach and Goldstein's liberal mens rea approach, proponents of the third school have called for the complete elimination of mens rea as an element necessary for conviction. Lady Barbara Wooton—the leading advocate of this approach—has been paraphrased as saying, "[M]ens rea must go because we cannot get inside a person's mind to really see intent at work."[72] Supporters of this view perceive abolition of the insanity defense as a first step toward reaching their goal of conviction without blame or stigma.

Under this proposal, the duty of the jury would be restricted to finding whether the defendant committed the criminal act or not. The mental state of the accused would be irrelevant until the dispositional stage of the trial. At this stage, the offender would meet with a "treatment tribunal," which would "investigate and weigh a number of factors including the possibility of dangerous behavior and the likely effect of a particular decision upon the offender."[73] Clearly, the issue of mental illness would weigh heavily in the determination of an individualized "treatment plan."

Opponents believe that this approach would be unconstitutional. In defense of their argument, they point to *Morrisette v. United States*,[74] in which the Supreme Court held on the facts presented that criminal intent is an essential element to a serious crime.[75] Still others believe that the creation of such a therapeutic state would not only subject the mad and the bad to state control, but would also seek to control all nonconformists. In the end—Richard Gerber has argued—"this kind of law encroaches on all, for once guilt is abolished, so too is innocence."[76]

The movement to abolish the defense of insanity gained momentum following the acquittal of John Hinckley, as it has done after every sensational trial in which a defendant has been found not guilty by reason of insanity. The passage by Congress of the 1984 Crime Control Act lends support to some of the movement's objectives; but, at the time of writing, only the state legislatures of Montana and Idaho have abolished the insanity defense. In all of the federal and in 48 of the state jurisdictions, modified versions of the defense of insanity are still applicable.

GUILTY BUT MENTALLY ILL STATUTES

The History and Purposes of the "Guilty But Mentally Ill" Verdict

In 1974, the Michigan Supreme Court decided *People v. McQuillan*,[77] holding that automatic civil commitment for persons found "Not Guilty by Reason of Insanity" (NGRI) violated both the Due Process and Equal Protection clauses of the United States Constitution.[78] The Court further held that a verdict of NGRI only applies to the defendant's mental condition at the time of the crime; a presumption of present insanity is insufficient. Each time a NGRI verdict is returned, a hearing on the issue of the defendant's present sanity must be held.[79]

The decision of the court applied prospectively as well as retroactively, affecting nearly 270 insanity acquittees who were presently confined.[80] Within several months of the *McQuillan* decision, approximately 64 insanity acquittees were found presently sane and were discharged from confinement.[81] A short time thereafter, one of the 64 murdered his wife and another committed two rapes.[82] Public outcry was enormous.[83]

In response, the Michigan legislature enacted the nation's first "Guilty But Mentally Ill" (GBMI) statute.[84] Lawmakers viewed the statute as serving a dual purpose. First, it would reduce the number of insanity acquittals. Second, it would provide greater protection to the public by offering an alternative verdict which ensures incarceration and provides treatment for the defendant's mental illness.[85] Michigan's GBMI law is the prototype and has been followed closely by statutes in Alaska, Delaware, Georgia, Illinois, Indiana, Kentucky, New Mexico, Pennsylvania, South Dakota, and Utah.[86]

The verdict of GBMI provides an alternative to the extreme verdicts of "guilty" and "NGRI." Under a GBMI verdict, the defendant is found guilty of the offense and mentally ill at the time of the act, yet not legally insane. This approach provides for the punishment of criminal conduct as well as for the treatment of the defendant's mental illness.[87] Thus, this verdict allows the court to impose a sentence that could be given to any defendant found guilty of the same crime. However, it differs from a regular guilty verdict because it offers the defendant the possibility of mental health treatment during the term of the sentence.[88]

How the Guilty But Mentally Ill Verdict Works

The model state for GBMI legislation is Michigan, which, in 1975, became the first state to adopt a GBMI statute. All other GBMI statutes were adopted in the 1980s, apparently in response to the *Hinckley* verdict.[89] Because Michigan is the model state for GBMI legislation, the discussion concerning GBMI will be based on the Michigan statute, unless otherwise noted.

The verdict of GBMI is available when the sanity of the defendant is at issue. In Michigan, this occurs when the defense of NGRI is raised at trial.[90] Once the defendant raises this defense, the judge may instruct the jury as to the availability of four possible verdicts: guilty, not guilty, not guilty by reason of insanity, or guilty but mentally ill.[91]

For a judge or jury to render a verdict of GBMI, specific findings of fact must be made. Several states' statutes provide that a defendant "who offers a timely defense of insanity" may be found GBMI if the judge or jury determines beyond a reasonable doubt that (1) the defendant is guilty of the offense, (2) the defendant was mentally ill at the time the offense was committed, and (3) the defendant was not legally insane at the time the offense was committed.[92] However, other states, such as Georgia, provide for the possibility of a GBMI verdict in all cases "in which the defense of insanity is interposed."[93] Thus, there are some variations among the states.

In applying this "test," questions arise concerning the applicable standard of proof to be used in determining whether someone is GBMI. Some states require proof that a defendant be GBMI "beyond a reasonable doubt."[94] Others only require that the prosecution prove the defendant's guilt "beyond a reasonable doubt" and that the defendant prove by a "preponderance of the evidence" that he was mentally ill at the time of the offense.[95] Still other states are silent regarding the standard of proof to be used in determining whether a defendant is GBMI.[96]

In order for a jury to render a verdict of GBMI, it must find, as stated above, that the defendant was *not legally insane* at the time of the offense and that he was *mentally ill* at the time of the offense. The key to such a determination is differentiating between the definitions of mental illness and legal insanity. These definitions are provided by each state in the respective states' statutes. For example, Pennsylvania's definition of "mental illness" follows the American Law Institute's standard:

> As a result of mental disease or defect, [the defendant] lacked substantial capacity either to appreciate the wrongfulness of his conduct or to conform his conduct to the requirements of the law.[97]

The "insanity" standard is based on *M'Naghten* as follows:

> [The defendant], laboring under such a defect of reason, from disease of the mind, as not to know the nature and quality of the act, or if he did know it, he did not know what he was doing was wrong.[98]

Lay jurors, hearing these definitions for the first time, could easily become confused. The problem of distinguishing between two somewhat similar standards can arise in any state having a GBMI law with similar standards of insanity and mental illness.

In *People v. DeWitt*,[99] an Illinois case, the defendants argued that the distinction between legal insanity and mental illness is likely to be incomprehensible to the average juror, particularly because the definitions overlap and are poorly conceptualized.

The state's response was that such distinctions had to be made prior to GBMI legislation. Jurors were compelled to distinguish between legal insanity and mental illness in order to determine whether a defendant's state of mind exceeded the threshold for legal insanity. Using a narrow standard of vagueness under the Due Process clause ("statute may not be so vague that men of common intelligence must necessarily guess at its meaning"[100]), the court held that the statutory language provided meaningful standards for a jury to make proper findings.

Whether GBMI statutes unfairly promote "compromise verdicts" is a related issue. GBMI appeals to jurors as an attractive alternative to a verdict of NGRI. In many instances, fearing that a dangerous criminal might be set free, the jury may reach such a compromise verdict. Where there is doubt over the question of the defendant's sanity, the jury may compromise and find him GBMI rather than NGRI, even though he may be legally insane. The jury is thus able to satisfy its concern for public safety while at the same time ensuring itself that the defendant will be given treatment for his illness.[101] When questioned after their decision in the *Hinckley* case, several jurors stated that they would have preferred to reach a GBMI verdict had that option been available to them.[102] Keilitz and Fulton argue that a major intent of GBMI legislation is to help prosecutors convict defendants who otherwise would be acquitted by reason of insanity.[103] Although the GBMI verdict provides a supplementary verdict, it is often seen in practical terms as supplanting the insanity defense.

In addition to the availability of a GBMI verdict upon a plea of legal insanity, a defendant also may enter a GBMI plea. In doing this, the defendant must waive his right to a trial by jury as well as other trial rights. With permission of the prosecuting attorney, the judge may accept the defendant's plea of GBMI as an alternative to a plea of guilty. However, in Michigan, the judge may not accept the plea until he has examined psychiatric reports, held a hearing on the issue of the defendant's mental illness, and determined that the defendant was mentally ill at the time of the offense.[104] If the plea is accepted, the defendant is treated just as if the jury had returned a GBMI verdict.[105] There is some variation among the states on this issue.

In Pennsylvania, consent of the prosecuting attorney is not necessary. Also, if the plea is not accepted, the defendant may withdraw the plea and have a trial by jury.[106] The Center of Forensic Psychiatry in Michigan found that GBMI statutes are used as a plea bargaining tool, and that the GBMI plea tends to be used by sex offenders. There is little evidence in these cases that tends to show mental illness, so a chance for an NGRI verdict is slight at best. These cases are therefore bargained down to a GBMI plea. According to the National Commission on the Insanity Defense, the defendants plead GBMI in an attempt to "soften" the effect of their criminal behavior on their friends, family, and even themselves.[107]

When a defendant is ultimately found GBMI, the court will impose on the defendant any sentence permitted by law for the crime of which the defendant is convicted.[108] This may take the form of a prison sentence, jail, or probation. After a conviction in Michigan and Kentucky, a pre-sentencing psychiatric evaluation of the defendant's present mental health is required by the court before the sentence is imposed.[109] In Pennsylvania, it is required by statute.[110]

If the defendant is sent to prison, an evaluation is given by the Michigan Department of Mental Health to determine if psychiatric treatment is appropriate. Treatment may then be given by either the Department of Mental Health or the Department of Corrections. If treatment is given by the Department of Mental Health, it is on an outpatient basis and upon completion of treatment, the defendant must return to the Department of Corrections to serve out the remainder of his sentence.[111] If treatment is given by the Department of Corrections, the defendant receives treatment while in prison or jail.

When a person is found GBMI, a prison or jail sentence is not automatic. Probation is also an alternative, if the court determines that it is appropriate. In most states, probation requirements are very rigid. For example, Michigan provides that treatment is a condition of probation. Failure to continue treatment is a violation of probation. The probation period is for a minimum of five years and will not be shortened without the consideration of psychiatric reports by the sentencing court.[112]

The procedures described above have been criticized by some scholars. Professor Richard Bonnie objects to the GBMI verdict on several grounds. He argues:

> It makes no sense for commitment procedures to be triggered by a jury
> verdict based on evidence which does not even relate to the defendant's
> present mental condition. . . . Decisions about the proper *placement* of
> convicted offenders should be made after, and independent of the entry
> of the conviction, and should be based entirely on the offender's need
> for therapeutic restraint in a mental health facility.[113]

Others similarly argue that under conventional sentencing procedures
already in place, judges may order treatment for convicted persons in
need of it, and that a jury verdict relating to past mental illness is an
awkward device for making dispositional decisions concerning a person's present need for mental health treatment.

Effectiveness of GBMI Statutes

GBMI has been formulated by lawmakers as a way of reducing the
number of insanity acquittals while at the same time providing treatment for incarcerated criminals suffering from mental illness.[114] But
the question still remains whether the statutes achieve those purposes.
Is there actually a reduction in the number of insanity acquittals,
and are those convicted as GBMI receiving the treatment promised?

Concerning the first goal of the lawmakers, there has not been a
reduction in the number of people found NGRI. As noted in Chapter 1, juries have traditionally been reluctant to reach NGRI verdicts.
Successful insanity defense verdicts usually occur in uncontested
cases, based on uncontroverted expert medical findings. Mickenberg
argues that GBMI is a supplement to the insanity defense and not a
replacement for it. Defendants who would have been found NGRI
before the GBMI verdict should still be found NGRI after it. Defendants found GBMI should come from those who would otherwise have
been found guilty.[115] Opponents of GBMI statutes argue that GBMI
verdicts simply add an option that unduly complicates disposition
and creates a special subpopulation of mentally ill offenders for the
already overburdened departments of mental health and corrections.[116]

There is evidence that supports Mickenberg's thesis. In a 1982
Michigan survey, the records of all 141 GBMI defendants who
received prison sentences between 1975 and 1981 were examined.
The records of 302 insanity acquittees and 211 defendants found
guilty were also examined, and 60 attorneys who defended GBMI

cases and 60 attorneys who defended NGRI cases were interviewed. The findings were that: (1) GBMI has not resulted in a reduction in the number of people found NGRI, (2) most people found GBMI would have been found guilty in the absence of the statute, and (3) the verdict in 60 percent of the GBMI cases is obtained through a plea arrangement.[117]

In another study, Keilitz and Fulton (1984) surveyed 11 states having GBMI laws. They too found that GBMI has not displaced NGRI, that the most frequent method of finding a defendant GBMI was through a plea, and that GBMI offenders are no more likely to receive treatment than mentally disordered offenders in the general inmate population.[118]

This last finding is particularly disturbing. One of the basic objectives of the GBMI verdict is to provide treatment for a defendant's mental illness. If this is not being provided, the effectiveness of the GBMI verdict must be questioned.

In states providing a GBMI verdict, there is no guarantee that psychiatric treatment will be provided to defendants found GBMI.[119] Michigan provides treatment as is "psychiatrically indicated."[120] Georgia only provides such evaluation and treatment within the "limits of state funds appropriated therefor."[121]

The American Psychiatric Association has also confirmed the findings that GBMI offenders are not guaranteed to receive treatment. In Michigan, felons have received no more treatment than they would have prior to the new law.[122] Dr. John Prelesnick, Superintendent of the Reception and Guidance Center at the Jackson (Michigan) State Penitentiary, asserted that "in reality, GBMI prisoners are treated like any other prisoners; they will receive extra treatment if they need it, but it is the same treatment afforded everyone else."[123]

In another study, this proposition was again supported. In Michigan, over 75 percent of GBMI defendants who were sentenced to prison received no treatment. The other 25 percent had received only an occasional examination.[124]

A GBMI bill in the Kansas legislature was "shelved because of the significant capital costs which the state would incur in providing the mental facilities for this type of criminal defendant."[125] Judge Irving R. Kaufman, author of the landmark opinion in *United States v. Freeman*, concluded: "[P]roper application of a GBMI verdict requires that the states commit the necessary resources to house and treat those recommended for psychiatric supervision. If we are serious about treating the ills of the insanity laws, we must be willing to pay the medical bills for the cures."[126]

Constitutional Issues

GBMI laws have been attacked in state supreme courts on several grounds. The response from the courts has consistently been to approve the statutes. The laws have been upheld as constitutional, and questions regarding public policy have been answered by deferring to the wisdom of the legislatures. Nevertheless, this litigation has provided a forum for raising both public policy and constitutional concerns about GBMI statutes.

Allegations of unconstitutionality have been made in several different areas. First, GBMI laws have been applied to defendants whose offenses occurred before passage of the laws, but whose trials occurred afterward. Defendants have argued that this is an *ex post facto* violation. Second, GBMI laws have been attacked on grounds that they constitute a denial of equal protection and due process. The third area of challenge is the argument alleging that the statutes are vague, have no legitimate purpose, and promote jury confusion.

Ex Post Facto Application of the Statutes

In Illinois, the courts have applied GBMI laws to defendants who were tried after the passage of the law, but whose alleged crimes were committed before the law was enacted. On appeal, defendants have argued that the statute is unconstitutional as an *ex post facto* law. It increases the penalty for the crime and disadvantages the defendant by diluting his statutory right to an insanity defense.[127] The increased punishment is that the defendant is adjudicated mentally ill as well as guilty.[128] This, in turn, arguably creates a stigma impairing his ability to find employment, to obtain certain licenses, or to retain custody of children, and increases the probability of future involuntary commitment.[129]

Further, the increased punishment is not counterbalanced by any benefit to the defendant. Studies found that of the 44 defendants found GBMI in Illinois, none was committed to a hospital for treatment.[130]

An Illinois appellate court used the U.S. Supreme Court case of *Weaver v. Graham*[131] to analyze the *ex post facto* argument in *People v. DeWitt*.[132] It applied a two prong test to the statute: to violate the *ex post facto* clause of the state constitution, the law must be retrospective or retrospectively applied, and the law must disadvantage the defendant affected; mere procedural changes are exempt. The court upheld the GBMI statute, finding the defendant not disadvantaged under the *Weaver* test.

Another Illinois appellate court considered whether the GBMI laws were a constitutionally applied procedural change. Citing *Dobbert v. Florida*[133] and *Weaver v. Graham, supra,* the court held that a procedural change, while it might adversely affect a defendant, is not necessarily an *ex post facto* violation. The court stated that any disadvantage imposed by GBMI laws does not materially alter the defendant's legal situation and therefore striking down the law would not be warranted.

In *People v. Smith,*[134] the court found that the defendant would not suffer from the alleged stigma of a GBMI adjudication. According to the court, "the fact that the defendant has been convicted of the most serious of crimes, murder, imposes the most dramatic stigma on the defendant and also engenders most of the collateral consequences that the defendant claims arise from the finding of mental illness."[135] Instead, "the additional finding of mental illness ameliorates the culpability attendant to a finding of murder."[136] Similarly, other state courts have also recognized an ameliorative effect resulting from the GBMI adjudication.[137]

Equal Protection

A frequent charge against the GBMI laws has been that they create an arbitrary classification of offenders, violating equal protection guarantees under the Constitution. This special class is comprised of defendants who unsuccessfully raise the insanity defense at trial. Thus, it is argued that they are subject to the stigma of an additional adjudication that they are mentally ill, and because they are provided no *quid pro quo* for this harsher form of adjudication, the GBMI statute is in violation of equal protection. This argument has not met with much success. In both Illinois and Michigan, where GBMI statutes have been challenged and decided by the highest state court, the argument has been rejected.[138]

In Michigan, the five year statutory probation period has been attacked on equal protection grounds. It is argued that other persons convicted of similar crimes are not subject to this minimum probation period. In *People v. McLeod,*[139] the court ruled that since no "suspect classification"[140] was introduced and no "fundamental interest"[141] was infringed, the legislation was rationally related to the state's interest of assuring supervised medical treatment for convicted individuals who suffer from mental illness.

Equal protection, in this context, demands only that differences in treatment bear a rational relationship to the purpose of the classification. Since GBMI offenders are not a suspect class nor is the interest at issue a fundamental one, the state need only meet a rational relationship standard. The court thus held that the combination of guilt and mental illness is enough to distinguish this group from others in society and that their different treatment will be found to further the state's interest in protecting society and providing mental health treatment to the mentally ill.

Due Process

Determination of Present Mental Condition. GBMI statutes do not usually provide for a hearing to determine present mental condition before treatment is imposed.[142] The GBMI verdict reflects only the mental condition of the defendant at the time of the crime. While most states judicially provide that mental condition is determined at some point after sentencing and before treatment is administered, present mental condition is usually not determined by a judge.[143] Because the need for treatment is determined by psychiatric examination rather than by a hearing conducted by a neutral judicial officer, in theory it can be arbitrarily administered, possibly even when it is not needed. In *People v. McLeod,*[144] the Michigan Supreme Court held that a sentencing court must obtain a psychiatric report evaluating a defendant's present mental health prior to sentencing, but specifically determined that due process did not require a hearing.[145]

Determination of Treatment. The lack of specificity in GBMI statutes about the determination of treatment creates a potential for arbitrariness that could have unfair consequences. Treatment, for instance, could be imposed for odd or antisocial behavior rather than for actual mental illness.[146]

Even when a defendant is sentenced, examined, and is determined not to need treatment, the statutes are silent as to the extent of jurisdiction over his "mental condition." It is unclear whether a defendant, once adjudged GBMI, can be subjected to treatment at any time during his sentence (even if he is initially found not to need it).

Prisoners who have not been found GBMI have a procedural due process right to a hearing prior to being transferred to a mental institution to determine whether they are suffering from mental illness.[147] In its 1980 decision in *Vitek v. Jones*,[148] the U.S. Supreme Court dealt with the constitutionality of an involuntary transfer of a prisoner (originally found guilty) to a state mental hospital. The Court held that involuntary transfer to a mental hospital implicates liberty interests protected by the due process clause of the Fourteenth Amendment. The Court held that while a conviction and sentence extinguish an individual's right to freedom from confinement for the term of the sentence, they do not authorize the state to classify a person as mentally ill and subject him to involuntary psychiatric treatment without affording him additional due process protections.[149]

While *Vitek* establishes a prisoner's right to some sort of due process, it is questionable whether an adjudication of GBMI allows for the same right. GBMI statutes assume there will be treatment, and simply specify that the state is to determine the kind of treatment that will be given.[150] The effect of this language is to merge the defendant's right to due process before commitment with his right to a trial. The defendant is allowed one proceeding for the adjudication of all rights, including the issue of determination of treatment. Once adjudicated as GBMI and sentenced, the defendant may be subjected to treatment at any time while serving his sentence without the opportunity to make further arguments to the contrary in a judicial proceeding.[151]

Jury Instructions on the Insanity Defense and GBMI. The courts have addressed two different arguments concerning due process violations. The first, similar to the equal protection argument, is that GBMI statutes penalize defendants who unsuccessfully raise the insanity defense. The second is that the jury may be instructed on the possibility of a GBMI verdict even though they are not instructed on the possibility of an insanity defense verdict.

Proponents of the first argument state that the GBMI statutes penalize those defendants who unsuccessfully raise the insanity defense—imposing the label of mental illness without compensation or mitigation—thereby creating a chilling effect on the assertion of the insanity defense.[152] An Illinois appellate court responded: "The legislature intended to provide a statute that reduced the number of persons who were erroneously found NGRI."[153] The Court thus appears to find that one of the purposes of the GBMI statute is to reduce NGRI verdicts—to discourage acquittals by reason of insanity—though it adds that the law does not significantly chill the defense. However, by limiting and discouraging insanity verdicts, the insanity defense would appear to be less attractive to defendants than it was prior to the GBMI legislation.

The second argument regarding due process and fundamental fairness—that the jury may be instructed on the possibility of a GBMI verdict even though they are not instructed on the possibility of an insanity defense verdict—has been addressed in two state cases: State v. Ball,[154] a Georgia Supreme Court case, and State v. Page,[155] a New Mexico Appellate Court decision.

The Ball court specifically rejected a jury instruction on insanity because of insufficient evidence and gave instead a jury instruction on GBMI. The Georgia Supreme Court found that the two instructions are separate and distinct. Where an insanity plea is not supported by minimal evidence, an instruction on insanity need not be given. At the same time, a GBMI instruction may be supported by sufficient evidence and may be given even though the insanity instruction is not.

In the Ball case, the defendant was convicted of illegal sales of marijuana and cocaine, resulting in a GBMI verdict. The defendant had begun medical treatment after the offense for control of seizures ("blackouts"), a condition that had apparently existed before the offense. In his testimony, the defendant denied both making the sales and the possibility that the sales were made during a blackout. The court found that an insanity charge was not supported by the evidence, presumably based on the lack of causal effect between the illness and the offense. It did find, however, that a GBMI charge was supported by the evidence.

The second case, State v. Page,[156] holds that where a defendant has not pleaded the insanity defense, but has requested that the jury be given instruction of what constitutes the ability to form requisite "specific intent" to commit a crime, in a jurisdiction permitting a defense of partial diminished capacity, the door is opened to a jury instruction on GBMI. In Page, the defendant was convicted of burglary with a GBMI verdict. The defendant testified at trial that he had been drinking, smoking marijuana, and had taken a number of pain pills due to back pain. Only his intoxication was corroborated by a companion. The defendant requested a jury instruction on the defense of insanity to which the prosecutor objected. The court upheld the prosecutor's objection. The court then instructed the jury regarding the defendant's ability or inability to form the "specific intent" to commit the offense due either to intoxication or mental disease or disorder. The jury was also instructed on a possible GBMI verdict.

The *Page* court considered the jury instructions adopted by the New Mexico Supreme Court following the enactment of the state's GBMI statute.[157] They found that the state supreme court had "broadened the instances wherein the instruction as to GBMI may be given, including instances where a defendant had asserted the defense of an inability to form specific intent" because of intoxication or mental illness.[158] Thus, a defense of lack of specific intent to commit a crime because of mental disorder may subject a defendant to a GBMI verdict, but it does not ensure an instruction on the insanity verdict.

CONCLUSION

At first glance, the GBMI verdict seems to be an attractive alternative to what the public perceives as an overused and overly broad defense of insanity.[159] The verdict permits an unequivocal statement to be made about the factual guilt, mental condition, and moral responsibilities of all defendants who raise a claim of insanity. The GBMI verdict provides a supplementary verdict to the stark choice of either NGRI or guilty. It may assist prosecutors in convicting defendants who otherwise would be acquitted by reason of insanity. The GBMI verdict protects the public from dangerous criminals by allowing the court to impose a sentence that could be given to any defendant found guilty of the same crime.

The available evidence suggests, however, that there has been no decrease in the number of persons found NGRI as a result of the GBMI verdict. This probably reflects the fact that juries have traditionally been reluctant to render NGRI verdicts, and that most NGRI verdicts are the result of agreements between prosecutors and defense attorneys that result in uncontested pleas of NGRI.

The available evidence also suggests that a major purpose of GBMI statutes is not being achieved: the treatment promised to GBMI defendants is seldom provided. The states adopting GBMI statutes have not committed the resources to house and treat those recommended for mental health treatment.

Opponents of GBMI statutes argue that the statutes add an option that unduly complicates disposition and creates a special subpopulation of mentally ill offenders for already overburdened correctional facilities. Under GBMI statutes, commitment procedures are triggered by a jury verdict based on evidence that does not relate to the defendant's present mental condition. Conventional sentencing procedures available in most states permit judges to order treatment for persons in need of it. Transfer procedures also allow prisoners in need of mental health treatment to be temporarily sent to secure mental health institutions. Decisions about the proper placement of convicted offenders should be made after the entry of a conviction based solely on the offender's need for treatment.

While 11 states have adopted "guilty but mentally ill" verdicts, this verdict form has been opposed by both the American Psychiatric Association and the American Bar Association[160] and has received little support from professionals outside those states.

NOTES

1. Norval Morris, "Psychiatry and the Dangerous Criminal," 41 *S. Cal. L. Rev.* 518 (1968).

2. Wash. Stat. 7(1909), as cited by Donald H. S. Hermann, "Assault on the Insanity Defense: Limitations on the Effectiveness and Effect of the Defense of Insanity," 14 *Rutgers Law Journal* 257 (1983).

3. Ibid., p. 257.

4. Samuel J. Brackel and Ronald S. Rock, eds., *The Mentally Disabled and the Law* (Chicago: University of Chicago Press, 1971), p. 378.

5. *State v. Strasbury*, 60 Wash. 106, 110 P. 1020 (1910).

6. Hermann, "Assault on Insanity Defense," p. 257.

7. Curtis D. Wilbur, "Should the Insanity Defense to Criminal Charges Be Abolished?" 18 *A. B. A. J.* 631 (1922).

8. Benjamin Cardozo, as cited by John Palimore, "The Insanity Defense Revisited," 11 *Northern Kentucky Law Review* 5 (1984).

9. Hermann, "Assault on Insanity Defense," p. 260.

10. Sheldon Glueck, *Mental Disorder and the Criminal Law* (Boston: Little, Brown, 1925), p. 486.

11. *Sinclair v. State*, 161 Miss. 142, 132 So. 581 (1931).

12. Brackel and Rock, *Mentally Disabled and Law*, p. 378.

13. Barbara Wooton, as cited by Alexander Brooks, *Law, Psychiatry, and the Mental Health System* (Boston: Little, Brown, 1974), pp. 226–27.

14. Norval Morris, as cited by Brooks, *Law and Mental Health*, p. 233.

15. American Medical Association (AMA), *The Insanity Defense in Criminal Trials and Limitations of Psychiatric Testing* (Chicago: AMA, 1983), p. 62.

16. Stanton Samenow, as cited by Jonathan Rowe, "Why Liberals Should Hate the Insanity Defense," *Washington Monthly* 42 (May 1984).

17. Thomas Szasz, *Law, Liberty, and Psychiatry* (New York: Collier Books, 1963), p. 136.

18. Norval Morris, *Madness and the Criminal Law* (Chicago: University of Chicago Press, 1982), p. 59.

19. Norval Morris, as cited by Richard G. Singer, "Abolition of the Insanity Defense: Madness and the Criminal Law," 4 *Cardozo Law Review* 693 (1983).

20. William Raspberry, as cited by Orin Hatch, "The Insanity Defense Is Insane," *Readers Digest* 204 (October 1982).

21. Herbert Goldstein, as cited by Brooks, *Law and Mental Health*, p. 223.

22. Hermann, "Assault on Insanity Defense," p. 261.

23. Ibid.

24. Baruch Brody, *Ethics and Its Applications* (New York: Harcourt, Brace, Jovanovich, 1983), p. 57.

25. Herbert Morris, "Persons and Punishment," in Richard Wasserstrom, ed., *Today's Moral Problems* (New York: Macmillan, 1979), p. 471.

26. T. L. Clanon, Louis Shauver, and Douglas Kurdys, "Less Insanity in the Courts," 68 *A. B. A. J.* 825 (1982).

27. Jonathan Rowe, "Why Liberals Hate," p. 45.

28. David Bazelon, as cited by Alan Dershowitz, "The Real Issue Is Free Will," *New York Times*, March 25, 1973, p. E6.

29. N. Morris, "Dangerous Criminal," p. 520.

30. Joseph Goldstein, as cited by Brooks, *Law and Mental Health*, pp. 222–23.

31. *United States v. Brawner*, 471 F. 969 (D.C. Cir. 1972).

32. Richard C. Allen, Elyce Zenoff Ferster, and Jesse G. Rubin, *Readings in Law and Psychiatry* (Baltimore: Johns Hopkins Press, 1957), p. 706.

33. Herbert J. Miller, chairman, *Report of the President's Commission on Crime in the District of Columbia* (Washington, D.C.: U.S. Government Printing Office, 1966), p. 549.

34. Rowe, "Why Liberals Hate," p. 42.

35. Seymour Halleck, *Law and the Practice of Psychiatry* (1980).

36. Rowe, "Why Liberals Hate," p. 43.

37. Ibid.

38. Curtis D. Wilbur, "Should the Insanity Defense to Criminal Charges Be Abolished?" 18 *A. B. A. J.* (1922).

39. Szasz, *Law, Liberty, Psychiatry*, p. 136.

40. John Palimore, "The Insanity Defense Revisited," 11 *Northern Kentucky Law Review* (1984).

41. Allen, Ferster, and Rubin, *Readings*, p. 707.

42. Harlow M. Huckabee, *Lawyers, Psychiatrists, and the Criminal Law* (Springield, Ill.: Charles C. Thomas, 1980), pp. 57–58.

43. David F. Leroy, "The Insanity Defense under Siege," 6 *Mentally Disabled Law Reporter* 342 (September 1982).

44. Huckabee, *Lawyers, Psychiatrists*.

45. Halleck, *Law and Psychiatry*, p. 222.

46. N. Morris, "Dangerous Criminal," p. 522.

47. *Sinclair v. State*, 161 Miss. 142, 132 So. 581 (1931).

48. Ibid., as cited by Hermann, "Assault on Insanity Defense," p. 265.

49. N. Morris, *Madness*, p. 74.

50. N. Morris, "Dangerous Criminal," p. 519.

51. Donald Hermann, as cited by Allen, Ferster, and Rubin, *Readings*, p. 713.

52. Huckabee, *Lawyers, Psychiatrists*, p. 71.

53. *Powell v. Texas*, 392 U.S. 514 (1968).

54. N. Morris, *Madness*, pp. 56–75.

55. *Leland v. Oregon*, 342 U.S. 790 (1952).

56. *Patterson v. New York*, 432 U.S. 197 (1977).

57. Joseph Goldstein and Jay Katz, "Abolish the Insanity Defense—Why Not?" 72 *Yale Law Journal* (1963).

58. Raymond L. Spring, "The End of Insanity," 19 *Washburn Law Journal* 32 (1979).

59. AMA, *Insanity Defense and Testing*, p. 71.

60. Ibid.

61. Richard G. Singer, "Abolition of the Insanity Defense: Madness and the Criminal Law," 4 *Cardozo Law Review* (1983).

62. AMA, *Insanity Defense and Testing*, p. 76.

63. Allen, Ferster, and Rubin, *Readings*, p. 710.

64. Jonas Robitsher and Andrew Ky Haynes, "In Defense of the Insanity Defense," 31 *Emory Law Journal* 36 (1982).

65. Alan Dershowitz, "The Real Issue Is Free Will," *New York Times*, March 25, 1973.

66. Act of May 14, 1979, ch. 713, 1979 Mont. L. 1979, as cited by Jeanne Matthews Bender, "After Abolition of the Insanity Defense in Montana," 45 *Montana Law Review* 133 (1984).

67. See Montana Code Ann., Stat. 46-14-102 (1979).

68. See Idaho Code, Stat. 18-207 (1982).

69. Bender, "After Abolition," p. 145.

70. Ibid.

71. AMA, *Insanity Defense and Testing*, p. 69.

72. Richard J. Gerber, "Is the Insanity Test Insane?" 20 *American Journal of Jurisprudence* 132 (1975).

73. Robitsher and Haynes, "Defense of Insanity Defense," p. 31.

74. *Morrisette v. United States*, 342 U.S. 246 (1951).

75. Brackel and Rock, *Mentally Disabled and Law*, p. 379.

76. Gerber, "Is Test Insane?" p. 135.

77. 392 Mich. 511, 221 N.W. 2d 596 (1974).

78. Sharon Morey Brown and Nicholas J. Wittner, "Criminal Law, 1978 Annual Survey of Michigan Law," 25 *Wayne Law Review* 335, 355 (1978).

79. Ira Mickenberg, "A Pleasant Surprise: The Guilty But Mentally Ill verdict has both succeeded in its own right and successfully preserved the traditional role of the insanity defense," 55 *University of Cincinnati Law Review* 943, 987–88 (1987). Present mental condition must be determined at a hearing substantially similar to other civil commitment proceedings. If sane, the defendant must be released. If still mentally ill, the defendant is treated like a civil committee. Judith A. Northrup, "Guilty But Mentally Ill: Broadening the scope of the criminal responsibility," 44 *Ohio State Law Journal* 797, 805 (1983).

80. Linda C. Fentiman, "Guilty But Mentally Ill: The real verdict is guilty," 26 *Boston College Law Review* 601, 618 (1985).

81. Brown and Wittner, "Criminal Law," p. 356.

82. Ibid. John McGee kicked his wife to death and Ronald Manlan raped two women.

83. Fentiman, "Guilty But Mentally Ill," p. 617.

84. Ibid.

85. "Guilty But Mentally Ill: A Legislative Response to the Insanity Defense," 8 *State Court Journal* 4 (Summer 1984).

86. Mickenberg, "A Pleasant Surprise," p. 987. Mickenberg also states that the verdict of GBMI has been followed by judicial decision in Maryland. Based on our research, this does not appear to be the case. See Appendix.

87. "Guilty But Mentally Ill," *State Court Journal*, p. 4.

88. Ibid.

89. See discussion in Chapter 1. As noted, there was a great outcry for insanity defense reform after the *Hinckley* verdict.

90. Mich. Comp. Laws Ann. sec. 768.36 (1)(2) (West 1982).

91. Mich. Comp. Laws Ann. sec. 768.29 (a)(2) (West 1982); Mickenberg, "A Pleasant Surprise," p. 987.

92. Mich. Comp. Laws Ann. sec. 768.36 (1)(2) (West 1982).

93. Ga. Code Ann. 17-7-131(b) (Supp 1985); Fentiman, "Guilty But Mentally Ill," p. 619. This may include the situation where the defendant initially

pleads NGRI, but there is insufficient evidence to convince a judge to permit the defense to be heard by the jury. It may also include the situation, permitted in some jurisdictions, where the judge or the prosecutor raises an insanity defense that is supported by the evidence even when the defendant does not desire to go forward with the defense.

94. Fentiman, "Guilty But Mentally Ill," p. 620.

95. Ibid.

96. Ibid.

97. 18 Pa. Const. Stat. Ann. sec. 314(c)(1) (Purdon 1983).

98. 18 Pa. Const. Stat. Ann. sec. 314(c)(2) (Purdon 1983).

99. 463 N.E.2d 742 (Ill. App. 1984).

100. Ibid.

101. Northrup, "Guilty But Mentally Ill," p. 815.

102. Ingo Keilitz and Junius P. Fulton, *The Insanity Defense and Its Alternatives: A Guideline for Policy Makers* (Williamsburg, Va.: Institute on Mental Disability and the Law, National Center for State Courts, 1984), p. 42.

103. Ibid.

104. Fentiman, "Guilty But Mentally Ill," pp. 624–25.

105. Mickenberg, "A Pleasant Surprise," p. 988.

106. 18 Pa. Const. Stat. Ann. sec. 314(b) (Purdon 1983).

107. National Mental Health Association, "Myths and Realities: A Report of the National Commission on the Insanity Defense" (March 1983), pp. 32–34.

108. Mich. Comp. Laws Ann. sec. 768.36(3) (West 1982).

109. Fentiman, "Guilty But Mentally Ill," note 4, pp. 624–25.

110. 42 Pa. Const. Stat. Ann. sec. 9727(a) (Purdon 1983).

111. Brown and Wittner, "Criminal Law," p. 357.

112. Fentiman, "Guilty But Mentally Ill," p. 628.

113. Keilitz and Fulton, *The Insanity Defense and Its Alternatives*, p. 41. Emphasis in original.

114. See Hermann, "Assault on Insanity Defense."

115. Mickenberg, "A Pleasant Surprise," pp. 991–92.

116. Keilitz and Fulton, *The Insanity Defense and Its Alternatives*, p. 43.

117. Gare A. Smith and James A. Hall, "Evaluating Michigan's Guilty But Mentally Ill Verdict: An Empirical Study," 16 *University of Michigan Journal of Law*, Ref. 77, 91–95 (1982); John Klofas and Ralph Weisheit, "Pleading Guilty But Mentally Ill: Adversarial Justice and Mental Health," 9 *International Journal of Law & Psychology* 491, 493 (1986).

118. Klofas and Weisheit, "Pleading Guilty But Mentally Ill," p. 493, citing Keilitz and Fulton, *The Insanity Defense and Its Alternatives*, p. 41.

119. Fentiman, "Guilty But Mentally Ill," p. 628.

120. Ibid., n. 139.

121. Ibid.

122. Ibid., p. 628.

123. Mickenberg, "A Pleasant Surprise," pp. 993–94.

124. Smith and Hall, "Evaluating Michigan's Guilty But Mentally Ill Verdict," p. 105, n. 137.

125. D. J. Heineman, "Legislation 1982," 51 *Journal of the Kansas Bar Association* 106-7, p. 106 (1982), as cited in Keilitz and Fulton, *The Insanity Defense and Its Alternatives*, p. 44.

126. Ibid.

127. *People v. DeWitt*, 463 N.E.2d 742, 749 (Ill. App. 1984) *see People v. Smith*, 465 N.E.2d 101, 103 (Ill. App. 1984).

128. *People v. Smith*, p. 103.

129. Ibid.

130. National Mental Health Association, "Myths and Realities," pp. 26–27, 32–34.

131. 450 U.S. 24 (1981).

132. *People v. DeWitt*, pp. 749–50.

133. 432 U.S. 282, 293 (1977).

134. 465 N.E.2d 101, 103 (Ill. App. 1984).

135. Ibid., p. 104.

136. Ibid., p. 105.

137. *See Kirkland v. State*, 166 Ga. App. 578, 304 S.E.2d 561 (1983), which finds that a GBMI adjudication has an ameliorative effect because it reduces or modifies the penalty of a guilty verdict, decidedly lessens the stigma of criminal guilt, and provides treatment for the mental illness.

138. Northrup, "Guilty But Mentally Ill," pp. 812–14.

139. 407 Mich. 632, 288 N.W.2d 909 (1980).

140. Suspect classification is based on race or national origin.

141. Fundamental interest is based on a right secured under the constitution.

142. Pennsylvania is the exception. A hearing is held to determine present mental condition prior to treatment. 42 Pa. Const. Stat. Ann. sec. 9727(a) (Purdon 1983).

143. Kenneth Slowinski, "Criminal Responsibility: Changes in the Insanity Defense and the Guilty But Mentally Ill Response," 21 *Washburn Law Journal* 515, 548.

144. 407 Mich. 632, 288 N.W.2d 909 (1980).

145. Northrup, "Guilty But Mentally Ill," p. 812.

146. Michael J. Churgin, "The Transfer of Inmates to Mental Health Facilities: Developments in the Law," *Mentally Disordered Offenders: Perspectives from Law and Social Science*, ed. John Monahan and Henry L. Steadman (New York: Plenum Press, 1983), p. 209.

147. *Vitek v. Jones*, 445 U.S. 480 (1980).

148. Ibid.

149. Ibid.

150. Examples: Alaska Stat. 12.47.050 (the Department "shall provide

mental health treatment to a defendant found GBMI"). Ga. Code. A. 17-7-131(g)
(further evaluated and then treated as is psychiatrically indicated for his mental
illness). N.M. Stat. Ann. 31-9-4 (the department shall examine the nature and extent of defendant's mental illness and shall provide treatment).

151. One state has a partial exception: Delaware allows a defendant to refuse to take prescribed drugs, although there is no mention in the statute of the
right to refuse any other type of treatment or treatment altogether. But this
refusal may be overridden when the defendant's life or the life of another is in
danger. Del. Code Ann. tit. 11, 408(b).

152. *People v. Smith*, p. 105.

153. Ibid., p. 106.

154. 251 Ga. 840, 310 S.E.2d 516 (1984).

155. 100 N. M. Appl 788, 676 P.2d 1353 (1984).

156. Ibid.

157. NMSA 1978, Section 31-93-3 (Cum. Supp 1983) provides in part:
E. When a defendant has asserted a defense of insanity, the court, where warranted by the evidence, shall provide the jury with a special verdict form of
guilty but mentally ill and shall separately instruct the jury that a verdict of
guilty but mentally ill may be returned instead of guilty or not guilty, and that
such a verdict requires a finding by the jury beyond a reasonable doubt that the
defendant committed the offense charged and that the defendant was not legally
insane at the time of the commission of the offense but that he was mentally ill
at that time.

158. 100 N. M. Appl. 788, 676 P.2d 1353 (1984), p. 1356.

159. Fentiman, "Guilty But Mentally Ill," p. 601.

160. Keilitz and Fulton, *The Insanity Defense and Its Alternatives*, p. 45.

7

How Other Countries
View the Insanity Defense

This chapter examines the legal criteria and the procedures surrounding the defense of insanity in several West and East European, African, Latin American, and Asian societies. John Q. La Fond's essay, "Observations on the Insanity Defense and Involuntary Civil Commitment in Europe," serves as the basis for much of the information we present on several of the current codes for European countries.[1]

HISTORICAL PERSPECTIVE

Before discussing the contemporary codes, we provide a brief summary—abridged from Oppenheimer's *The Criminal Responsibility of Lunatics*[2]—on the insanity statutes in the criminal codes of 47 nations, as they appeared up to 1907. Oppenheimer summarized the differences among the codes as follows:

> The first important class of codes which claims our attention comprises those which go the whole length of declaring the victims of mental alienation incapable of committing a crime in any circumstances. The test is here a purely medicopathological one, and as soon as the question of disease of the mind is answered in the affirmative, an acquittal must follow as a matter of course. The text which has served as a model to all members of this group is Art. 64 of the French Code, and the plan of thus identifying insanity and immunity may justly be termed the French plan. The article is reproduced, with or without slight and unimportant terminological alterations, in the codes of Belgium, Guatemala, Hayti, Luxemburg, Monaco, and of two of the Swiss cantons,

Geneva and Neuchatel. The texts of Argentine, Bolivia and Peru [also] embody the principle laid down therein. Closely akin to it are further the provisions of those codes which, following the lead of Spain and Portugal, adopt its subject only to a reservation if favour of acts committed during a lucid interval; this which may be called the Iberian modification of the French plan we meet with in the criminal law of Chili, Costa Rica, Honduras, and Uruguay.[3]

Oppenheimer's next major classifications are those codes that insist on a description, a type, or a degree of severity of the mental illness, before the accused may be exempt from responsibility. Such codes contain phrases such as "*completely* deprived of the full use of reason," rather than just "deprived."

Into a third group, he places codes that grant to the judge absolute discretion in the determination of responsibility. In Oppenheimer's words, "it leaves the matter entirely in the hands of the judge without supplying him with any help in the solution of the problem."[4]

The fourth category are those codes that rely on a knowledge test—most often the *M'Naghten* right–wrong criterion. Here are included Great Britain, most of the United States, and many of the British colonies.

A fifth—and small—category is the codes that determine responsibility by the actor's capacity to determine his or her own will in the matter.

A combination of the knowledge and the will tests—so that "a madman who satisfies either the one or the other will escape"—was contained in the codes of several U.S. states, Norway, Bulgaria, Russia, Italy, and Mexico.[5]

Finally, a few codes anticipated the diminished responsibility notion prevalent today, and sought to establish "a mathematical ratio between reduction of punishment and diminution of responsibility, fixing one fourth of the ordinary minimum punishment as the limit below which the judge must in no case descend."[6]

WESTERN EUROPE

Turning to the present, we first examine the following West European countries: France, Great Britain, Greece, West Germany, Holland, Sweden, Spain, and Switzerland.

The French code of today reads much like the French standard in 1907 as cited by Oppenheimer: namely, that the presence of mental illness is a "sufficient basis for excusing a defendant without regard to specific incapacitating consequences of mental illness."[7]

Article 64 of the French Penal Code provides:

> If the person charged with the commission of a felony or misdemeanor was then insane or acted by absolute necessity, no offense has been committed.

The defense need not establish any causal relationship between the mental illness and the behavior.

If insanity is raised as an issue, the court appoints an attorney as an officer of the court to conduct an inquiry into the state of the defendant's mental health at the time of the offense. The attorney arranges for psychiatric examination of the defendant, usually by two forensic psychiatrists who are selected from a list of experts approved by the court. The defendant may request examination by more than two experts, but the examination may not be carried out by experts whom the defendant wishes to select. The court-approved psychiatrists make their evaluation as to the sanity of the defendant, and report their findings to the judge. The judge has the final say as to the defendant's sanity or insanity. The defendant found to be insane then undergoes further examination to determine whether he or she is mentally ill and dangerous at the present time. The defendant so found is sent either to a prison or to a hospital, where he or she remains until both the medical experts and the civil authorities give approval for release. A defendant may appeal a negative release decision to a special judicial tribunal, which can release him or her over the objections of the medical and civil authorities. According to La Fond, "this evidently does not occur often."[8]

Great Britain still uses *M'Naghten* as the criterion of nonresponsibility. La Fond makes the point that "very few defendants invoke the defense, and of those who do, very few are successful."[9] In 1982—according to La Fond—there were only three or four successful insanity acquittals in England and Wales.

More popular is the partial defense of "diminished responsibility" for persons charged with first degree murder. Mental illness (which does not involve use of the *M'Naghten* right–wrong criterion) is introduced as a partial defense, to reduce a charge of first degree homicide to manslaughter—which carries with it a mandatory life sentence. La Fond reports:

> A convicted criminal defendant who is considered mentally ill, although not legally insane, can be sent either to a prison or to a hospital. If a person is sent to a mental health hospital, it is usually for an indeterminate period. The court can and usually does impose a "restriction order" on such a person if it considers him dangerous. If a person is not subject to a restriction order, the hospital staff can release a mentally ill offender when they determine that he is safe enough to be in the community. If a person is subject to a restriction order, however, the Home Secretary must concur in the decision to release. Thus, the release of a mentally ill offender from a psychiatric facility or from a prison in England is usually a combined medical-political decision. Courts have virtually no control over the decision.[10]

The criterion for nonresponsibility in Greece bears a strong resemblance to the *M'Naghten* rule. According to the Greek Penal Code:

> An act shall not be imputable to its perpetrator if, at the time of commission, by reason of a morbid disturbance of his mental activity or of his conscience, he was unable to understand the unjustified character of his act or to act in accordance with such understanding. [Article 34][11]

The code also allows for diminished responsibility, by stating:

> If, due to mental conditions described in Article 34, a person's capacity for imputability has been substantially reduced, but not entirely removed, a lesser punishment shall be imposed. [Article 36]

The treatment such defendants receive is described in Article 37:

> Whenever a condition of diminished responsibility as to imputability, defined in Article 36, makes special handling or care necessary, the imposed punishment or incarceration shall be executed in a special psychiatric institution or annex to the penitentiary. [Article 37]

A later article specifies that the defendant's release "shall be determined with the counsel of special advisors by the misdemeanors court in the jurisdiction in which the punishment was executed."[12]

The West German Penal Code drafted in 1972 reads much like the criteria spelled out in the American Law Institute test. It states:

> Whoever is incapable, at the time of committing the offense, of appreciating the wrongfulness of the offense or of acting according to such appreciation because of a pathological mental defect, a seriously disturbed consciousness, feeblemindedness, or another serious form of mental deviance, acts without blameworthiness. [Article 20][13]

The code also allows for diminished responsibility when it states:

> If the actor's capability to appreciate the wrongfulness of the offense or to act according to such appreciation is, at the time of committing the offense, significantly reduced for one of the reasons named in § 20, the punishment can be reduced in accordance with § 49. [Article 21]
>
> If the defendant meets the criteria defined in Articles 20 or 21, the court will order an evaluation of his/her act and a determination of his/her dangerousness to the public. If the offender is found to be dangerous, he/she will be committed to a psychiatric hospital.
>
> The court can, at any time, examine whether the further execution of detention is to be suspended on parole.

Such examination would occur after the offender has been in a psychiatric hospital for one year.

The Dutch system combines the principles of a guilty but mentally ill verdict and the lack of specific criterion for determining nonresponsibility. The terms "defective development" or "impairment of mental facilities" are mentioned as conditions that may absolve an offender from responsibility. It is the judge who makes the decision, "although a psychiatrist is consulted if the judge thinks there is any possibility of a mental disorder."[14] The defendant does not enter a plea of insanity; but if—at the end of the trial—he or she is found guilty of having committed the offense, the defendant may then be found not liable to punishment because of mental illness or mental deficiency. The crucial issue is whether it has been proven that the defendant's mental disorder was the main factor leading to the offense. The judge has the option, "but not the obligation, to order restrictive measures."

The psychiatrists' role in these proceedings is that of providing medical diagnosis; the determination of responsibility is in the hands of the judge. On the matter of what should be done with the defendant, the psychiatrist may also offer an expert opinion. He or she may point out that detention would be detrimental to the defendant, and may propose special conditions.

Switzerland—like West Germany—applies a criterion for determining insanity that is similar to the American Law Institute's test. It states:

> If a defendant was mentally ill at the time of the offense and had no capacity to appreciate the wrongfulness of his act or to conform his conduct to the requirement of the law, he has a personal excuse which precludes his being punished for his conduct.[15]

When the insanity issue is raised, the court appoints an expert to examine the defendant. The expert submits an opinion to the court in the form of a written report—unless there is a jury trial, whereupon the expert is likely to testify in person. The defendant may also retain his own expert, but—according to La Fond—"the report of this expert is frequently greeted with a fair degree of skepticism. The judge invariably follows the opinion of its own appointed expert."[16]

If the defendant is declared not guilty by reason of insanity, he or she may be released or committed to a prison or a hospital. Release is usually a medical decision, which needs approval by an executive authority.

The Spanish code drafted in 1982 has the breadth and lack of specificity noted in the French code. It states that—if a person is considered mad or in a state of temporary mental confusion, and has committed an act that the law has sanctioned as a criminal offense—the person is exempt from criminal responsibility. A tribunal will decree the offender's committal into a mental hospital, where he or she will remain until otherwise authorized by the same tribunal.

Sweden abolished the insanity defense in 1965. In its place, it passed legislation applicable to all mentally ill persons, including those charged with committing criminal offenses.

La Fond summarizes the system as follows:

If a person charged with a crime is suspected of having suffered from mental illness at the time of the offense, the court can order a psychiatric evaluation of the defendant in a public facility. This examination, however, cannot be conducted unless the prosecutor has proven that the defendant has committed the criminal act or unless the defendant has confessed to the act. At the public health facility, psychiatrists will examine the defendant and submit in writing to the court their opinion as to whether the defendant was suffering from mental illness at the time of the offense. Invariably, the court accepts the opinion of the independent mental health experts concerning the defendant's mental health at the time of the offense. The defendant can appeal the court's finding to a national review board.

If the court finds that the defendant committed the criminal act but was suffering from mental illness, the defendant is found guilty but he cannot be sent to jail. Rather, the court is limited to choosing from among the following dispositional alternatives: (1) confinement in a closed hospital; (2) probation; or, (3) pecuniary penalties. If the court further finds, based on the experts' opinion, that treatment is necessary or appropriate, it can send the offender to a closed hospital for psychiatric treatment. This commitment to a psychiatric facility is for an indefinite period and the court does not determine when the mentally ill offender will be released. That decision is exclusively a medical decision to be made by the medical staff. Usually two psychiatrists must agree that release is appropriate. A mentally ill offender can appeal a negative release decision to a hospital review board and, if unsuccessful, to a national review board.[17]

A comparison of the West European countries described in the preceding paragraphs against the United States reveals that many of the former are less concerned about attributing specific individual blame and responsibility than the United States, where the emphasis is much more on the relationship between specific characteristics of the defendant's mental state and the act committed. The European systems tend also to focus more on treatment of the offender and on protection of society. In the United States, the system works harder to establish blame or the lack of it, and expends less energy on treatment.

The West European countries are also more likely to defer to medical opinion and to extract medical testimony from the partisan system. Experts' views have greater influence in European courts than in U.S. proceedings—not only on the issue of the defendant's responsibility, but also in decisions concerning commitment and subsequent release.

EASTERN EUROPE

Turning to Eastern Europe, we look first at the 1978 Criminal Code of the Hungarian Peoples' Republic, which states that the basic condition of criminal responsibility is the accountability of the person. A person—it reasons—can only be regarded as accountable if he or she possesses the ability of recognition, and is capable of developing willful intent and of acting accordingly. A person who is not accountable cannot be punished. Article 24 of the Hungarian code reads as follows:

> Whoever commits the act in a state of mental deficiency, particularly insanity, mental debility, intellectual decline, schizophrenic or personalistic troubles, that render him unable to realize the consequences of the act or to proceed in accordance with such realization, cannot be punished.[18]

According to La Fond, any participant in the proceedings (the police, the judge, the prosecutor, or the defendant) can raise the insanity defense. Once raised, the criminal proceedings are delayed while the court arranges for a psychiatric examination.

> Two psychiatrists will evaluate the defendant and submit their opinion in writing to the court. If the experts cannot agree, additional experts may be requested to examine the defendant. If the judge disagrees with the expert opinion, he may send the defendant to a legal-medical committee for further evaluation. A defendant can also request, but cannot demand, that another expert examine him. Normally, the judge follows the recommendation of the experts.
>
> If the defendant is found by the court to have been insane at the time of the offense, the criminal proceedings are terminated and the focus shifts to considering what disposition should be made of the defendant. If the defendant is still mentally ill and (1) the crime was one of violence against the person, or (2) the crime created a public danger, or (3) the punishment for the crime would have been confinement in prison for more than a year, the defendant may be sent to a psychiatric hospital for treatment. A violent offender may also be treated in a hospital within a prison. Alternatively, a defendant may be released on

probation and treated as an out-patient. Commitment to an in-patient psychiatric facility is for an indeterminate period. Except for one hospital in Hungary, release from a psychiatric facility is exclusively a medical decision to be made by the staff. Release from this one other hospital requires approval of the court.[19]

Hungary also allows for a reduction of punishment on grounds of diminished responsibility. As in Great Britain, the diminished responsibility defense may be introduced if a defendant is charged with first degree murder and seeks to have it reduced to manslaughter.

The Polish Penal Code—adopted in 1973—states:

> Whoever, at the time of the commission of an act was incapable of recognizing its significance or of controlling his conduct because of a mental deficiency, mental illness or other disturbance of the mental function, does not commit an offense. [Article 25, par. 1][20]

Allowing for diminished responsibility, paragraph 2 states:

> If at the time of the commission of an offense the ability to recognize the significance of the act or to control the conduct was diminished to a significant extent, the court may apply extraordinary mitigation of the penalty.

The Romanian Penal Code—adopted in 1968 and amended in 1973—employs a concept similar to the irresistible impulse test.

> If the perpetrator, at the moment of committing an act proscribed by the penal law, could not be well aware of his actions or omissions or was unable to control them due to mental illness or some other cause, the act does not constitute an offense. [Article 48][21]

The legal standard applied in the Soviet Union—employing an emphasis on cognitive as well as volitional influences—reads much like the ALI criteria.[22] The Soviet Criminal Code states:

> A person who was in a state of irresponsibility when committing a criminal offense—that is, when he could not be aware about his actions or could not govern them as a result of chronic mental disease, temporary disorder of mental activity, feeblemindedness, or some other

malady—is relieved from legal responsibility. To such a person, compulsory medical treatment, envisaged by the legislation of the Union Republics may be applied if the court so rules. [Article 11][23]

Soviet legislation also relieves from responsibility persons who become mentally ill after they commit an offense, and who are thus unaware of their prior actions and of controlling their behavior. Such persons, however, "may be liable to punishment" after they have received medical treatment.

The role of forensic psychiatrists (who may be called by both the prosecutor and the defense) in such cases involves making judgments not only about the status of the defendant at the time of the examination, but also about the history of the defendant's disease and about his condition during any previous periods of hospitalization.

Defendants who are found not responsible for their criminal acts are committed to psychiatric institutions. The medical board of the hospital makes the determination about when a patient may be released. Patients are subject to reexamination at least every six months in order to decide whether "prolongation or shortening of the period of compulsory treatment is advisable, or whether transfer of the patient to an ordinary hospital, to outpatient treatment, or to placement under the observation of his relatives would be indicated."[24]

Soviet law states:

Compulsory treatment is not a penal measure; the decision, although given by a court, is not a sentence but a ruling. This ruling, however, is given not in a preparatory session but in open court—that is, the court must establish the identity of a person who has committed an offense and determine to what extent he constitutes a danger to others. To this end, the court procedure is essential.[25]

Hungary, Poland, and Romania apply standards that are more inclusive and less precise than the British, West German, Swiss, or Dutch standards. The Hungarian code—particularly—seems to focus on the treatment of *any* offender who suffers from mental illness. There appears to be no need to establish any relationship between the illness and the criminal act. The Soviet Union standard resembles the ALI criteria used in the United States, West Germany, and Switzerland. Both the Soviet and Hungarian codes—like those in some of the West European countries discussed earlier—grant more authority to medical experts in the determination of insanity and of subsequent commitment and treatment than the United States does.

LATIN AMERICAN, ASIAN, AND AFRICAN SOCIETIES

The article bearing on the defense of insanity adopted by Argentina in 1963 reads much like the American Law Institute's standard. Article 34 of the penal code states that the following persons are not criminally liable:

> Anybody who at the time of the commission of the crime could not appreciate the unlawfulness of the deed or control his actions by reason of insufficiency or diseased disturbance of his mind, or by unconsciousness, or by error of fact or ignorance for which he is not responsible.[26]

A defendant found not guilty by reason of insanity is automatically committed to an insane asylum. Release is dependent on a judicial hearing in the presence of a public prosecutor and on the presentation of a medical experts' report that, in their view, the patient no longer constitutes a danger to self or others.

Most of the African and Asian countries have adopted the same legal standard for determining responsibility as the colonial power under which they were ruled. Thus, until recently, Nigeria and Israel employed the *M'Naghten* standard. In 1983, the Israeli Penal Law was updated to read as follows:

> A person shall not bear the criminal responsibility for an act that he has committed if, by reason of a mental illness or defect, he is incapable of choosing between performing the act and refraining from doing so.[27]

Israel has thus shifted from a purely cognitive standard to one that takes volition into account and that reads much like the American Law Institute standard.

In 1965, Tanzania adopted a statute that bears strong resemblance to *M'Naghten*. It notes first that every person is presumed to be and to have been of sound mind until the contrary is proved. It then states:

A person is not criminally responsible for an act or omission if at the time of doing the act or making the omission he is through a disease affecting his mind incapable of understanding what he is doing or of knowing that he ought not to do the act or make the omission.

But a person may be criminally responsible for an act or omission, although his mind is affected by disease, if such disease does not in fact produce upon his mind one or other of the effects above mentioned in reference to that act or omission.[28]

Kenya's standard—adopted originally in 1959 and revised in 1982—also reads much like *M'Naghten.*

Where an act or omission is charged against a person as an offence, and it is given in evidence on the trial of that person for that offence that he was insane so as not to be responsible for his acts or omissions at the time when the act was done or the omission made, then if it appears to the court before which the person is tried that he did the act or made the omission charged but was insane at the time he did or made it, the court shall make a special finding to the effect that the accused was guilty of the act or omission charged but was insane when he did the act or made the omission. [Article 166][29]

If a defendant is found to be insane, the case is reported to the president; the accused is placed in custody—in either a mental hospital or a prison—and remains under the jurisdiction of the court.

[T]he President may, at any time after a person has been detained by order of the President under subsection (3), make a special report to the Minister for transmission to the President, on the condition, history and circumstances of the person so detained, and the President, on consideration of the report, may order that the person be discharged or otherwise dealt with, subject to such conditions as to his remaining under supervision in any place or by any person, and to such other conditions for ensuring the safety and welfare of the person in respect of whom the order is made and of the public, as the President thinks fit. [Article 166, par. 6][30]

The Zambian Criminal Code bearing on insanity reads much like the code adopted by Kenya:

Where an act or omission is charged against any person as an offence, and it is given in evidence on the trial of such person for that offence that he was insane so as not to be responsible for his actions at the time when the act was done or omission made, then, if it appears to the court before which such person is tried that he did the act or made the omission charged but was insane as aforesaid at the time when he did or made the same, the court shall make a special finding to the effect that the accused was not guilty by reason of insanity.

Where a special finding is made under subsection (1), the court so finding shall order the person to whom such finding relates to be detained during the President's pleasure.[31]

The Turkish Criminal Code (1965) contains the breadth of generality found in the codes of some of the East European countries. It states:

Anybody afflicted with mental disease which causes a complete loss of consciousness or of freedom of action, at the time of commission of the act, shall not be punished.

However, during the preparatory investigation, the decision subjecting such person to custody and medical treatment must be rendered by the Justice of the Peace, during the preliminary investigation by the investigating judge, and during the final investigation by the competent court.

The custody and medical treatment continues until such person is cured. But a defendant accused of a crime entailing heavy imprisonment shall not be released prior to one year. [Article 46][32]

A decision concerning the defendant's release is made by the court on the basis of a report from the hospital board of the institution in which the defendant was a patient. The report must state that the patient has recovered, and must give its opinion about whether the defendant should be examined on a regular basis to be sure that his or her symptoms have not recurred. The prosecution has the responsibility for carrying out and checking on the defendant's compliance with these requirements. Should there be signs of mental illness, the defendant must be recommitted.

The Turkish code also allows for diminished responsibility in the following manner:

1. the punishment of death shall be reduced to heavy imprisonment of not less than fifteen years;
2. life imprisonment shall be reduced to heavy imprisonment of fifteen to nineteen years; and

3. permanent disqualification to hold public office shall be reduced to temporary disqualification to hold public office.
Other punishments shall be reduced by one third to one half.[33]

The Japanese Criminal Code—amended in 1954—states simply:

An Act of a person of unsound mind is not punishable. Punishment shall be reduced for acts of weak-minded persons. [Article 39][34]

The Korean Criminal Code—amended in 1960—reads as follows:

A person is not punishable if, because of mental disorder, he is unable to pass rational judgment or to control his will.[35]

Korea also allows for diminished responsibility.

The punishment of a person who, due to a mental disorder, is deficient in the capacity mentioned in the preceding Section, shall be mitigated. [Article 10, sec. 3][36]

CONCLUDING REMARKS

All of the above discussion is admittedly superficial and lacks important empirical and practical data and tests about how the courts and other criminal justice institutions interpret and respond to the defense of insanity. We offer—for example—no information about the numbers of such pleas in the different countries, the verdicts reached by the courts, the role that the expert witnesses actually play in defense of insanity trials, the number of persons committed, and the average length of their confinement. We have tried to obtain such information from secondary sources in the United States and by writing to various individuals and organizations in different countries, and were not successful in gaining any additional data. Thus, the chapter provides the reader with little more than the formal criteria—as contained in the legal codes—about the standards for determining responsibility or insanity, with some occasional information about verdict forms and commitment procedures. For those who wish to delve further, this information is at least a framework.

A point worth mentioning is that we are not so naive as to assume that the formal criteria necessarily reflect how the system in fact functions. Thus—while we note that, on paper, several of the East European countries have the most enlightened criteria—in the absence of real data, we must withhold judgment about how the system actually functions. Indeed, we recognize that, in presenting only the formal criteria, we may be providing a distorted perspective—one that covers over, rather than elucidates, the real state of affairs. As scholars, we must believe that our readers will recognize the usefulness of the skeletal scheme, and will withhold judgment about its functioning, until such data are available.

NOTES

1. John Q. La Fond, "Observations on the Insanity Defense and Involuntary Civil Commitment in Europe," *University of Puget Sound Law Review* (Spring 1984).
2. Heinrich Oppenheimer, *The Criminal Responsibility of Lunatics* (London: Sweet and Maxwell, 1909).
3. Ibid., p. 82.
4. Ibid., p. 89.
5. Ibid.
6. Ibid., p. 90.
7. La Fond, "Observations," p. 531.
8. Ibid.
9. Ibid., p. 532.
10. Ibid., p. 533.
11. Nicholas Lolis, *The Greek Penal Code* (Hackerman, N.J.: Rothman, 1973), pp. 47–48.
12. Ibid., pp. 48–49.
13. Gerhard O. W. Mueller and Thomas Buergenthal, *The German Penal Code* (of the German Federal Republic of May 15, 1871, R.G. Bl. 127; as republished August 25, 1953, B.G. Bl. I 1083; corrected 1954 I 33; as of January 1, 1961).
14. Michael Zeegers, "Diminished Responsibility," *International Journal of Law and Psychiatry* 433 (Summer/Fall 1981).
15. La Fond, "Observations," p. 540.
16. Ibid., p. 541.
17. Ibid., pp. 535–36.
18. Ibid., p. 538.
19. Ibid.
20. William Kenney and Jadeusz Sadowski, *The Polish People's Republic Penal Code* (Hackerman, N.J.: Rothman, 1973), p. 40.

21. Simone-Marie Vrabiesch Kleckner, *The Romanian Socialist Republic Penal Code* (Hackerman, N.J.: Rothman, 1976), p. 36.

22. The discussion of the Soviet standards is adapted from E. A. Babayan, *Legal Aspects of Psychiatry in the Soviet Legislation*, published in the Soviet Union in 1979.

23. Ibid., p. 21.

24. Ibid., pp. 23–24.

25. Ibid., p. 25.

26. Emilio Gonzalez-Lopez, *The Argentine Penal Code* (Hackerman, N.J.: Rothman, 1963), p. 28.

27. S. Z. Feller, "Factual Tests for Identification of Volitional Insanity." 19, 1 *Israel Law Review* 20 (1984).

28. Nicholas Lolis, *Tanzania Penal Code* (Hackerman, N.J.: Rothman, 1965), p. 22.

29. Nicholas Lolis, *Kenya Penal Code* (Hackerman, N.J.: Rothman, 1983), p. 61.

30. Ibid., p. 62.

31. Nicholas Lolis, *Zambia Penal Code* (Hackerman, N.J.: Rothman, 1965), p. 63.

32. Nicholas Lolis, *Turkey Penal Code* (Hackerman, N.J.: Rothman, 1965), p. 27.

33. Ibid., p. 28.

34. Thomas Blakemore, *The Criminal Code of Japan and Minor Offenses Law of Japan* (Rutland, Vt.: Charles E. Tuttle, as amended in 1954), p. 35.

35. Paul Ryn, *Korean Criminal Code* (Hackerman, N.J.: Rothman, 1960), p. 27.

36. Ibid., p. 35.

8

Depictions of the Insanity Defense in Fiction and Theater
(with the assistance of Peter Darvas)

Fictional literature and drama serve both as a mirror and as a repository for society's behavior. They have also been used as barometers for measuring the climate of social values in a given society or culture. The novel—particularly—is a unique discipline that combines artistic movement, intellectual thought, and—at its best—an illumination of social values from the perspective of the artist in his or her relationship to society. On the other hand, drama has historically established itself as the most "social" of the written arts, both in form and content. While its form (that is: production, acting, staging, audience interaction, and so on) obviously lends itself to social interpretation, its content—from the social morality plays of Aeschylus to the revolutionary work of Ibsen and Brecht—has a deeply imbedded social consciousness.

Adopting the format that Simon used in her edited volume *The Jury System in America*,[1] we decided to include a chapter on how the defense of insanity has been portrayed in fiction and drama. Traditionally, the courtroom has been a rich source of material for both the novelist and the playwright. In her chapter on "The Jury in American Literature"[2] in the aforementioned work, Emily Watts had no dearth of materials from which to select themes about how the jury interpreted its responsibility and about the interpersonal dynamics among the 12 persons charged with determining a defendant's guilt or innocence. But in our search for scenarios in which novelists and playwrights focus on the defense of insanity, we could find only a few examples. Indeed, Jon Breen's volume, *Novel Verdicts:*

A Guide to Courtroom Fiction—an exhaustive and detailed bibliography that includes hundreds of titles—offered only two books that touched on the insanity defense.[3]

In trying to understand why there was such a dearth of materials on what would appear to be a rich and meaty subject, we arrived at the following explanation. Novelists and playwrights shy away from the defense of insanity, because it detracts or interferes with their portrayal and development of character. If an author allows the fictional agent to invoke a defense of insanity, the author is robbing him of responsibility for his actions—and thus depriving him of those emotions, pains, and internal conflicts that build and vitalize characters. To put it more bluntly, invoking an effective defense of insanity results in the demise of the character as a complex and interesting subject. The author in so doing does away with the fictional agent.

To jump ahead a bit for purposes of illustration of this theme, we look at Levin's treatment of the two characters in *Compulsion*—both of whom have committed a heinous, brutal act. The author provides separate portrayals of Artie Straus and Judd Steiner; and, as the novel develops, Judd becomes not only the deeper and more sympathetic character, but also the one who appears more and more sane. Artie is consistently portrayed as a hollow shell, devoid of character, and unwarranting of sympathy—but also seemingly the one who is least responsible for their crime. In such a situation, the author must thus deprive a character of humanness—and perhaps, thereby, of interest.

Having made this discovery about the dearth of materials on the defense of insanity--and having arrived at an explanation—we then thought it of interest and importance to go ahead and present the materials we did find and to analyze how successful the authors were in their artistic endeavor as well as in their portrayal of a meaningful protagonist. In carrying out this task, we decided to spread a rather wide net, and include examples ranging from classic Greek tragedy to contemporary U.S. fiction. We also stretched the phrase "defense of insanity" to include deviant acts that have been judged outside the courtroom and in the absence of specific legal violations. It is in this spirit, then, that we examine how novelists and playwrights have treated the defense of insanity specifically, and—more generally—how they have managed the tension between the individual's freedom and personal responsibility and society's need to control and punish.

GREEK TRAGEDY

While Aristotle did not express the dilemma of moral responsibility per se in *The Poetics*, his comments on the subject of character are helpful to this discussion.[4] Aristotle understood the requirement of moral and psychological integrity for the effectiveness of character in literary form.

> [A]ny speech or action that manifests moral purpose of any kind will be expressive of character: the character will be good if the purpose is good.[5]

This is not an ascription of moral goodness, but rather of literary quality. Aristotle believed that characters must be grounded in action and, more generally, in life. While his ideal character-heros may be flawed, may suffer unjustly, and may act from other than reason, they still must be viewed as self-contained moral agents in order to be dramatically effective.

Examining Sophocles's *Oedipus*, we find a hero plagued by circumstance, but in no way exonerated of his guilt. While any modern court would find Oedipus innocent of any intentional wrongdoing, the court of the gods unleashes on Thebes a punishment of terrible proportions, and—ultimately—destroys the hero himself. Oedipus and the entire house of Laius are not guilty of murder or of any crime with intent, but—rather—of ignorance of circumstances. While Oedipus becomes the ruler of Thebes as a result of his mental alacrity, his downfall is a result of his unintentioned acts, to which the gods ascribe guilt and retribution in no less harsh sanctions.

In probably the most influential of the Greek tragedies—in terms of Western culture—*Oedipus* represents the guilt conscience of the literary hero. The best of human development, reason, intelligence, and the courage of independent action bring nothing but ruin and suffering. In this context, irrationality and capricious action can best be ascribed to the gods, for visiting this destruction on good men and women. But in what Aristotle terms the perfect tragedy, Sophocles purposefully offers a hero who falls from fortune to tragedy; and,

from stability in form, the play moves toward instability and—finally—
to the wrenching catharsis of denouement.

Oedipus's "crime" is his ignorance of circumstances. To separate
a character from his or her responsibility—as an effective insanity
defense must do—suggests that the story is robbed of what Aristotle
has described as purposive action. Or—stated somewhat differently—
if Aristotle is correct in describing effective drama as made up of
intentional characters or agents who "manifest moral purpose," then
to emasculate that moral purpose is to sabotage the effectiveness of
the drama.

What is important to note in this structure is that dramatic energy
seems to flow from characters meeting and coping with responsibility
for acts that are not morally theirs alone. On learning of his predicament, Oedipus could have raised his hands and cried, "Look at what
the gods have done to me!"—and left things at that. But that would
have made for poor tragedy and shallow character. Tragedy evolved
from the early irrational anger of man shaking his fists at the heavens
for his fate. By the time of Sophocles and the development of good
drama, it had evolved far past that primeval stage. Dramatic action
and the development of character had transcended the externaliza-
tion of conflict and the mourning of fate. Drama as portrayed in
Oedipus had evolved to the internalization of conflict and the
coming to terms with a harsh external world.

Tragedy thrives on the justification of rationality. It denigrates
fate and the irrational. As Aristotle pointed out, the writer requires
a character with sufficient depth and integrity—even to do evil.

DR. JEKYLL AND MR. HYDE

While no insanity plea is offered in *The Strange Case of Dr. Jekyll
and Mr. Hyde*,[6] it provides an interesting illustration of the principal
character's failure to exercise moral and rational choices—a failure
that leads to murder and, ultimately, to suicide. The story is told
from the point of view of Dr. Jekyll's attorney—Utterson—who is
puzzled at the distinguished and respected doctor's association with
the vile and repugnant Edward Hyde. Hyde is first presented as the
heir to Jekyll's estate and intimate friend—so close that he shares in
the liberties of the doctor's household and enjoys his financial
support.

With the popularization and mythologizing of Robert Louis Stevenson's tale, the surprise element of the story—Jekyll's and Hyde's oneness—becomes mundane and expected. But this Hoffmann-like tale could not have anticipated its ultimate notoriety. With the advent of the psychological model, *Jekyll and Hyde* became the classic account of criminal personality dissociation—or in more popular terms, the schizophrenic killer.

Hyde was an evil persona. Stooped and deformed, dark and ill-featured, he moved in quick and furtive strides; and—almost expectedly, as in a fateful nightmare—Hyde was a brutal psychopathic killer. Without dwelling on the familiar story, what is striking is that Hyde is never offered as an excuse—as an explanation for the character's whole behavior. Indeed, Jekyll revels in his ability to assume the anonymity and base behavior that Hyde's character offers, through the intake of a strange apothecary mixture. The story is a moral allegory; Utterson the attorney passes no judgment, and offers no clue as to what we should make of Jekyll. In fact, the story ends with the opening of sealed letters written by an associate of Jekyll's and a statement from the doctor himself. Here the reader finds the nineteenth-century drug addict, who—for this experience—taps into the primeval, brutal personality element within himself and falls prey to an addiction. By the story's end, Jekyll's experiments had led to irreversible and spontaneous metamorphosis into the persona of Mr. Hyde.

What is key is the integrative element of the narrative. Jekyll is flawed and commits murder not for reasons of insanity, but rather for falling prey to the dark figure he found within himself. Hyde—then—is not an excuse, but rather a damning evidence of Jekyll's culpability. The dramatic device of not reconciling the two personas until the very end makes this point. Stevenson spends no time building sympathy for the "good" character of Dr. Jekyll being led astray by the terrible behavior of his Mr. Hyde. Quite the contrary, the story's circumstances suggest the contrived nature and personal culpability of the doctor. Jekyll's own final sanction is to take his own life—now irreversibly in the form of Hyde.

While many see the story as a Victorian parable concerning the repressed id of man (and, perhaps, a justification for this repression), one cannot overlook the author's treatment of his character, who might have been presented as absolved of crime committed under powerful mind- and body-altering drugs. But instead, responsibility for the character's acts falls squarely on the moral and rational choices made by the scientist-doctor, who could have discontinued his long series of fateful self-experiments.

Although one might wonder what Stevenson's trial for Dr. Jekyll/ Mr. Hyde would have looked like, it is important to note that no such trial takes place, nor seems appropriate. Again, the author—even with a character of radically split personality—is unwilling to allow for exoneration of the character's acts on psychological grounds. Even a Mr. Hyde—the sinister half of a normal, unified person— cannot be isolated and utilized to imply freedom from moral blame. Instead, this evil agent brings on the inevitable destruction of the whole person. Once again, robbing the hero of rationality or the trappings of a moral self seems counterproductive to effective story- telling and the creation of character.

THE BROTHERS KARAMAZOV

The chapter in the *Brothers Karamazov*[7] that we discuss here is the one in which the medical testimony is examined in the trial of Mitya for his father's murder. It is entitled "The Medical Experts and a Pound of Nuts," and concerns the testimony of three doctors as to the mental stability of the defendant.

Dostoevsky offers three experts: two doctors who find the defendant mentally impaired, but for different and conflicting rea- sons; and a third who finds the defendant sane. Dostoevsky presents the doctors' testimony as comic, irrelevant, and out of place. Indeed, writing about the novel in reference to the trial, R. P. Blackmur re- marks: "The medical experts . . . no doubt fuddled the jury as much as they annoyed Dostoevsky and outraged the prisoner."[8]

Even with this irrelevant atmosphere surrounding the psycho- logical testimony, the third doctor's findings of the defendant as sane and responsible for the alleged murder is embraced by the conviction-hungry public inside the courtroom: "[T]he young doctor's opinion had a decisive influence on the judges and on the public, and, as appeared afterwards, everyone agreed with him."[9]

The context of the trial is all important. We shall return to this theme in our discussion later of Robert Traver's *Anatomy of a Murder*. While Dostoevsky trivializes the expert testimony as inaccessible infighting, the receptiveness of the public and the jury to observations supporting popular sentiment is not overlooked by the author. In describing the action, he notes parenthetically, "(It must be noted that I report this [the testimony] in my own words; the doctor made use of very learned and professional language.)" But the effect of the testimony that corroborates public sentiment is not passed over.

Concerning the trial as a whole, Ralph Matlaw observes that "the townspeople desire to see Mitya convicted and, by extension, all of Russia and humanity, since the trial becomes a cause celebre, creating interest throughout the land."[10]

Where, in *Anatomy of a Murder*, Traver presents a sympathetic public (and jury) searching to acquit the murderer of a disliked member of the community by an outsider, Dostoevsky—80 years earlier—offers a hostile public eager to convict an innocent member of the community for an alleged act of patricide. In either case, the substantive value of the insanity plea is minimized, and the social dynamics are similar.

THE GOOD SOLDIER SVEJK

Turning now to the realm of the absurd, an examination of the use of an insanity plea or competency test in early twentieth-century literature shows a similar unwillingness on the part of an author to relinquish a character's action to such a device. On the contrary, the absurdist author emphasizes the irrationality of a society that is oppressive and deaf to reason.

Jaroslov Hasek—author of *The Good Soldier Svejk*[11]—may perhaps be best characterized as a latter-day beatnik, a political anarchist, and a social outcast. The stories that he produced satirized a particularly violent and absurd period in European history. Hasek depicts a dull irrational bureaucracy making pronouncements upon the mind-sets of its citizens. While still couched in fable form and softened by the clownlike Svejk, Hasek's story offers "expert" doctors who make no sense, along with policemen who make arbitrary and unfounded arrests. As in most situations that Svejk encounters, his stupidity in the face of mindless bureaucracy confounds and illuminates the medical experts and their functions.

Svejk is arrested for conspiracy in the assassination of the Archduke Ferdinand—a charge that was widespread at the time and blatantly unfounded. After his arrest, interrogation, and confession,

Svejk is sent to the court and interviewed by a kindly magistrate. The magistrate recommends a medical examination for Svejk and he is taken into custody to await the examination. His fellow inmates relate their separate experiences with medical experts. The first describes his good fortune:

> "I've been examined by those medical experts too," said a young man. ... "They certified me as feeble-minded. Now I've embezzled a steam threshing machine and they can't do anything to me. My lawyer told me yesterday that once I've been certified feeble-minded, I'll have the benefit of it for the rest of my life."[12]

The second inmate commiserates on the unpredictability of such expert opinions:

> "I don't trust those medical experts at all," observed the man with the intelligent appearance. "Once when I forged some bills of exchange I prepared myself for all eventualities and went to lectures by the psychiatrist Dr. Heveroch, and when they caught me, I pretended to be a paralytic, exactly as Dr. Heveroch had described one. I bit one of the medical experts on the commission in the leg, drank ink out the ink pot and relieved myself, if you'll pardon the expression, gentlemen, in the corner in the view of the whole commission. But because I bit one of them through the calf they certified me as completely fit and so I was done for."[13]

The story offers alternative views of men fully wishing to manipulate competency decisions in order to gain diminished responsibility status. This sharply contrasts with Svejk, who seems quite content whatever the outcome. Finally, the third man in the cell proclaims:

> Medical experts are swine. ... Not long ago quite by chance they dug up a skeleton in my meadow, and the medical experts said that it was murdered forty years ago by some blunt object on the head. I'm thirty-eight and I've been gaoled, although I have my birth certificate, and extract from the parish register and my identity card.[14]

However, competency is the issue, and Svejk himself meets the experts who will "decide whether his mental horizon did or did not correspond to all the crimes with which he was charged." In order to determine his sanity, the doctors direct a series of questions to Svejk, such as: "Is radium heavier than lead?" and "Do you believe in the end of the world?" and, finally, "How much is 12,863 times 13,863?"—to which Svejk answers "729 . . . without batting an eyelid." With the examination complete, the doctor's report reads:

> The undersigned medical experts certify the complete mental feebleness and congenital idiocy of Josef Svejk, who appeared before the aforesaid commission and expressed himself in terms such as: "Long live our Emperor Franz Joseph I," which utterance is sufficient to illuminate the state of mind of Josef Svejk as that of a patent imbecile. The undersigned commission accordingly recommends:
> 1. That the investigation of Josef Svejk be quashed.
> 2. That Josef Svejk be sent to a psychiatric clinic for observation to establish how far his mental state is a danger to his surroundings.[15]

On the basis of the report, Svejk is remanded to the custody of the lunatic asylum. His stay at the asylum is—in his view—disappointingly brief, as the doctors accuse him of malingering and send him on his way. Having not had lunch, however, Svejk raises such a scene that a policeman is called to remove him, and places him under arrest once again for breach of the peace.

Medical experts appear periodically throughout the story, but invariably have little or no concern with accurate diagnosis or sensible treatment. Svejk suffers from terrible rheumatism, but gains no sympathy from the army or its doctors. Even his documented certification as a "patent idiot" only draws accusations of "malingering." In any case, the state and its agents constantly take and manipulate medical classifications for their own, often capricious use.

COMPULSION

Levin's *Compulsion*[16] offers the dramatization of factual circumstances, in this case the notorious Loeb–Leopold murder of 1930s Chicago. From the outset, it should be stressed that—while *Compulsion* takes perhaps the most accepting stance of integrating psychological analysis into a criminal justice system—it is not a work of pure fiction, and insanity is treated in the context of sentencing, not in assigning guilt. During the trial, the defense makes a plea of guilty, and—in hopes of avoiding a capital sentence—pleads mitigating circumstances of mental incapacity.

The subject of the book is the cold-blooded and shocking murder of a millionaire's eight-year-old child by two wealthy young men—Artie Straus and Judd Steiner—in an affluent, predominantly Jewish Chicago suburb. The story depicts the planning stages of the kidnapping-murder, offering personality sketches of the boys, and laying the foundation for later analysis of the crime. The actual murder, subsequent investigation, and public reaction are detailed—leading to the inevitable discovery of Artie and Judd, their interrogation, and trial.

Told in the first person from the point of view of a young reporter and former classmate of the two, the story has the feeling of an inquiry throughout. Expert testimony and its shrewd use by an eloquent defense counsel save the boys from execution. Several factors are at work. More than in any other story examined so far, the sense of public outrage and horror at the crime is emphasized. The murder carried with it overtones of sodomy; and, as publicized by the media, the homosexual relationship between the boys stirs public emotion to the boiling point. The crime is against the family of a prominent, respected, and wealthy member of the community. In addition, it is soon known that the suspects in the crime are of the same social standing. In effect, this works to fuel both public reaction to the crime, and outrage at the criminals. Interestingly, the narrator's father remarks, "One thing is lucky in this terrible affair, Sid. It's lucky it was a Jewish boy they picked."[17]

Levin devotes much time to the psychic world of the boys—particularly the more sympathetic Judd Steiner. We are given the picture of two wealthy and exceptionally intelligent boys, who are years ahead of their classmates and are college graduates at 18. Artie is popular, attractive, and sociable; Judd is introverted and shy, and devotedly in love with Artie. The author creates a complex symbiosis between the two. Later in the book, one of the prosecution's psychiatrists will state that he had trouble differentiating between the two in interviews—noting statements made by the one as made by the other. But the similarities between the boys serve as a literary device to emphasize their differences. While Artie is the attractive and accessible character, Judd—who is disliked for his reclusive introversion and reproachful elitism—becomes the character of interest and development. Through the psychological inquiry, it is discovered that—although the two are both significantly disturbed—Artie's is the truly destructive disorder. Judd's character develops; and the reader experiences his turmoil over his actions, and the establishment of a healthy love relationship with a girl in the story. Artie is progressively seen to be impotent and destructive, paranoid and sadistic—with this personality disorder worsening over time. On the other hand, Judd seems to be making emotional progress: from infantile fantasy to stages of turbulent growth.

The act of murder itself is complex. Painstakingly planned and yet clumsily performed, they have numerous opportunities to back out of what seems just a dangerous fantasy. The fantasy is realized, however; and Judd leaves crucial physical evidence at the scene—leading the authorities to them. While creating an ingenious plan to receive the ransom—replete with various stages of transfer, including throwing the money from a moving train—the boys leave the victim's body where it will be discovered before the ransom is paid; and they type the ransom note on Judd's portable typewriter, virtually ensuring the failure of their plan. Levin clearly implies a subconscious desire for capture—reinforcing the argument for mental disorder.

After some investigation and interrogation—where Artie is the first to break down—the police obtain full confessions from the boys. Horn, the prosecutor, promises a death penalty for the two. With this, the boys' parents employ the most famous defense attorney in the country—Jonathan Wilk, renowned for his defense of the poor and the underclass. The lawyer is characterized as an aged humanist—a "Lincolnesque figure." With their parents orchestrating the defense, the boys initially enter a plea of not guilty, hoping to prove their case on the grounds of insanity. The plea is changed almost immediately after initial consultation with the primary expert "alienist" to one of guilty, in order to avoid trial by a jury who would be sure to call for a death penalty. Their witness explains:

> Juries invariably regard the insanity plea as a dodge. They discredit the experts. What they really base their verdict on is whether society has been threatened by the accused. If they feel his act to be against society they will find him guilty; if they feel it has been against himself, as sometimes in a murder of passion, say the Thaw case, then they will tend to pity the murderer, and send him to an asylum.[18]

The plan of the defense, then, is to keep the case as far from public control as possible. While fully admitting guilt—and even calling for severe penalty in the form of life imprisonment (which the parents and defense both do)—the defense seeks only to present mitigating reasons to spare the lives of the two boys. The major problem that faces the defense is a legal one. At the time, Illinois law stated that any insanity plea must be heard by a jury—a point that the prosecutor Horn raises repeatedly as the defense attempts to introduce psychiatric testimony in the trial proceedings. As the defense confers on this paradoxical problem of how to present evidence of mitigating psychological nature without broaching insanity issues, its expert witness Dr. McNarry expresses

> his lifelong disgust with this curious situation in which a jury of laymen, the persons least equipped for it, were always the ones who had to decide whether a person was insane. Bring in the most learned men in the world to testify, and all their learning, all their special knowledge could be erased by people who had no understanding of it.[19]

Still, however, the defense is put in the uncomfortable position of having to go before a judge with a plea of guilty and attempt to influence a judgment of leniency without resorting to a jury trial. Early on, the defense—led by Wilk and McNarry—address the issues of competing expert psychiatric testimony and the fact that the decision might be left to persons who lack the skill and intelligence to understand the expert testimony. Wilk suggests a joint panel of "scientific inquiry" to determine the causes of the crime. As might be expected, the prosecutor flatly refuses such an exercise, because he believes he already has a "hanging case."

Levin portrays the public's responses to the trial as reflecting deep-seated antipathies rooted in class distinctions, and in disgust at the homosexuality implicit in the relationship between the two defendants. The courtroom action is heavily influenced by this, although in curious ways. The judge—Chief Justice Mathewson—had "precisely the bearing for his role. He had the fullness of years, but with no suggestion of frailty of age. He looked considerate, firm, and aware of the meaning of his position."[20] Wilk implores him not to let the wealth of the boys influence his opinion adversely—a curious plea from an attorney noted for representing the poor and oppressed. But perhaps more telling is the prosecutor's error in repeatedly cautioning the judge as to the public reaction to a less than harsh sentence. Horn intimates suspicions of graft and catering to the wealthy—which, in his closing statement, proves to be a fatal mistake, because it elicits in reaction a more lenient sentence from the judge.

At the risk of deliberating too long on a work that does not actually invoke an insanity defense, certain points are yet worth noting. With such overwhelming and predictable public reaction, a jury proceeding is vehemently avoided on the advice of psychiatric experts and defense lawyers alike. But possibly more important is the circumstance of the testimony itself. Guilt or innocence are not (or only for the briefest period) in question in *Compulsion.* Motive, personality, interpersonal dynamics, and social circumstances all come into play, including psychological evidence; but most have no bearing on the question of guilt per se—only in adjusting degree and gauging social response. Ultimately, in the judge's decision, it is the age of the defendants (18 and 19) that wins them mercy—a point that Wilk concentrates on primarily in conjunction with the psychiatric testimony.

Public climate and community reaction are also stressed. Harsh sentencing is never at question, although perhaps—at least for one of the murderers—it should be. But rather, psychiatric testimony as partial mitigation is put in its place both legally and in literary form. The judge in his sentencing decision remarks:

> It would have been the task of least resistance to impose the extreme penalty of the law. . . . In choosing imprisonment instead of death, the court is moved chiefly by the consideration of the age of defendants, boys of 18 and 19 years.[21]

One could even see this as a complete failure of the insanity strategy, as the factor of age is what Wilk chooses to emphasize in his closing arguments.

Literature is concerned with understanding the person as a whole, and *Compulsion*—told from the perspective of a newsman years later—attempts to assemble the puzzle that led to such destruction of three young and promising lives. The reason that sympathy is found for Judd Steiner—one of the killers—is precisely that his psychological character is developed, and enables him to confront his crime and his condition soon after the murder. Artie is forever obscure—a psychopath suspected of other unsolved murders in the area. He is killed in prison—we are told—by a jealous lover; the reader is left with not a character, but an enigma. The occasion of the telling of the story is the upcoming parole hearing date for Judd, some 30 years later—and the once young newsman/friend's retrospection. The reader leaves Judd alive and imbued with interest, not destroyed by insanity both in life and in story. The path of an insanity plea could not have led to this interest, in any imagined outcome.

ANATOMY OF A MURDER

In the social laboratory that literature creates, critical issues are seen to play themselves out—offering examination and commentary not found in the real world. The insanity plea finds its most explicit laboratory in Robert Traver's *Anatomy of a Murder*.[22] This popular novel of the late 1950s was written by a former Michigan Supreme Court justice, and carries with it the authentic flavor of expertise. Although the book is primarily concerned with the legal battle conducted by its hero—defense attorney Paul Biegler—it nevertheless also offers insight into the problems of the insanity plea.

Especially from our point of view, what makes *Anatomy* interesting is the hesitancy with which the author treats the insanity plea.[23] Biegler is a retired local district attorney in a small town in Michigan's upper peninsula. He takes on the case of a temporarily assigned army lieutenant, Frederic Manion, who has admittedly killed a local bar owner. The circumstances suggest a simple revenge killing in response to the victim's brutal rape of the lieutenant's wife. With a wealth of eyewitnesses and the defendant's own admission, the case against him seems depressingly complete. It is at this point that our hero delivers what he terms "the lecture," apprising the defendant of his legal predicament and his only possible recourse. Explaining to the lieutenant the possible responses to a charge of murder, Biegler names three alternatives: (1) a mistake in the charge—that there was no murder; (2) a mistake in identification—that there was a murder, but his client was not the killer; or (3) that his client's actions were somehow legally justified. The defense attorney then explains:

> You see, Lieutenant, it's not the act of killing a man that makes it murder; it is the circumstances, the time, and the state of mind or purpose which induced the act.[24]

Here is the beginning of the attorney's gentle prodding of an acceptable defense from the defendant. At this point in the story, artifice is shown to be the originator of the insanity plea. The plea is not in itself the original justification for the crime; ironically enough, it is a rational response by both lawyer and client to a severely limited menu of legal alternatives to the charge. The author seems to suggest from the outset that the insanity plea is inevitably a plea of convenience for the otherwise helpless defense attorney in an otherwise hopeless case. Calling something a convenience is not necessarily a condemnation; however, by structuring the plot in this manner, the author is implicitly preparing the reader for the eventual resolution of dramatic conflict.

As the story unfolds, Traver is careful to emphasize two related points. The first is the complete condemnation of the murder victim, Barney Quill. Although this is perhaps unusual in a defense of insanity, Traver has given us a victim who displayed antisocial tendencies and was thoroughly disliked by the community. Through depiction of popular sentiment and by description of the character himself, the author offers an overwhelmingly deserving murder victim. Quill is depicted as a powerful and resourceful man, a bully and a braggart who has managed to disaffect the entire town. The reader quickly learns that public opinion is decidedly for the defense, although not out of any great attachment to the transient army lieutenant. Rather, it is a combination of a general feeling of moral justification for the killing, along with the community dislike for the murder victim.

The second point of emphasis has to do with the irritating character of the prosecuting attorney, Claude Dancer—the district attorney from the state capital, who takes over the prosecution from the local district attorney (who, in turn, was Biegler's successor to that office). Dancer is a caricature of the physically small prosecuting attorney—mean and abrasive, although evidently quite capable in his profession. This contrast with the hero's general amiability and low-key legal style fuels the already partisan public opinion.

Through this attention paid to deficiencies of character in both the victim and the state's counsel, the author shifts the reader's attention away from the actual crime, and toward the prevailing feelings of the community. Throughout the book, we are reminded that the verdict will ultimately rest in the hands of the jury—a local jury—and any reader can tell that local favor in *Anatomy* lies with both the defendant and his counsel—or, perhaps more importantly, against the murder victim and "his" counsel.

While Traver turns the insanity plea into a legal tool in the hands of the story's hero, Paul Biegler, the ironies of Biegler's methods do not descape the defendant.

> This insanity business is pretty damned unscientific. . . . We can't prove insanity without a medical expert, you tell me. Yet you and I have already decided I was insane, we know that we're going to plead insanity—you tell me it's the only legal defense I've got. And even I can see that now. In other words, you a mere lawyer, and I a dumb soldier, have between us decided that I was medically and legally insane. Having decided that, we must now go out and shop around for a medical expert to confirm *our* settled conclusion. Yet you tell me an ordinary medical doctor won't do. It all sounds damned unscientific to me.[25]

There are certainly two levels at which the defense is working in the case. The first is the formal level of excusing the offense by the lieutenant in some legally justifiable terms. This must be done within the framework of the court and the rules therein. Part of this framework entails the examination and expert testimony provided by the psychiatrist (a young army doctor) for the defense. While Traver offers us the image of a youthful but highly intelligent and competent psychiatrist, his actual role in the story is notably brief. His examination of the defendant—while presented as quite exhaustive—is not given great attention. Prior to trial, the lieutenant is accompanied down state for clinical evaluation by the army doctor. Quite atypically, defense attorney Biegler has no knowledge of the psychiatrist's evaluation other than indirectly through the defendant, until the night prior to presentation of the doctor as an expert witness. In other words, we have the impression that there is no relationship whatsoever between attorney and psychiatrist—even for the purpose of outlining what the doctor is likely to testify to, as Biegler questions the doctor on his arrival the night before he is to testify:

> "And do I assume from what you've just said that you still are of an opinion that the Lieutenant was legally and medically insane when he fired the fatal shots?"
> The Doctor glanced at me quickly. "Yes. There is not the slightest doubt about that. What you've told me tonight only serves to clinch it."
> "Would you feel disposed to discuss it more now?" I said.
> He shook his head. "I would rather do so in court, if you don't mind. It might lend my testimony a little more spontaneity, if nothing else,

and at the same time spare you from being bored twice instead of once."[26]

Indeed, Biegler's interview with the doctor occupies less than three pages prior to trial; and the doctor's testimony during the trial, about eight short pages of dialogue. This seems somewhat brief in a 437-page book—half of which is trial action—for the most crucial part of the lieutenant's defense. And while the army doctor's expert testimony is crucial to the story, the decisive factor is not the veracity of his testimony, but rather its relative merits compared to the expert testimony offered by the prosecution. The state's expert witness seems inept and pompous. He has not examined the defendant prior to trial, and we are given to believe that he is basing his testimony solely on his in-court observation of the defendant.

By setting up the conflict in this manner, the author highlights the issue of conflicting expert testimony and its importance in the eventual outcome of the trial—as well as calling attention to the importance of counsel, and their role in impeaching the credibility of opposing expert testimony. This reduces the significance of expert testimony to a contest-like war of counsels, involving their adroitness in cross-examination and their ability or luck in obtaining sound expert witnesses.

Biegler is careful to warn his client that there is no such thing as "natural law" inside the courtroom; but, ironically, he must sell just such a natural law or right to the jury, by presenting a rationale for the lieutenant's insanity. His overwhelming problem is to somehow introduce and prove the alleged rape of the lieutenant's wife. The dramatic meaning in *Anatomy* is clear: The insanity plea by itself won't get the lieutenant off, but it will provide the legal framework for an amenable jury to bring in a not guilty verdict. One is almost compelled to wonder what the verdict would have been had Lieutenant Manion shot a more popular member of the community—or, alternatively, acted from less extreme provocation. Interestingly, in Dancer's summation as the people's attorney, he calls the jury's attention to the fact that it is not the victim who is on trial, as the defense attorney would have us believe. The night before the crucial expert testimony, the sensible young psychiatrist for the defense says:

Yes, to me the dead man is by far the most fascinating character in the whole drama, . . . I would have loved to try and find out just what made *him* tick.[27]

In the end, the defense wins a not guilty by reason of insanity verdict from the jury. And in all of the excitement and public celebration of the outcome, the judge and counsel for the people agree to suspend any civil or criminal commitment proceedings against the lieutenant. The thrust of their decision stems not from their belief that Lieutenant Manion's insanity should excuse his crime, but from the community's approval of his actions as morally acceptable.

SHORT STORIES BY NORVAL MORRIS

[I]njustice and inefficiency invariably flow from a blending of the criminal-law and mental health powers of the state. Each is sufficient unto itself to achieve a just balance between freedom and authority; each has its own interested constituency; when they are mixed together, only the likelihood of injustice is added.[28]

Norval Morris's book on the subject—*Madness and the Criminal Law*—suggests the necessity of separating the legal and psycho-medical models in the criminal justice system. In the text, Morris incorporates two short stories that serve to highlight and dramatize the argument he presents. Perhaps encountering the same difficulty that we did in locating relevant examples of the insanity plea in literature, Morris has—in effect—turned our task on its head, and written his own fiction dealing with the insanity plea. Where we have searched for and attempted to analyze the fictional and dramatic treatment of the plea, Morris created his own.

Morris's creations support our contention about the lack of materials from which to draw and also support our subsequent explanation, but they also offer the interesting opportunity to examine what occurs when fiction is created for the express purpose of providing material for a thesis concerning the NGRI plea.

In the first story—"The Brothel Boy"—a young man of diminished mental capacities rapes and inadvertently kills a young girl in his Burmese village. It is common knowledge in the village that the boy has been brought up in the whorehouse where he was conceived. He does small menial chores in order to earn his keep there, but is generally considered mentally incompetent. An observer in the story—Eric Blair—sees the boy as a product of his environment, with strange examples of sexuality all around him and with no sense not to commit the sort of crime he did. The story is basically a narrative of the discussions between Blair—the English magistrate in the village—and the local doctor, Dr. Verswami—an English-educated Indian national. What follows is a parade of philosophical argumentation for and against punishment of the boy, with Dr. Veraswami—himself an unaccepted stranger in the village, although to a lesser degree than Blair—strongly persuading the Englishman from interceding in the affair. In short, Veraswami argues for the external nature of justice.

The important elements here—as will also be seen in the story that follows—are the social dynamics that exist as a context for the murder. The young girl who was attacked seems to have been a valued and accepted member of the community, in sharp contrast to the brothel boy. Furthermore, the crime took place between two members of the same community—although of unequal rank. In terms of how the community views itself and its concepts of justice and legal remedies, the judgment is without question. Community sentiment—and this is what is really at the heart of the story—cannot afford such mercy as Blair advocates; it is too costly.

Just as in *Anatomy of a Murder*, individual guilt must be balanced and weighed by the society at large. Where in *Anatomy* the public used the defense to excuse an act that they tacitly—at least—wished to condone, so in "The Brothel Boy" do the interests of the integrity of tribal justice outweigh the sophisticated mercy of the English magistrate. Justice—Blair decides—is a social act.

The second story—"The Planter's Dream"—offers the same magistrate and, again, Dr. Veraswami; this time, they are discussing the case of an Englishman, Taylor, who killed his native mistress. Now, with a more intelligent and competent defendant pleading a form of not guilty by reason of insanity, we witness the inevitable lack of sanction taken against him for his act. Here the context is entirely changed. Now the victim—a low-status village woman—has been a marginal member of the community, as mistress to the Englishman. Taylor—the self-admitted killer—is totally removed from the community. As an Englishman, he has none of the community ties that invoke responsibility. But he has committed a bloody and violent act: shotgunning the native woman who was his mistress, prior to his wife's joining him from England. The story is unclear on this point, but it is perhaps suggested that the murder was committed in an unconscious, irrational state. However, what is clear throughout the story is that the same community pressure for justice evidenced in "The Brothel Boy" is absent. The magistrate—Eric Blair—is once again put in the uncomfortable position of arguing against the community mood—which says that the Englishman is unaccountable for his actions—and somehow attempting to apply an individualistic morality to the situation.

Again, the story recalls *Anatomy*. While the justification for the lack of public outcry is somewhat different, the context is the same. Here again, the defendant is an outsider—not considered a true member of the tribe or society. He is also an elite—an Englishman—in much the same way as the war hero Lieutenant Manion may have been viewed by the town in *Anatomy*. Notice also that, in both fictional cases the victims were marginal members of the societies, at best. Although Morris's work can be said to be contrived, both scenarios offer the same fictional grounds for an insanity plea: The victims are marginal members of society; the defendants are removed from the responsibility-invoking circle of the community; and the acts are placed into an acceptable moral framework. Indeed, the states of "madness" that overcome both Taylor and Lieutenant Manion are quite subjective and legally flimsy excuses for murder. Society can accept such an act under the correct circumstances; under other—perhaps even more compelling—ones such as occurred in "The Brothel Boy," the community cannot or will not accept any amelioration of the crime, in order to protect its communal integrity.

"EXECUTION OF JUSTICE"

Emily Mann's "Execution of Justice"[29] dramatizes the trial of Dan White for the murder of San Francisco Mayor George Moscone and City Supervisor Harvey Milk, and the surrounding circumstances. The play utilizes trial transcripts, interviews, and news reportage loosely structured around the trial proceedings. The play is strongly political in tone; it emphasizes the miscarriage of justice done in allowing Dan White to be exonerated of first degree murder charges, and instead handed a token sentence. It is an angry play—which sees the incident as an example of publicly sanctioned murder, and an insult to the gay community in San Francisco.

While keeping in mind the political context of the work, certain elements of the play are relevant to this discussion. Again, as was the case in Traver's *Anatomy of a Murder*, the insanity plea is seemingly used by the jury—representing society—as a device to at least partially exonerate the defendant from public sanction for his crime. As the play's title suggests, justice is sacrificed to the popular will through the instrument of a diminished capacity defense.

Here, however, the safety valve phenomenon discussed in *Anatomy* seems to be far less tolerable to the author. Once again, the psychiatric witnesses are presented as tools of the lawyers. In Act II, the witnesses for the defense are presented as a chorus, delivering evaluations simultaneously. Testimony is disorganized and incoherent.

Testimony centers around the premeditation element of the first degree murder charge. The heart of the expert testimony in the play is delivered by a Dr. Jones. He elaborates on his own version of a *M'Naghten*/ALI test and its application in the present case.

> *Jones*: In order to have malice, you would have to be able to do certain things, to be able to be intent to kill somebody unlawfully. You would have to be able to do something for a base and anti-social purpose.
>
> You would have to be aware of the duty imposed on you not to do that, not to unlawfully kill somebody or do something for a base, anti-social purpose, that involved a risk of death, and you would have to be able to act, despite having that awareness that, that you are supposed to do that, and so you would have to know that you are not supposed to do it and then also act despite—keeping in mind that you are not supposed to do it.
>
> *Jones then concludes*: I think he had the capacity to know that there was a duty imposed on him not to do that, but I don't think he had the capacity to hold that notion in his mind while he was acting; so that I think that the depression, plus the moment, the tremendous emotion of the moment, with the depression, reduced his capacity for conforming conduct.[30]

Following this testimony, the prosecutor—Mr. Norman—brings out the key issues for the state: (1) White eluded the metal detector at the city administration building's entrance; (2) he reloaded his gun between the killings of Moscone and Milk; and (3) White fired execution-style close-range shots to the head after his victims had initially fallen. The witness for the defense practically ignores Norman's arguments—repeatedly asserting his initial testimony. Norman's frustration is noteworthy, as an attorney confronted with expert testimony that defies rationality. In presenting the psychiatric testimony in this manner, Emily Mann emphasizes the inherent conflict that such testimony entails in criminal proceedings. The opposing attorney is reduced to arguing judgments instead of facts—something that is not only a hopeless task for the nonprofessional, but is also the job of the jury, not the attorney.

With the presentation of the prosecution's psychiatric witness in Act III, another judgment is presented—this time, predicated on a postshooting interview with the defendant by a Dr. Levy.

> *Levy*: At that time it appeared to me that Dan White had no remorse for the death of George Moscone. . . . I had the feeling that there was some depression but it was not depression that I would consider as a diagnosis. . . . At that time I saw him, it seemed that he felt himself to be quite justified.
>
> I felt he had the capacity to form malice. I felt he had the capacity to premeditate. And . . . I felt he had the capacity to deliberate, to arrive at a course of conduct weighing considerations.[31]

Again, Emily Mann makes a poignant statement in contrasting the cross-examination styles of the opposing counsels. When cross-examining witnesses for the defense, the prosecutor has been evidently frustrated in having to argue the facts leading to the professional judgments of diminished capacity made by the psychiatrists. Counsel for the defense—Mr. Schmidt—pursues an entirely different track in cross-examination of the prosecution's witness. Instead of addressing the merits of the evaluation on the facts of the case, Schmidt merely makes assertions and questions impugning the competency of the witness himself, and the circumstances of his interviews with the defendant. While the prosecution seemed to argue facts in vain, the defense simply argued testimony. Here—as in *Anatomy*—the defense wins the battle of expert testimony not on substance, but by tactic.

While still fiction, "Execution of Justice" not only is based on— but draws much of its dialogue from—real life and the actual trial of Dan White. Here, the literary dynamic involving the characters' or actors' responsibility in literature begins to edge its way into the real world.

NOTES

1. Rita J. Simon, *The Jury System in America* (Beverly Hills: Sage Publications, 1975).

2. Emily Watts, "The Jury in American Literature," in Simon, *Jury System*, pp. 159–78.

3. Jon Breen, *Novel Verdicts: A Guide to Courtroom Fiction* (Metuchen, N.J., and London: Scarecrow Press, 1984).

4. Aristotle, *The Poetics* (New York: Hill and Wang, 1961).

5. Ibid., p. 81.

6. Robert Louis Stevenson, *The Strange Case of Dr. Jekyll and Mr. Hyde* (New York: Heritage Press, 1952).

7. Fyodor Dostoevsky, *The Brothers Karamazov* (New York: Norton, 1976).

8. R. P. Blackmur, "The Peasants Stand Firm: Tragedy of the Saint," in Dostoevsky, *Brothers Karamazov*, p. 881.

9. Dostoevsky, *Brothers Karamazov*, pp. 639-40.

10. Ralph E. Matlaw, "Myth and Symbol," in Dostoevsky, *Brothers Karamazov*, p. 864.

11. Jaroslov Hasek, *The Good Soldier Svejk, and His Fortunes in the World War* (New York: Thomas Crowell, 1973).

12. Ibid., p. 26.

13. Ibid.

14. Ibid., p. 27.

15. Ibid., pp. 29-30.

16. Meyer Levin, *Compulsion* (New York: Signet, 1965).

17. Ibid., p. 301.

18. Ibid., p. 336.

19. Ibid., p. 337.

20. Ibid., pp. 303-4.

21. Ibid., p. 462.

22. Robert Traver, *Anatomy of a Murder* (New York: St. Martin's Press, 1958).

23. More than 20 years later, Traver again used the courtroom as the focus of his novel *People versus Kirk*. This time, the defendant is charged with the murder of the woman he loved, and is found by a jury to be "not guilty by reason of unconsciousness." The defense attorney—with the help of a retired country doctor—successfully argued that the defendant had acted under a hypnotic trance.

24. Traver, *Anatomy*, p. 37.

25. Ibid., p. 67.

26. Ibid., p. 336.

27. Ibid., p. 337.

28. Norval Morris, *Madness and the Criminal Law* (Chicago: University of Chicago Press, 1982).

29. Emily Mann, "Execution of Justice," unpublished script, Arena Stage, Chicago, August 1983.

30. Ibid. Act II, p. 14.

31. Ibid., Act III, p. 2.

9

Summary and Concluding Remarks

Intellectually, the defense of insanity is alive and well. It continues to be the subject of numerous law review articles and symposia. It is a favored topic of debate among social scientists and legal scholars. As a practical matter, the defense of insanity continues to be offered in less than 1 percent of all criminal trials. However, it is greatly over-represented in sensational trials involving the assassination of a public figure or the indictment of a defendant for a particularly heinous act.

This book has reviewed the historical origins, the moral basis, and the changing definitions by which the defense has been applied and identified. It has also traced reactions to the use of the insanity defense in trials involving assassination or attempted assassination of English sovereigns, prime ministers, and U.S. presidents—from George III to Ronald Reagan. It has reviewed the major precedent-setting cases by which the standards for determination of responsibility have been interpreted and changed—from the wild beast test enunciated by Justice Tracey in England in 1723 to the Insanity Defense Reform Act passed by the U.S. Congress in 1984.

Commenting on the changes that have been introduced during the past 160 years, we noted that the initial emphasis was on cognition and—specifically—on the defendant's ability to distinguish good from evil, or right from wrong. With few variations and altera-tions (as represented by the *Hadfield* case in 1800, and two New Hampshire cases in the 1890s), the courts retained that emphasis until the *Durham* rule was enacted by the Court of Appeals of the District of Columbia in 1954 and the American Law Institute standard was adopted by all of the federal jurisdictions and many of the states in the 1960s. *Durham* and the American Law Institute test included volitional along with cognitive factors in determining whether a defendant should be held responsible for his or her criminal acts. The 1984 Insanity Defense Reform Act emphasizes cognition exclusively, and is thus patterned along the lines of the earlier *M'Naghten* standard.

Along with criteria for the determination of insanity, cases and statutes were examined to show changes in the burden and standard of proof and in verdict forms. In separate chapters, we described the intellectual and political bases for the movement to abolish the defense of insanity, and assessed its strength following the acquittal of John Hinckley. We have also provided statutory data on the standards employed by other societies in different parts of the world for assessing criminal responsibility or the lack of it, as well as the procedures employed for determining conditions for commitment and release from custody.

The role of expert witnesses and their presumed influence on the court and the jury's determination of the defendant's guilt was traced from English courts in the eighteenth century up to the present time in the United States. Disagreement between experts testifying on behalf of the defense and the prosecution, the function of experts in such trials, and their usefulness in responding to the legal and moral issues involved in a defense of insanity case are some of the questions considered in Chapter 3, devoted to expert testimony.

In addition to relying on the traditional form of legal scholarship with its focus on the analysis of important precedent-setting cases, we also collected empirical data by conducting a survey of judicial experts—the results of which were reported in Chapter 5. Views on such matters as the preferred standard for determining responsibility, burden of proof, verdict forms, commitment procedures, and whether the defense of insanity should be retained were compared against each other. Judges (state and federal, trial-level and appellate), prosecution and defense attorneys (both public and private), and medical experts comprised the target population for our survey. The biggest sources of controversy and disagreement on the major defense of insanity issues (legal standards, burdens of proof, verdict forms, and so on) were reflected in the response patterns of the various experts, with the prosecution and defense attorneys representing the greatest areas of disagreement on all the important issues.

How the defense of insanity has fared in the hands of the U.S. jury is explored in Chapter 4, with attention paid to the interaction of different types of jurors as represented by social class, sex, age, and race and to the issues posed in such trials. The jury's competence to understand the issues, its willingness to abide by the rules of law and evidence, and its reactions to expert testimony were considered in that chapter.

For reasons explained in Chapter 8, the defense of insanity is a theme not frequently used by novelists or playwrights. We found only one relatively recent U.S. novel and one new play that were based on real events and that dealt directly with the insanity defense. Traver's *Anatomy of a Murder*—which is rich in courtroom drama and behind-the-scenes strategy—is purely fiction. Themes closely associated with the insanity defense—morality, responsibility, free will, and responses to adversity—are naturally favored topics around which a hero's personality and character can be developed. However, the declaration of insanity as a defense for one's antisocial behavior is viewed by novelists and playwrights as an abdication of responsibility; and such abdication is not consistent with the heroes they wish to portray. Indeed, one might extend that argument to real defendants in real defense of insanity trials, and recognize that such defendants are never even grudgingly depicted by the press as heroes. For some other defendants—no matter how distasteful their act—there may be some bit of respect for their demeanor in the courtroom or for the manner in which they accept their fate. Not so with a defendant who pleads insanity. He has lost a crucial part of his humanness, along with any respect he may have acquired from the public observing such events.

We end on the same note on which we began—namely, that the defense of insanity is applied in less than 1 percent of all criminal trials, but often gains national attention when it is the defense to a particularly heinous crime and/or an attack on a public figure. The outcry that follows an acquittal in such a trial also leads to more systematic efforts to abolish the availability of the defense, or else to tighten the criteria by which defendants may be declared not responsible for their acts. The results of our survey support impressionistic data that the legal profession holds strong and differing views about almost all of the important issues surrounding the defense—from its validity, to the criteria concerning responsibility that ought to be applied, to which side should have the burden of proof and by what standard, to the verdict forms, and to the processes that ought to be applied in the posttrial phase. Abolition of the defense is an idea that attracts discussion and scholarly articles; but it has not become a widespread movement that is likely to result in legislative and judicial action at the federal level or by many of the states.

The best explanation for why the United States and many other societies in the world perpetuate the defense of insanity is that it tests the societies' ultimate social values, which hold individuals accountable for their actions because they are capable of making rational and voluntary choices. The moral test comes when a legal system judges that individuals who lack the ability to make such choices should be exempt from punishment. The United States is not likely to give up that distinction.

Appendix:

Insanity Defense Standards, Burdens of Proof, and Verdict Forms

Alabama

Test: ALI Section 13A-3-1
   Year established: 1977
Burden of Proof: Defendant must prove insanity by a preponderance of the evidence.
   Year established: 1958 (Ala. Code, tit. 15, sec. 422)
Verdict Form: NGRI
   Year established: 1940 (Section 15-16-24)

Alaska

Test: ALI
   Year established: 1982 (Alaska Stat., sec. 12.47)
Burden of Proof: Defendant, by a preponderance of the evidence
   Year established: 1982
Verdict Form: Guilty but mentally ill
   Year established: 1982

Arizona

Test: M'Naghten
   Year established: 1970 (*State v. Shaw*, 106 Ariz. 103, 471 P.2d 715). Codified in 1977
Burden of Proof: Defendant, by clear and convincing evidence
   Year established: 1983 (A.R.S. Section 13-502(B). Supp. 1984)
Verdict Form: NGRI
   Year established: 1956

Arkansas

Test: ALI
    Year established: 1976
Burden of Proof: Defendant, by a preponderance of the evidence
    Year established: 1979
Verdict Form: NGRI
    Year established: 1975

California

Test: ALI
    Year established: 1978
Burden of Proof: Defendant, by a preponderance of the evidence
    Year established: 1872. Codified in 1982.
Verdict Form: NGRI
    Year established: First codified in 1927.

Colorado

Test: *M'Naghten* (and irresistible impulse)
    Year established: 1963 (amended in 1978 and 1983)
Burden of Proof: Prosecutor, beyond a reasonable doubt
    Year established: 1973
Verdict Form: NGRI
    Year established: 1973

Connecticut

Test: ALI Section 53a-13 (found guilty but not criminally responsible). Excludes defense where caused by voluntary ingestion of liquor or unprescribed drugs or manifested by compulsive gambling
    Year established: 1977 (Gen. Stat. Section 53a-13, rev. to 1979)
Burden of Proof: Defendant, by a preponderance of the evidence
    Year established: 1983 (Public Acts 1983, no. 83-486)
Verdict Form: Guilty but mentally ill
    Year established: 1982

Delaware

Test: *M'Naghten* rule. Excludes defense where caused by voluntary ingestion of liquor or unprescribed drugs
    Year established: 1982 (amendment to 11 Del. Code, sec. 401)
Burden of Proof: Defendant, by a preponderance of the evidence
    Year established: First stated in 1903 (*State v. Jack*, 58 A. 833). Codified in 1953

Verdict Form: Guilty but mentally ill
 Year established: 1982

District of Columbia

Test: ALI
 Year established: 1972
Burden of Proof: Defendant, by a preponderance of the evidence
 Year established: 1973 (D.C. Code 1973, sec. 24-301(j))
Verdict Form: NGRI
 Year established: 1970 District of Columbia Court Reform and Criminal Procedure Act of 1970, Pub. L. No. 91-358, sec. 207

Florida

Test: *M'Naghten* modified ("A person is considered to be insane when he had a mental infirmity, disease or defect; and because of this condition he did not know what he was doing or its consequences; or although he knew what he was doing and its consequences, he did not know it was wrong.")
 Year established: 1977 (*Wheeler v. State*, 344 So.2d 244, 246). Test was first mentioned in 1973 (*Anderson v. State*, 276 So.2d 17)
Burden of Proof: Prosecution, beyond a reasonable doubt
 Year established: 1986 (In *Yohn v. State*, 476 So.2d 123 (Fla. 1985), the Florida Supreme Court held the standard jury instruction on the insanity issue to be legally incorrect with respect to the state's burden of proof concerning insanity. The Committee on Florida Standard Jury Instructions in Criminal Cases submitted a revised instruction, which was adopted in 1986 by the Supreme Court of Florida.)
Verdict Form: NGRI
 Year established: 1977 (*Wheeler v. State*, supra)

Georgia

Test: ALI
 Year established: 1968
Burden of Proof: Defendant, by a preponderance of the evidence
 Year established: 1977
Verdict Form: Guilty but mentally ill
 Year established: 1982

Hawaii

Test: ALI. Language expanded to include physical or mental disease, disorder, or defect
 Year established: 1972

Burden of Proof: Defendant, by a preponderance of the evidence
                        Prosecutor, beyond a reasonable doubt
   Year established: 1980
Verdict Form: NGRI
   Year established: 1972

Idaho

Test: Idaho has effectively abolished the insanity defense. Section 18-207. Mental condition is not a defense to any charge of criminal conduct.
   Year established: 1982
Burden of Proof: State must prove criminal intent.
   Year established: 1982
Verdict Form: None
   Year established: 1982

Illinois

Test: ALI
   Year established: 1962
Burden of Proof: Defendant, by a preponderance of the evidence
   Year established: 1962
Verdict Form: Guilty but mentally ill
   Year established: 1981

Indiana

Test: ALI
   Year established: 1976
Burden of Proof: Defendant, by a preponderance of the evidence
   Year established: 1976
Verdict Form: Guilty; not guilty; not responsible by reason of insanity at the time of the crime; guilty but mentally ill at the time of the crime
   Year established: 1981

Iowa

Test: M'Naghten
   Year established: 1981 (*State v. Donelson*, 302 N.W.2d 125)
Burden of Proof: State, beyond a reasonable doubt
   Year established: 1978
Verdict Form: Guilty; not guilty; not guilty by reason of insanity; not guilty by reason of diminished responsibility
   Year established: 1978

Kansas

Test: M'Naghten
　　Year established: 1977 (*State v. Smith*, 223 Kan. 203, 574)
Burden of Proof: State, beyond a reasonable doubt
　　Year established: 1971 (*State v. Chase*, 206 Kan. 352, 362, 480 P.2d 62)
Verdict Form: NGRI
　　Year established: 1979

Kentucky

Test: ALI
　　Year established: 1963 (*Terry v. Commonwealth*, Ky., 371 S.W. 2d 862; with some refinement since then)
Burden of Proof: Defendant, to the satisfaction of the jury
　　Year established: 1977 (*Edwards v. Commonwealth*, Ky., 554 S.W.2d 380)
Verdict Form: Guilty but mentally ill
　　Year established: 1982

Louisiana

Test: M'Naghten
　　Year established: First stated in 1931 (*State v. Tapie*, 138 So. 665). Codified in 1942
Burden of Proof: Defendant, by a preponderance of the evidence
　　Year established: 1980
Verdict Form: NGRI
　　Year established: 1966

Maine

Test: ALI
　　Year established: 1983 (Maine Rev. Stat. Ann., tit. 17-A, sec. 39. This is the last official codification of the defense, although it appeared in the same form in 1979.)
Burden of Proof: Defendant, by a preponderance of the evidence
　　Year established: 1972 (*State v. Collins*, Me., 297 A.2d 620). Codified in 1979 (17-A.M.R.S.A. Section 58(3) (Supp.))
Verdict Form: NGRI
　　Year established: 1870 (First time court instructed that the accused could be relieved of criminal responsibility if he was laboring under a sufficient defect of reason). Codified in 1968.

Maryland

Test: ALI. Mental disorder, rather than disease or defect

Year established: 1967 (Chapter 709 of the Laws of Maryland, Md. Code (1957, 1964 repl. vol., 1967 cum. supp.), art. 59, sec. 9. Refined in 1970 by Chapter 407, where "mental disorder" was substituted for "mental disease or defect")
Burden of Proof: Defendant, by a preponderance of the evidence
   Year established: 1964 (*Bradford v. State*, 234 Md. 505)
Verdict Form: Not criminally responsible
   Year established: 1985

Massachusetts

Test: ALI
   Year established: 1967 (*Commonwealth v. McHoul*, 352 Mass. 544, 546–48)
Burden of Proof: State, beyond a reasonable doubt
   *Year established:*1976 (*Commonwealth v. Kostka*, 370 Mass. 516, 531–32)
Verdict Form: NGRI
   Year established: 1967

Michigan

Test: ALI (Mental illness is defined as "a substantial disorder of thought or mood which significantly impairs judgment, behavior, capacity to recognize reality, or ability to cope with the ordinary demands of life.")
   Year established: 1975
Burden of Proof: State, by a preponderance of the evidence, beyond a reasonable doubt
   Year established: 1966 (*People v. Krugman*, 377 Mich 559,563; 141 N.W.2d 33)
Verdict Form: Guilty but mentally ill
   Year established: 1975

Minnesota

Test: M'Naghten
   Year established: 1971 (Minn. Stat. Section 611.026) Trial must be bifurcated—established 1983.
Burden of Proof: Defendant, by a preponderance of the evidence
   Year established: Codified in 1971
Verdict Form: NGRI
   Year established: 1977

Mississippi

Test: M'Naghten ("[A] person shall be deemed insane if the court finds the convict does not have sufficient intelligence to understand the nature of the proceedings against him, what he was tried for, the purpose of his punishment, the impending fate which awaits him, and a sufficient understanding to know any fact which might exist which would make his punishment unjust or unlawful.")

Year established: 1974 (*Bean v. State*, 297 So.2d 903). Codified in 1984 (Mississippi Code Ann. Section 99-19-57 (Supp.); but the earliest case in which *M'Naghten* was used was *Bovard v. State*, 30 Miss. 600 (1856))

Burden of Proof: Prosecutor, beyond a reasonable doubt

Year established: 1983 (*Edwards v. State*, 441 So.2d 84; *en banc*, Miss. 1983)

Verdict Form: NGRI

Year established: Verdict first used in 1856 in *Bovard*, supra. Codified in 1972

Missouri

Test: ALI. Alcoholism or drug abuse without psychosis excluded
   Year established: 1963

Burden of Proof: Defendant, by preponderance or greater weight of evidence
   Year established: 1963

Verdict Form: Not guilty by reason of mental disease or defect
   Year established: 1963

Montana

Test: Montana has abolished the insanity defense. In 1969, the state had adopted a modified version of the ALI standard; but, in 1979, the legislature repealed that provision—only allowing evidence of a mental disease or defect to be admissible prior to trial in order to prove the defendant incapable of proceeding. During trial, such evidence is admissible to prove the defendant lacked a particular state of mind that is an element of the crime. The concept of inability to appreciate the criminality or to conform conduct to the requirements of law is contained only in the sentencing statute.

   Year established: 1969 (Title 46, ch. 14, pt. 1, Section 46-14-101 ff.)

Burden of Proof: See above

Verdict Form: See above

Nebraska

Test: M'Naghten
   Year established: 1876 (*Wright v. People*, 4 Neb. 407; articulated more recently in *State v. Smith*, 190 Neb. 722, 211 N.W.2d 922 (1972))

Burden of Proof: Defendant, by a preponderance of the evidence
   Year established: 1984 (Section 29-2203)

Verdict Form: NGRI
    Year established: 1876 (See Section 29-2203)

Nevada

Test: M'Naghten
    Year established: Originally announced in 1889 (*State v. Lewis*, 20 Nev. 333, 22 P.241). Adopted as state common law in 1969 in *Williams v. State*, 85 Nev. 169k, 451 P.2d 848.
Burden of Proof: Defendant, by a preponderance of the evidence
    Year established: 1889 (*State v. Lewis*, supra)
Verdict Form: NGRI
    Year established: 1889 (*State v. Lewis*, supra)

New Hampshire

Test: No specific test; factual determination for the jury (re: not criminally responsible)
    Year established: 1982 (RSA 628:2, II (Supp. 1983))
Burden of Proof: Defendant, by a preponderance of the evidence
    Year established: 1982 (RSA 628:2, II)
Verdict Form: NGRI
    Year established: 1982

New Jersey

Test: M'Naghten
    Year established: 1954 (*State v. Huff*, 14 N.J. 240, 250). Codified in 1978
Burden of Proof: Defendant, by a preponderance of the evidence
    Year established: 1975 (*State v. Lewis*, 67 N.J. 47, 48) Codified in 1978
Verdict Form: NGRI
    Year established: 1978

New Mexico

Test: M'Naghten and irresistible impulse
    Year established: 1954 (*State v. White*, 58 N.M. 324, 330, 270 P.2d 727, 731). Codified in 1978
Burden of Proof: State, beyond a reasonable doubt
    Year established: 1936 (*State v. Roy*, 40 N.M. 397, 60 P.2d 646)
Verdict Form: Guilty but mentally ill
    Year established: 1982 (NMSA 1978, sec. 31-9-3 (Cum. Supp. 1983))

New York

Test: M'Naghten (modified), ALI, and irresistible impulse

Year established: 1965
Burden of Proof: Defendant, by a preponderance of the evidence (Section 40.15 Supp. 1984)
  Year established: 1965
Verdict Form: Not responsible by reason of mental disease or defect
  Year established: 1980

North Carolina

Test: M'Naghten
  Year established: 1973 (*State v. Humphrey*, 283 N.C. 570, 196 S.E.2d 516)
Burden of Proof: Defendant, to the satisfaction of the jury
  Year established: 1943 (*State v. Harris*, 223 N.C. 697, 28 S.E.2d 232; see also *State v. Ward*, 301 N.C. 469, 272 S.E.2d 84 (1980))
Verdict Form: Acquitted on grounds of insanity
  Year established: 1943

North Dakota

Test: M'Naghten modified ("lack substantial capacity to comprehend the harmful nature or consequence of his conduct, or conduct was the result of a loss or serious distortion of capacity to recognize reality")
  Year established: 1977. *M'Naghten* first used in 1922 (*State v. Thronstadson*, 49 N.D. 348, 191 N.W. 628)
Burden of Proof: Defendant, by a preponderance of the evidence
                    Prosecutor, beyond a reasonable doubt
  Year established: 1973
Verdict Form: NGRI
  Year established: 1973

Ohio

Test: ALI, *M'Naghten*
  Year established: 1969 (*State v. Staten*, 18 Ohio St.2d 13; see also *State v. Brown*, 5 Ohio St.3d 133, 449 N.E.2d 449 (1983))
Burden of Proof: Defendant, by a preponderance of the evidence
  Year established: Codified in 1977
Verdict Form: NGRI
  Year established: 1953

Oklahoma

Test: M'Naghten
  Year established: 1974 (*Hair v. State*, 532 P.2d 72 (Okla. Crim. App.))
Burden of Proof: State, beyond a reasonable doubt

Year established: 1983 (*Munn v. State*, 658 P.2d 482)
Verdict Form: NGRI
    Year established: 1981 (See Title 22 O.S. 1981, sec. 1161)

Oregon

Test: ALI
    Year established: 1971
Burden of Proof: Defendant, by a preponderance of the evidence
    Year established: 1971
Verdict Form: Not responsible by reason of mental disease or defect
    Year established: 1971

Pennsylvania

Test: M'Naghten
    Year established: 1960 (*Commonwealth v. Woodhouse*, 401 Pa. 242, 249–50, 164 A.2d 98, 103
Burden of Proof: State, beyond a reasonable doubt
                   Defendant, by a preponderance of the evidence
    Year established: 1966 (Mental Health and Mental Retardation Act of 1966)
Verdict Form: Guilty but mentally ill
    Year established: 1982

Rhode Island

Test: ALI modified
    Year established: 1979 (*State v. Johnson*, 121 R.I. 254, 399 A.2d 469)
Burden of Proof: Defendant, by a preponderance of the evidence
    Year established: 1986 (*State v. Robert Smith*, Slip Opinion, Supreme Court of Rhode Island, June 17)
Verdict Form: NGRI
    Year established: 1956

South Carolina

Test: M'Naghten
    Year established: 1956 (*State v. Byrd*, 260 S.C. 537, 197 S.E.2d 678)
Burden of Proof: Defendant, by a preponderance of the evidence
    Year established: 1961 (*State v. Young*, 238 S.C. 119, 119 S.E.2d 504, cert. den. 368 U.S. 868)
Verdict Form: Guilty but mentally ill
    Year established: 1956. Codified in 1962

South Dakota

Test: M'Naghten modified ("[A]n accused's sanity is measured by his capacity and reason to enable him to distinguish between right and wrong with regard to the act charged")
> *Year established:* 1983

Burden of Proof: State, beyond a reasonable doubt
> *Year established:* 1961 (*State v. Violett*, 79 S.D. 292, 111 N.W.2d 598)

Verdict Form: Guilty but mentally ill
> *Year established:* 1983

Tennessee

Test: ALI
> *Year established:* 1977 (*Graham v. State*, 547 S.W.2d 531)

Burden of Proof: State, beyond a reasonable doubt
> *Year established:* 1973 (*Collins v. State*, 516 S.W.2d 179)

Verdict Form: NGRI
> *Year established:* 1977

Texas

Test: ALI, *M'Naghten*, and irresistible impulse
> *Year established:* 1974 (Texas Penal Code, sec. 8.01)

Burden of Proof: Defendant, by a preponderance of the evidence
> *Year established:* 1974

Verdict Form: NGRI ("The jury shall state in their verdict whether the defendant was sane or insane at the time the offense is alleged to have been committed and whether the defendant is sane or insane at the time of the trial")
> *Year established:* 1974

Utah

Test: Utah has abolished the insanity defense (Section 76.2-305(1)), but has adopted a guilty but mentally ill verdict
> *Year established:* 1983

Burden of Proof: State, beyond a reasonable doubt
> *Year established:* 1925 (*State v. Hadley*, 234 P. 940)

Verdict Form: Guilty but mentally ill (Sections 77-13-1, 77-35-21, 77-35-21.5)
> *Year established:* 1983

Vermont

Test: ALI
> *Year established:* 1974 (Vt. Stat. Ann., tit. 13, sec. 4801). Amended in 1983 to allocate burden of proof

Burden of Proof: Defendant, by a preponderance of the evidence

Prosecutor, beyond a reasonable doubt

Year established: 1983 (Section 4801(b))

Verdict Form: Plea of NGRI was abolished upon adoption of the Rules of Criminal Procedure; see *State v. Lapham*, 135 Vt. 393, 377 A.2d 249, 251 (1977). Defendant must still give notice of intention to rely on the defense, and insanity as a defense is usually raised in the omnibus hearing (B.R. Cr. P. 11(a)).

Year established: 1984 (Section 4822)

Virginia

Test: M'Naghten and irresistible impulse (only if defendant can distinguish right from wrong)

Year established: 1974 (*Davis v. Commonwealth*, 214 Va. 681, 204 S.E.2d 272). *M'Naghten* was first used in 1881 in *Dejarnette v. Commonwealth*, 75 Va. 867.

Burden of Proof: Defendant, by a preponderance of the evidence, to satisfaction of jury

Year established: 1960 (*Jones v. Commonwealth*, 202 Va. 236, 117 S.E.2d 67; repeated in *Shifflett v. Commonwealth*, 221 Va. 760, 274 S.E.2d 305 (1981).

Verdict Form: NGRI

Year established: 1950

Washington

Test: M'Naghten

Year established: 1973 (*State v. Ferrick*, 81 Wash.2d 9142, 506 P.2d 860). Codified in 1975.

Burden of Proof: Defendant, by preponderance of the evidence

Year established: 1973

Verdict Form: Special verdict form—mental disease or defect excluding responsibility

Year established: 1973

West Virginia

Test: ALI

Year established: 1973 (*State v. Grimm*, 195 S.E.2d 637)

Burden of Proof: State, beyond a reasonable doubt

Year established: 1979 (*State v. Milam*, 260 S.E.2d 205)

Verdict Form: NGRI

Year established: 1973

Wisconsin

Test: ALI (If defendant chooses Model Penal Code definition, then burden of proof remains on him or her. According to *Schleisner v. State*, 58 Wis.2d 605, 207 N.W.2d 636 (1967), defendant has option to choose *M'Naghten*—in which case, prosecution must prove sanity beyond a reasonable doubt.)

    Year established: 1971 (Wis. Stat. Ann., sec. 971.15). The Wisconsin Criminal Code, which became effective in 1983, added that "As used in this section, the terms mental illness or deficiency mean only those severely abnormal mental conditions that grossly and demonstrably impair a person's perception of understanding or reality and that are not attributable primarily to self-induced intoxication."

Burden of Proof: Defendant, by the greater weight of the credible evidence (bifurcated trial)

    Year established: 1967 (*LaFollette v. Raskin*, 34 Wis.2d 607, 150 N.W.2d 318)

Verdict Form: Bifurcated trial—both issues of guilt and sanity are tried before the same jury in a continuous trial. Verdict is NGRI, or not guilty by reason of mental illness or defect

    Year established: First announced in 1905 (*Steward v. State*, 124 Wis. 623, 102 N.W. 1079). Codified in 1967 in Section 957.11(1)

Wyoming

Test: ALI

    Year established: 1972 (*Reilly v. State*, 496 P.2d 899 (Wyo.)). Codified in 1975

Burden of Proof: Defendant, by a preponderance of the evidence

                      Prosecutor, beyond a reasonable doubt

    Year established: 1975

Verdict Form: Not guilty by reason of mental illness or deficiency (bifurcated, continuous trial)

    Year established: 1975

Selected Bibliography

Allen, Francis. *The Borderline of Criminal Justice.* Chicago: University of Chicago Press, 1964.

Biggs, John. *The Guilty Mind.* New York: Harcourt, Brace, 1955.

Brackel, Samuel J., and Ronald S. Rock, eds. *The Mentally Disabled and the Law.* Chicago: University of Chicago Press, 1971.

Dershowitz, Alan. "Abolishing the Insanity Defense: The Most Significant Feature of the Administration's Proposed Criminal Code—An Essay." 9 *Crim. L. Bull.* 434 (1973).

Glueck, Sheldon. *Mental Disorder and the Criminal Law.* Boston: Little, Brown, 1925.

Goldstein, Abraham S. *The Insanity Defense.* New Haven: Yale University Press, 1967.

Guttmacher, Manfred. *The Mind of the Murderer.* New York: Farrar, Strauss, and Cudahy, 1960.

Halleck, Seymour. "Insanity Defense in the District of Columbia—A Legal Lorelie." 49 *Geo. L. J.* (1950).

———. *Law and the Practice of Psychiatry.* 1982.

Huckabee, Harlow M. *Lawyers, Psychiatrists, and the Criminal Law.* Springfield, Ill.: Charles C. Thomas, 1980.

Kaufman, Irving. "The Insanity Plea on Trial." *New York Times Magazine*, August 8, 1982.

Kelitz, I., and J. Fulton. *The Insanity Defense and Its Alternatives: A Guide for Policy Makers*. Williamsburg, Va.: Institute on Mental Disability and the Law, National Center for State Courts, 1984.

La Fond, John Q. "Observations on the Insanity Defense and Involuntary Civil Commitment in Europe." *University of Puget Sound Law Review* (Spring 1984).

Low, Peter W., John Calvin Jeffries, Jr., and Richard J. Bonnie. *The Trial of John W. Hinckley, Jr.: A Case Study in the Insanity Defense*. Mineola, N.Y.: Foundation Press, 1986.

Miller, Herbert J., chairman. *Report of the President's Commission on Crime in the District of Columbia*. Washington, D.C.: U.S. Government Printing Office, 1966.

Morris, Norval. *Madness and the Criminal Law*. Chicago: University of Chicago Press, 1982.

Simon, Rita J. *The Jury and the Defense of Insanity*. Boston: Little, Brown, 1967.

Steadman, Henry J. "Empirical Research on the Insanity Defense." *Annals of American Academy of Political and Social Sciences* (1985).

Stone, Alan. *Mental Health and Law: A System in Transition*, DHEW pub. no. (ADM) 75-176. Rockville, Md.: NIMH, 1975.

—— "The Insanity Defense on Trial." *Harvard Law School Bulletin* (Fall 1982).

Szasz, Thomas. *Law, Liberty, and Psychiatry*. New York: Collier Books, 1963.

Weihofen, Henry. *The Urge to Punish*. New York: Farrar, Strauss, and Cudahy, 1956.

Weiner, Barbara A. "Not Guilty by Reason of Insanity: A Sane Approach." *Chicago-Kent Law Review* (1980).

Wooton, Barbara. *Law, Psychiatry and the Mental Health System*. Boston: Little, Brown, 1974.

Index

accountability: and free will, 4–5; mental illness reducing, 4–5

Adelman, Roger: on attorney's responsibility to jurors, 104; on expert testimony, 102–3; on expert witnesses, 96–97

adverse social conditions, and compulsion to commit crimes, 7, 177

Ake, George, 89–90

Ake v. Oklahoma, 89–90, 94; Rule 706 as vehicle for implementing mandate of, 106

Allen, Francis, 7

Allen, Richard, 179

American Bar Association: policy statement on definition of "appreciate," 54; recommendation on burden of proof, 59–60; on restrictions on expert testimony, 101–2; standard for jury instructions, 103; statement on insanity defense, 20

American Law Institute test, 19, 22; abolishment of, 45; adoption of, 44–45; "caveat" paragraph rejected by *Smith, Wade* and others, 41–42; "cognitive prong" excluded by *Currens*, 41–42; "cognitive prong" modified by Insanity Defense Reform Act of 1984, 53–54; criticism of, 45; degrees of incapacity recognized by, 39, 40, 41; departures from, 42, 43; designed to avoid causation problem of "product" approach, 38–39; differentiated from previous insanity tests, 38; modifications of, 41–44, 194; not approved by Judge Bazelon, 85; not universally approved, 85; operative concepts of, 37–38; preferred to

[American Law Institute test] *M'Naghten* rule, 39–42; replacing *Durham* rule, 36–37; volitional component of, 38, 40; "volitional prong" eliminated by Insanity Defense Reform Act of 1984, 49–53; "wrongfulness" substituted for "criminality," 44

American Medical Association: criticising liberal mens rea approach, 183, 185; statement on insanity defense, 21

American Psychiatric Association: comments on dropping "volitional prong," 50; diagnostic manual, 83; filing amicus brief in *Brawner*, 182; statement on burden of proof, 60; statement on insanity defense, 8, 20

Anatomy of a Murder, 228–29, 236–40, 241, 242, 243

Anglo-Saxon law, 10

Argentina: insanity defense in, 217

Aristotle, 225–26

Arizona: requiring defendant to prove insanity by clear and convincing evidence, 63

Arnold, Edwin, 19–11

Bazelon, David L.: American Law Institute test not approved by, 85; on compulsion to commit crime, 177; dissenting from *Brawner* decision, 85; instructions for expert witnesses, 84, 103; perception of function of jury, 85; ruling in *Durham* allowing expert witnesses, 83; stating *Durham* rule, 18

Bender, Jeanne Mathews, 185

Blake v. United States, 40–41

ABOUT THE AUTHORS

RITA J. SIMON is Dean of the School of Justice at the American University. She recently coauthored *Transracial Adoptees and Their Families: A Study of Their Identity and Commitment* with Howard Altstein. Her other works include *The Jury and the Defense of Insanity, Women and Crime,* and *Public Opinion and the Immigrant: Print Media Coverage, 1880–1980.*

DAVID E. AARONSON is a Professor of Law at the Washington College of Law at the American University with a joint appointment at the University's School of Justice. He is a member of the American Law Institute. His authored or coauthored books include *Maryland Criminal Jury Instructions and Commentary, Public Policy and Police Discretion, Decriminalization of Public Drunkenness: Tracing the Implementation of a Public Policy,* and *The New Justice, Alternatives to Conventional Criminal Adjudication.*